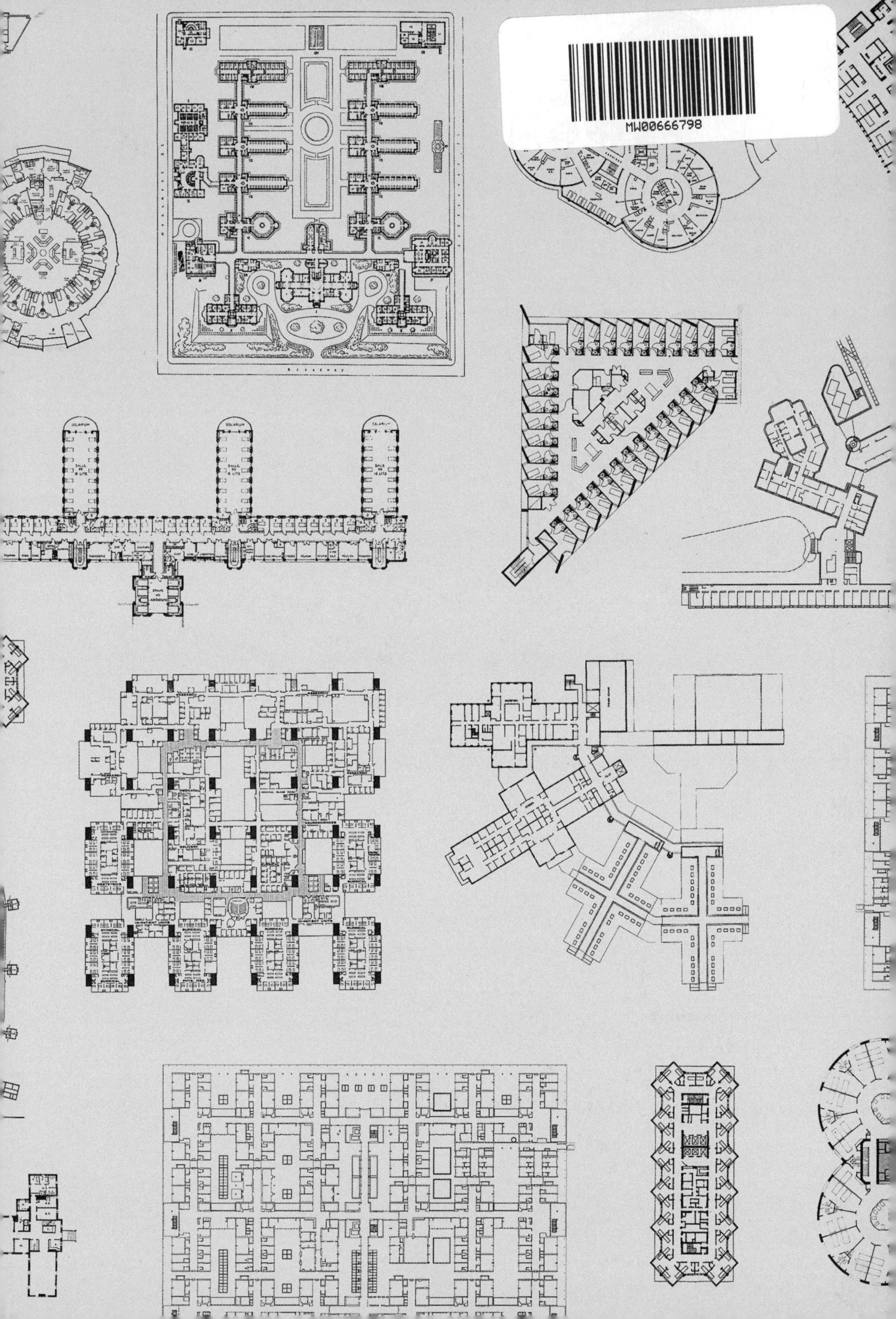

The Architecture of Health

Hospital Design and the Construction of Dignity

The Architecture of Health
Hospital Design and the Construction of Dignity

Michael P. Murphy Jr. with Jeffrey Mansfield
and MASS Design Group

COOPER
HEWITT

Published by Cooper Hewitt, Smithsonian Design Museum
2 East 91st Street, New York, NY 10128 USA cooperhewitt.org

Distributed (North America) by Artbook | D.A.P., 75 Broad Street, Suite 630, New York, NY 10004 USA artbook.com

Distributed (Worldwide) by Thames & Hudson UK
181A High Holborn, LONDON, WC1V 7QX UK
thamesandhudson.com

This publication is made possible in part by Furthermore: a program of the J. M. Kaplan Fund.

Furthermore: a program of the J.M. Kaplan Fund

Research was supported by the Robert Wood Johnson Foundation.

ISBN 978-1-942303-31-2

Library of Congress Control Number: 2021944429

Director of Cross-Platform Publishing Pamela Horn

Cross-Platform Publishing Associate Matthew Kennedy

Developmental Editor Daniel Murphy

Copy Editor Rebecca Roberts

Book Design Rick Valicenti, Bud Rodecker, Alyssa Arnesen

Typefaces: Headings, captions, and notes are set in Theinhardt from Optimo Type Foundry, body copy is in GT Sectra from Grilli Type, and display type is GT Flexa from Grilli Type

2021 2022 2023 2024 2025/
10 9 8 7 6 5 4 3 2 1

Printed in Italy

COOPER HEWITT Smithsonian Design Museum MASS.

Contents

Publisher's Note

In 2018, Cooper Hewitt, Smithsonian Design Museum initiated a series of projects examining the intersection of design and health, a topic of deep importance given the inevitable role that health care systems play in all our lives. With *Health Design Thinking*, by Ellen Lupton and Bon Ku, MD, scheduled for publication in April 2020, we began collaborating with MASS Design Group and Michael P. Murphy Jr., the group's founding principal and executive director, on an exhibition on a related subject, *Design and Healing: Creative Responses to Epidemics* (December 2021–August 2022). During the course of our research for the exhibition, it quickly became evident — through an extensive body of archival material, articles, renderings, and architectural studies concerning the design of hospitals, past and present — that many historical eras developed their own unique hospital types, and, further, that these structures were closely related not only to the medical practices of each period but also to the social behaviors and political ideals of those periods.

This publication, one of the fruits of that research, explores the evolution of hospital architecture through a behavioral lens, an approach largely absent from the discipline's scholarship and one that contributes an important perspective to Cooper Hewitt's focus on design and health. Hospitals, in their various services and functions, touch many lives, and — like all designed spaces — they not only reflect but also shape their social, political, and ecological environments. As the authors of this volume make evident (and the COVID-19 pandemic has amply demonstrated), health care infrastructure has not always been accessible to all communities, nor has it often been designed to meet the true range of human needs. It is our hope that *The Architecture of Health* will contribute to an expanding understanding of the role of human-centered design in creating an architecture of dignity and social good.

The Architecture of Health: Hospital Design and the Construction of Dignity is made possible in part with the support of Furthermore, a program of the J.M. Kaplan Fund.

Pamela Horn
Director of Cross-Platform Publishing and Strategic Partnerships
Cooper Hewitt, Smithsonian Design Museum

Preface

Since March of 2020, when the number of COVID-19 cases rose exponentially around the globe, discussions of hospital design have become increasingly charged and complex. The virus was the catalyst, but the debate is indicative of larger issues. As the pandemic revealed embedded inequities in public health, hospitals as spaces of care — and spaces of dignity — have found themselves more and more in the spotlight. Rightfully so, as medical professionals have transformed into essential workers, and — as we anticipate further disruptions in the form of pandemics and climate-related crises — our hospitals continue to reflect social values and commitments. *The Architecture of Health* enters into this charged space, describing the formal templates and organizational patterns of hospital design over the centuries, but keeping us tightly focused on the importance of these institutions to upholding, and reaffirming, the values of democratic, equitable societies. We will weather the coming storms according to the strength of our health facilities.

And storms are coming. From an architectural perspective, one of the essential challenges introduced, or exacerbated, by COVID-19 is the politicization of ventilation. In hospitals and schools in particular, the transmission of an aerosol virus may be reduced by increasing the volume of outside air that enters the space. Moving more air around leads to a greater demand on heating, ventilation, and air-conditioning systems and thus, with the existing electrical grid, to increased carbon emissions. In other words, mitigating the life-threatening effects of one public health crisis — the pandemic — exacerbates the near- and long-term effects of another — the climatic instabilities wrought by global warming.

The Architecture of Health is thus unrelenting on what might at first seem to be a secondary aspect of hospital design: the effective management of air. In chapter 2, author Michael Murphy quotes Florence Nightingale: "The very first canon of nursing... is this: to keep the air [the patient] breathes as pure as the external air." This may seem anachronistic, in that the air surrounding many of today's urban hospitals is often more toxic than would be preferred, but the premise remains: one of the primary tasks of hospital design is the provision of breathable air, of an interior atmosphere conducive to health and well-being. Today, this entails filtering, ventilating, and conditioning air; indeed, "air conditioning, in the literal sense, will establish itself as the main space-political theme of the coming era," the philosopher and cultural theorist Peter Sloterdijk wrote in 2014, in the second volume of his *Spheres* trilogy. There will be battles over air, in other words, debates about the value of a healthy environment. Hospitals will be — are already — at the center of these debates.

This book thus traces an essential historical arc: from open pavilion hospital to the closed, air-conditioned block and, perhaps, back again. For as societies begin to attend more aggressively to a very limited carbon budget, hospitals will remain one of the few places that air-conditioning is warranted: some amount of fossil-fueled ventilation or thermal isolation is likely to remain necessary for the provision of dignifying care. Murphy clarifies that the design of hospitals will increasingly involve debates around the right to breathe: in the hospital, breath is valued above all else.

But who gets to breathe? The challenge of hospital design is to maintain a space of atmospheric exclusivity that is nonetheless available to all. *The Architecture of Health* helps us to see that our current health care spaces are a legacy of colonial and postcolonial regimes of population management. The hospital was born, at least in part, not from an impulse of care but from the necessities of war and the desire to optimize an oppressed workforce — that is, through the same calculations of use value that are evident in the baroque mystifications of contemporary insurance regimes. Lives are, to some, numbers. Murphy's careful analysis encourages an approach to spaces of care that resists this legacy, demonstrating that we might learn the lessons of operational and atmospheric management while refusing the depersonalization of the human body; we might refuse to see public health as an agent of economic and racial stratification.

Indeed, to design dignifying spaces is to affirm and encourage a respect for all bodies, all souls, equally. *The Architecture of Health* is in this sense itself a breath of fresh air, insisting that architects recognize the importance of the hospital as a space of dignity — a provision that will challenge both existing and newly built spaces, and that will be increasingly difficult to achieve though ever more necessary to maintain in coming decades.

Daniel A. Barber
Associate Professor of Architecture
Waltzman School of Design, University of Pennsylvania

Prentice Women's Hospital, designed by Bertrand Goldberg, 1975, overlooking the Chicago skyline [fig. 4]

Prologue
Consider the Hospital

At some point, facing tragedy or joy, most of us will spend days, if not weeks, in a hospital, coping with the existential realities of birth and death. When I was a young architecture student, I sat with my father as he lay in a Manhattan hospital near the end of his life. Taking in the scene around me, I was shocked to see how few of the design lessons I was taught to honor had made their way into the spaces of care. As the equipment beeped and blinked, I asked myself, What has made this place so indifferent to the human experience? Why the indignity? Where is the design?

Later, I faced the flip side of this challenge, as part of a team tasked with designing a hospital for epidemic disease in Butaro, a remote district of Rwanda. Modern mechanical systems were too costly to purchase and maintain, and so we looked back at historical medical facilities for strategies to manage the movement of air, waste, and water. That research exposed me to a history of buildings and to foundational architects I had never before encountered. It also awakened me to the contradictions involved in the design of spaces that serve both the public and the individual. Looking back at that time spent with my father, I reflected that his hospital provided care that few in the world could access: not only leading science but also restorative moments, like the view of the East River from his double room. But the hallways filled with beeping equipment, the windowless waiting rooms, the maze-like sequence from street to patient room, the sense of being lost in the institution — those experiences will never leave me. My father's hospital journey probably served both his humanity and his medical condition, but rarely at the same time. The role of design is to manage this conflict. It softens the blow of our irrelevance to the systems around us, reminding us that we still matter. My friend and mentor Dr. Paul Farmer has called this "dignity construction," and the search for it in architecture is the purpose of this book.

The history of hospitals is not merely an account of changes in style, form, and auteur. Instead, it is a lineage of buildings that were designed to shape social conditions for others, that represented key milestones in political eras, and that were composed as systems by many authors. It includes brilliant and visionary creators — hospital architects, but also systems designers — driven by the aim of social change. They found innovative ways to resolve the medical dilemmas of their eras, and at times they also discovered universal truths. They acknowledged that a hospital is the visible manifestation of a vast network of services, politics, and people. The characters in this book are all polymaths and provocateurs, but probably none is quite as essential as Florence Nightingale, who, in laying out her guidelines for hospital design in 1859, demonstrated that the architecture of a medical facility can influence an entire political and social order. She showed us why buildings matter.

Hospital architecture illustrates the contradiction inherent in nearly all public built spaces: the tension between an imagined population that will need public services — *charity* — and the systems' overt need to shape that public's behavior so its members may attain it — *control*. The principles of charity and control pertain to architecture more broadly, but they were birthed in the clinic, and they can never be disentangled from the spaces of medical treatment. They help shape our understanding of architecture's ambivalence toward its public role and clarify that — whether we acknowledge it or not — buildings can determine our behavior as individuals and advance our rights as members of a society.

Michael P. Murphy Jr.

Patient tower, Prentice Women's Hospital, designed by Bertrand Goldberg, 1975 [fig. 2]

Introduction
The Rise and Fall of Prentice Women's Hospital

In the fall of 2014, the final latticework of scaffolding came down from around Prentice Women's Hospital, and with it fell the sinuous poured-concrete sections of the building's controversial petal-shaped floors. A last-minute campaign by preservationists and by Chicago's mayor had raised the hope that this brutalist icon might find a new purpose, but the effort had ultimately failed. The building's strange, elliptical windows were, for the first time, glassless, open to the air, breathing in and breathing out the dust of an architecture that had for forty years communicated ideas to the public about its relationship to health. These ideas had ceased to be legible, and Prentice had fallen.

In 1971, when Bertrand Goldberg (1913–1997), an idiosyncratic paragon of late American modernism, began designing a new facility for Prentice in downtown Chicago, he was consumed with the idea that architecture could change society. "My message," he wrote, "is more important either than myself personally, or than the quick identification as the round-building architect. I am talking about the performance of people in a social system, about the performance of people in the city."[1]

The building was evidence of a distinctive formal thesis — the curved concrete tower — that Goldberg would test in subsequent hospital and residential projects into the late 1980s (figs. 1, 2).[2] As in his distinctive masterpiece a few blocks away, Marina City (1968; fig. 3), Prentice featured a curvilinear form in its upper stories, and he gave each patient room a window looking out over the city (fig. 4), some with views of the beautiful expanse of Lake Michigan beyond.

Prentice was an engineering marvel. It was one of the first buildings developed with computer-aided-design (CAD) tools borrowed from aeronautics, which enabled the design team to perform complex parametric modeling of structural conditions (fig. 5). The upper part of the building, rising above a rectilinear base, was clover-shaped in plan (fig. 6), but instead of the post-and-beam stacked floorplates of a typical tower, its "leaves" were cantilevered from a single central stem. Four column-free bays — a quatrefoil — provided uninterrupted space inside (fig. 7).

By the 1970s, when Goldberg was designing Prentice, the single-patient room had already replaced the large open wards that had dominated medical architecture since Florence Nightingale first theorized them in her *Notes on Hospitals* in 1859. The single-patient room requires design solutions different from the ward: notably, each room must have a window and be in observational proximity to a nurses' station (fig. 8). Goldberg's solution was geocentric. A circle both minimizes the distance to the center from any point and maximizes the surface area of the perimeter (fig. 9). Rounded forms, he theorized, might offer an efficient solution for single-patient rooms (fig. 10). Similar to Jeremy Bentham's circular panopticon (or "all-seeing") prison design of 1791 (fig. 11), Goldberg's plan placed nurses' stations in the center of the quatrefoil; each semicircle of rooms was therefore observable from a single point, reducing staff needs. A thickened central stem incorporated vertical shafts for elevators, wastewater, and goods, easily overseen by staff and surrounded by the load-bearing structure.

Goldberg would continue his geometric experiments in hospital bed towers for the rest of his career. Renderings, often bird's-eye views, imagine alluringly wavy towers launching from thin columnar legs that seem to have paused midstride as they stepped over blank, rectilinear boxes below. In Prentice, the rectilinear base building rose up five stories from the street, a banal, expressionless, concrete post-and-beam extrusion that took up an entire block of North Fairbanks Court, between East Superior and East Huron Streets. It stood in stark contrast to the curvilinear mass and whimsical detailing of the bed tower spiraling above. The formal contrasts were severe, almost jarring.

1 Bertrand Goldberg, in "Bertrand Goldberg: Reflections," The Arts Club of Chicago, https://www.artsclubchicago.org/exhibition/bertrand-goldberg-reflections.

2 See "Selected Projects," in Zoë Ryan and Allison Fisher, *Bertrand Goldberg, Architecture of Invention* (New Haven, CT: Yale University Press, 2012), 170–88. In addition to Prentice Women's Hospital, notable projects by Bertrand Goldberg Associates include Elgin State Hospital, Elgin, Illinois (1967; see chapter 8); Stony Brook University Medical Center, Stony Brook, New York (1980; see chapter 5); Harvard Affiliated Hospitals (1980; see chapter 8); St. Joseph Medical Center, Tacoma, Washington (1974); St. Mary's Hospital, Milwaukee (1976); Good Samaritan Hospital, Phoenix (1982); and Providence Hospital, Mobile, Alabama (1987).

1

2

3

4

5
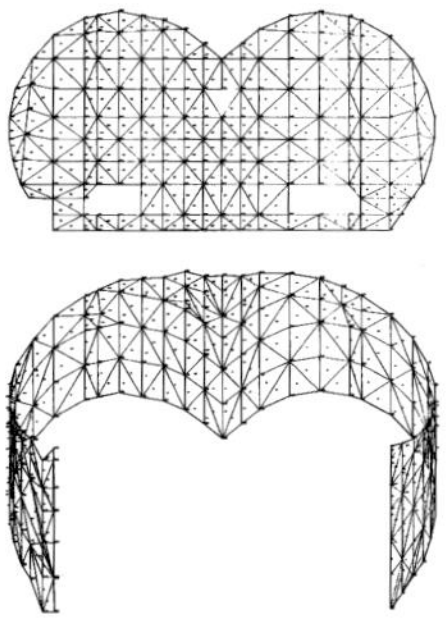

6
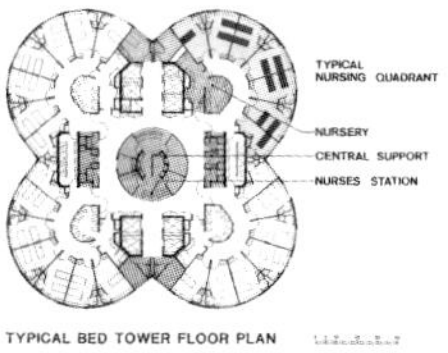

7

8
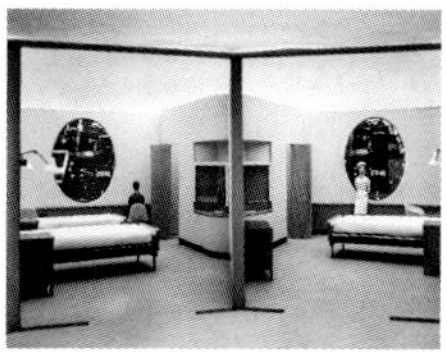

9
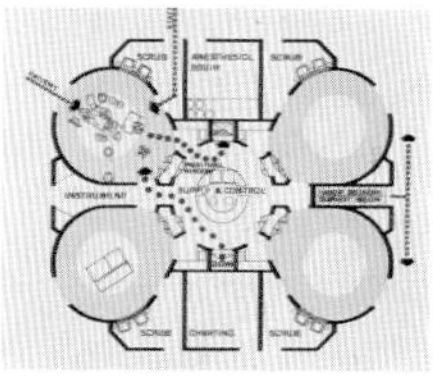

10

11
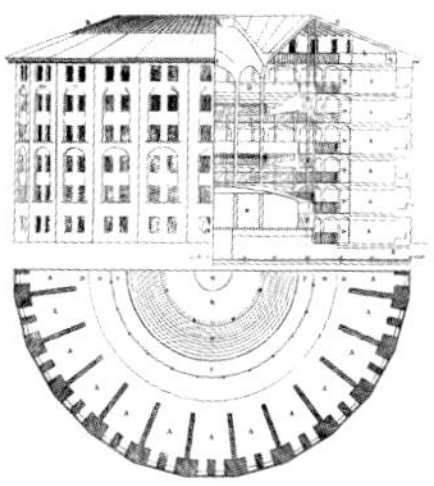

Prentice Women's Hospital,
Chicago, designed by
Bertrand Goldberg, 1975
[fig. 1]

Typical bed-tower floor plan,
Prentice Women's Hospital,
Chicago [fig. 6]

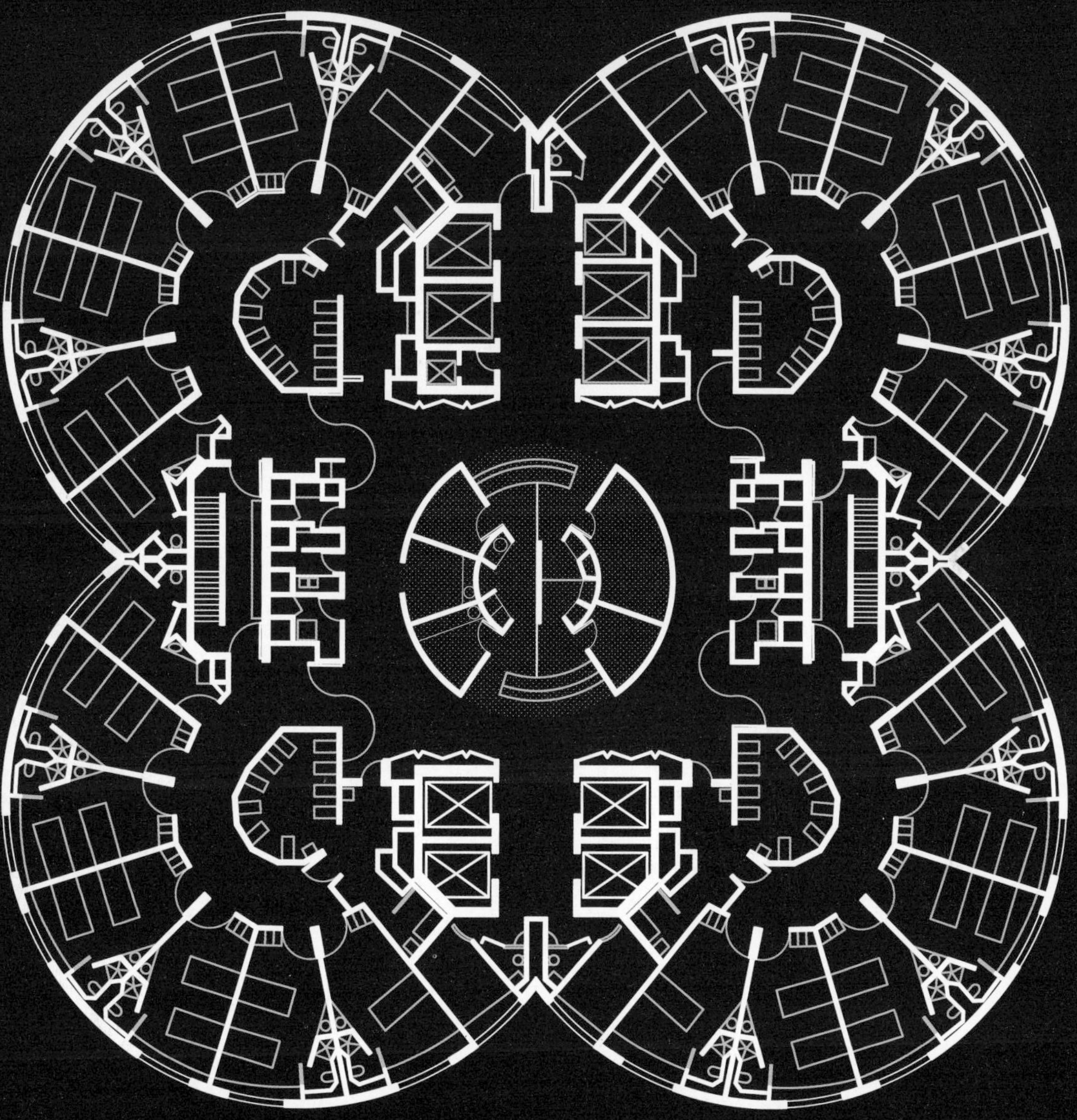

TYPICAL BED TOWER FLOOR PLAN

Prentice Women's Hospital
under construction [fig. 7]

As an architectural form, Prentice's base building was a familiar sight in 1970s Chicago. Made of black-tinted glass, it resembled the glass-and-steel structures of corporate modernism that had proliferated around the world at midcentury. The glass box had a particular resonance in Chicago, where Ludwig Mies van der Rohe, maybe its most vociferous advocate, built a career after leaving Germany during World War II **(fig. 12)**.[3] Functionally, the modernist box allowed for a deep, extendable floorplate. Deployed in hospitals, it prioritized *flexibility* in order to accommodate the rapid shifts in postwar medical technology and practice.

By 1970, however, the technological and service requirements of the hospital had become so complex that the systems took over the hospital. The spaces were now dependent on functioning mechanical systems, making these rational spaces inflexible to change. Cheaper air-handling systems allowed indoor air environments to balloon the building, taking up entire city blocks, with temperature and ventilation controlled from inside. All the functions and services of the hospital — patient procedures, power and electrical services, the distribution of food, and the elimination of waste — required precisely controlled environments. Operable windows, no longer necessary, were often avoided altogether so the entire building could be hermetically sealed and controlled. In Prentice's base building, interior hallways surrounded windowless rooms and equipment bays. The flexible modernist box had allowed for growth, but the complex workings of the 1970s hospital pushed it to its limits, and required new configurations to elevate the patient experience.

Split Personality

As Goldberg himself admitted, Prentice was really two different buildings, placed one on top of the other: a split personality **(fig. 13)**.[4] The lower building was a box with a rationalist grid, conservative spans, a preordained order, and vast, indeterminate, flexible space, a form supported by the universalizing theories of early international modernism and disseminated through global institutional and corporate adoption. This was the block hospital. The upper building, atop the block, was the sculptural result of Goldberg's spatial research into the patient's individual experience of care.

The design of the lower building imagined a user whose specific human needs could be reduced to shared, universal needs. This universality also lent the architecture a perceptible quality of imprecision and apathy. Rationalist modernism was critiqued for being alienating: it was designed for all, but for no one in particular. The block was designed for the machine, not for people. The upper building was almost the opposite, both in architectural statement and in function. Goldberg's sculptural forms, though in appearance malleable and free, were purposeful and inflexible, a result of their precise engineering and the use of concrete. The structure was both wholly unique and completely inalterable: frozen in an era formally, obstinately opposed to amendment, and adverse to adaptation.

3 Goldberg had been a student of Mies's at the Bauhaus—the art and design school founded in Weimar, Germany, and active from 1919 to 1933—and later an employee in Mies's Chicago office. Goldberg's obituary in the *Chicago Tribune* recounts the relationship between the two in anecdotal detail. See Blair Kamin, "Architect Bertrand Goldberg, 84," *Chicago Tribune*, October 9, 1997.

4 Susannah Ribstein, *Prentice Women's Hospital Report for Landmark Illinois* (July 2012), 3, cited in Paola Aguirre and Michelle Ha Tucker, "When the Future Was Here," *MAS Context*, nos. 25–26 (Spring–Summer 2015), 22.

12

13

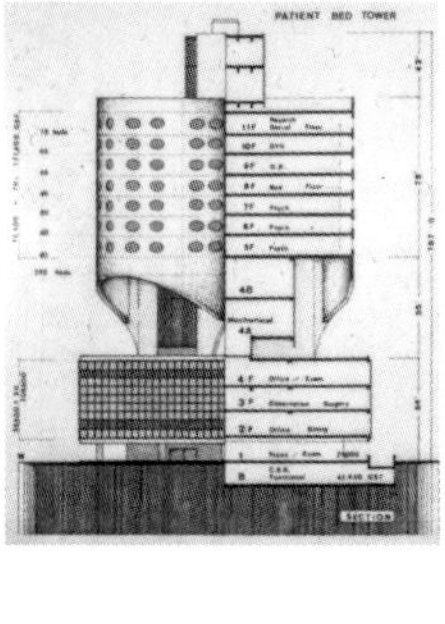

And yet it is the design of the bed tower that made Prentice exemplary and influential. The rounded quatrefoil was a formal innovation based on an elemental spatial rule: the ratio that delineates the distance from the nurses' station to the bed is the primary ratio of all hospitals. Goldberg's design was a clever expression of that rule. It also responded with precision to the medical methods of the era, leading to a solution that was both sophisticated and functional. But Prentice embodied a geometric rule as well: the rectangle is expandable; the circle is, at best, replicable. The rectangle is designed from the outside in, the circle from the inside out. As the institution grew, this rounded space resisted alteration. Goldberg could not add more beds or more floors, for example, without radically changing the structural equations that defined its elegance. The institution was evolving, but the building could not. Prentice reveals an elemental parameter: for the building to fully function, design must balance both flexibility *and* rigidity.

Form and Function

Historical hospital architecture can easily be interpreted as a measure of an era's particular essence of form. Architects experiment with variations of new formal ideas; enough similarity makes a type, enough type a movement. Goldberg's oeuvre of bulbous concrete towers fits neatly into a narrative of late heroic modernism, and his forms exemplify some key aspects of that era. Marina City, along the Chicago River, consists of twin, corncob-like icons of the city. Goldberg referred to their form as a "tremendous sunflower **(fig. 14)**."[5] These towers are rare examples of an architecture that transcends style to become symbolic and historic. Transcendent architecture, like Marina City, communicates cultural meaning over time and records the social order of a place, its shared values, beliefs, and history. Prentice was a demonstration of the evolution of a master builder and an example of his design in the city his work represented and spoke for — for this alone it deserved preservation.

But Prentice was not a masterpiece. It was at best a "wonderful oddball," as Michael Kimmelman has written, and at worst clunky.[6] Its two forms sat awkwardly together, like sections of a totem pole. Attempts to save the building included proposals for adapting the structure to meet contemporary needs. A last-ditch preservation effort by Chicago architect Jeanne Gang imagined the addition of a glass residential tower above the quatrefoil — a scheme more revealing of Prentice's inelegance than its timelessness. More precisely, the scheme made evident Prentice's elegance on top and its averageness below. Goldberg was right: it was two buildings. One was a powerful stylistic statement and the other wasn't a statement at all.

History has a tendency to simplify architecture into types, styles, and forms — a taxonomy that is often dismissive of structures' raisons d'être — and popular perceptions of architecture share this predilection. Why do structures look the way they do? And why should they be preserved, especially when they fall out of favor and enter functional obsolescence? (This takes, on average, forty years.) The task of answering these questions is left to an increasingly embattled frontline of architects and professional preservationists, who fight unbridled

5 Goldberg, "On the City," 1985, http://bertrand goldberg.org/resources /view/on-the-city-essay.

6 Michael Kimmelman, "A Vision to Avoid Demolition for a '70s Pioneer," *New York Times*, October 17, 2012.

14

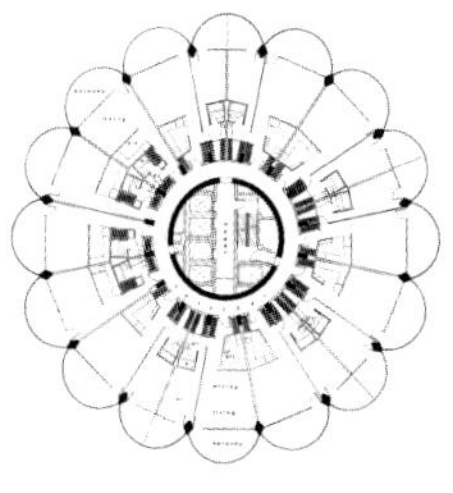

Chicago Federal Center, designed by Ludwig Mies van der Rohe, 1970 [fig. 12]

Section drawing, Prentice Women's Hospital, Chicago [fig. 13]

Prentice was really two different buildings, placed one on top of the other: a split personality.

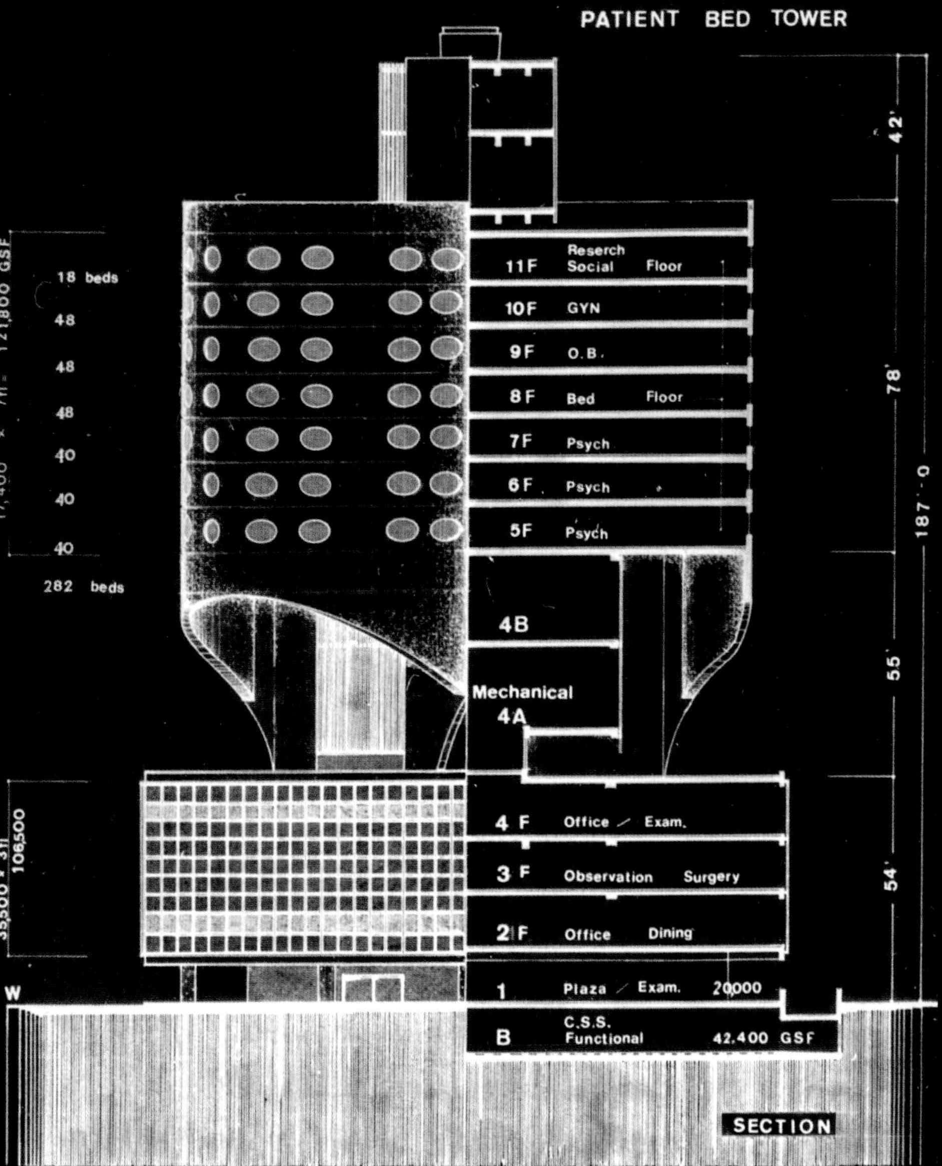

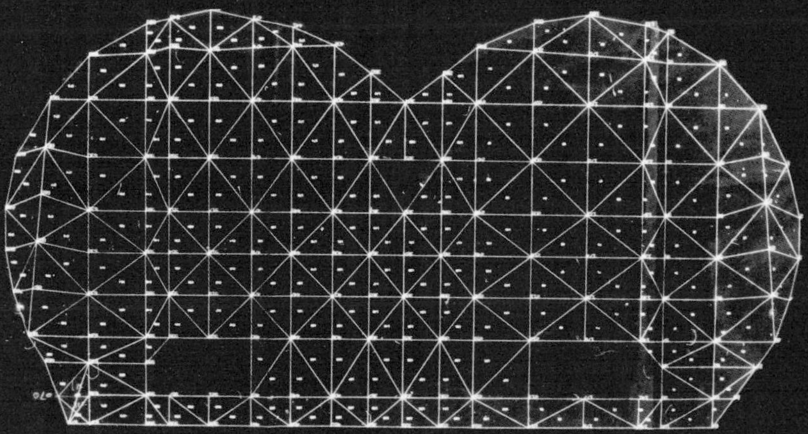

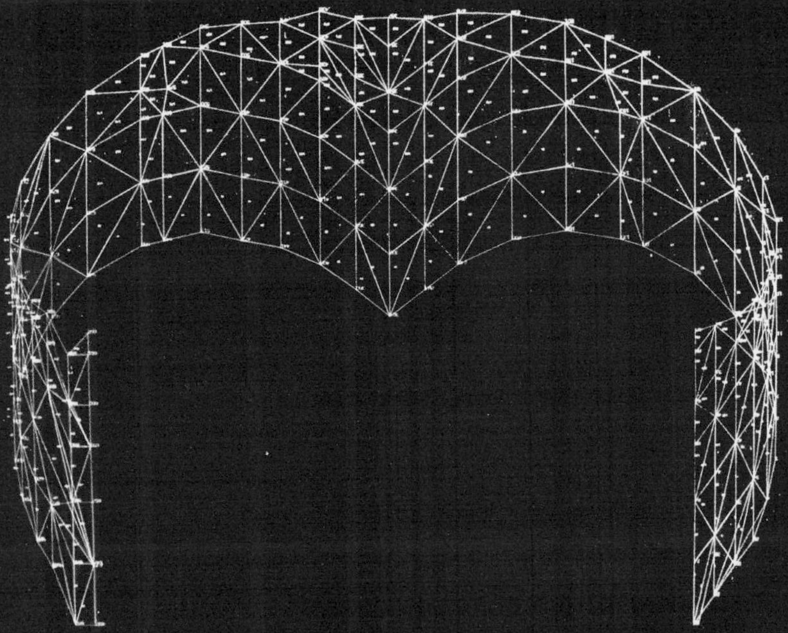

AutoCAD drawing for Prentice Women's Hospital, Chicago, designed by Bertrand Goldberg, 1971 [fig. 5]

Section and plan view of the panopticon prison, designed by Jeremy Bentham with Willey Reveley, 1791 [fig. 11]

Patient rooms, Prentice Women's Hospital, Chicago [fig. 8]

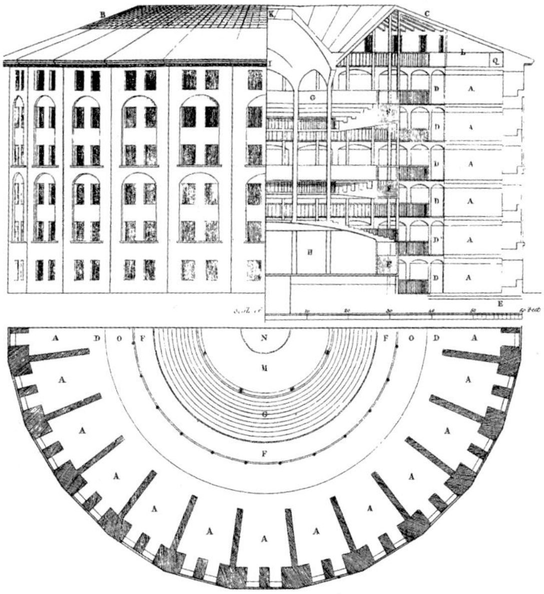

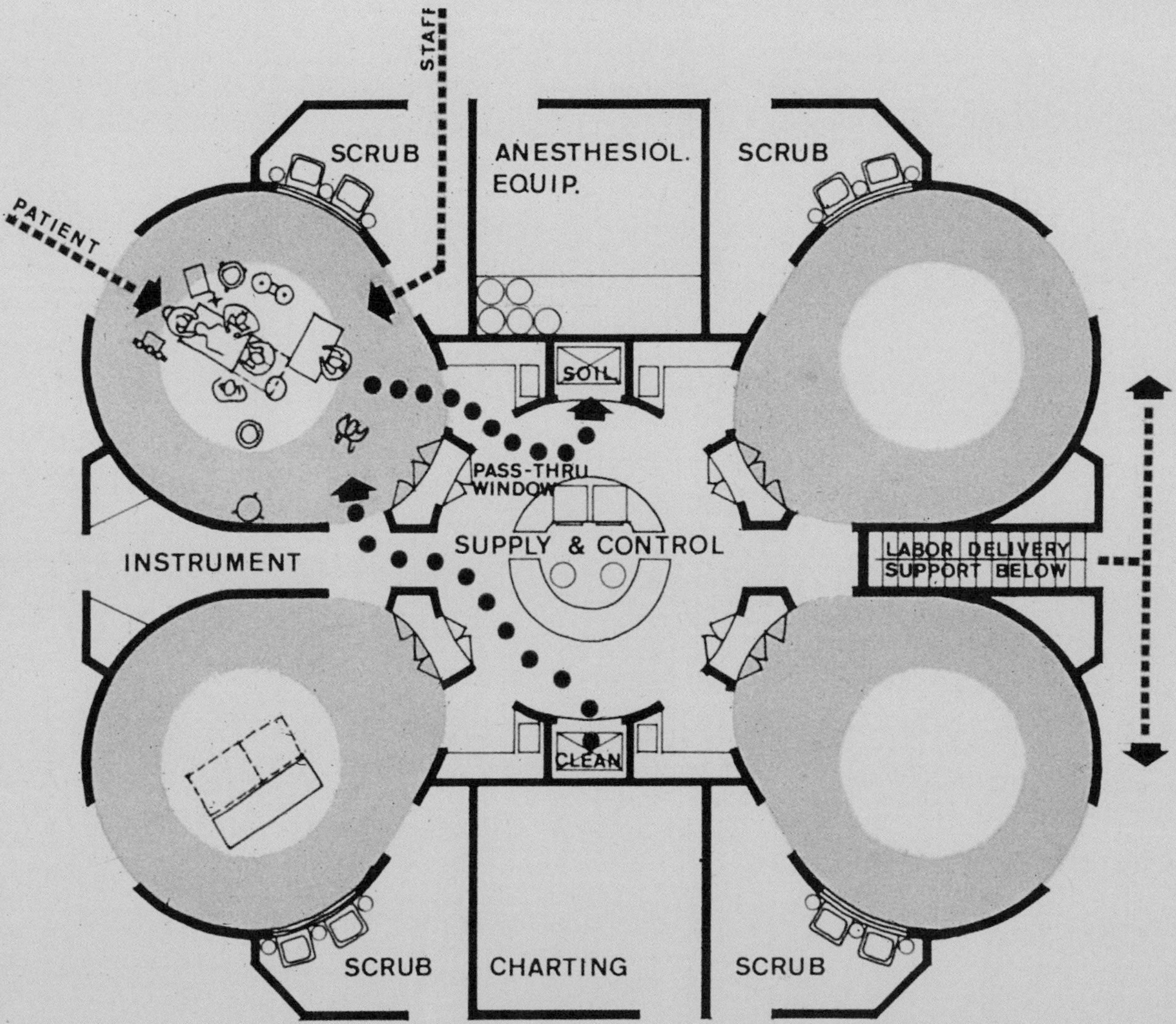
STAFF
PATIENT
SCRUB
ANESTHESIOL. EQUIP.
SCRUB
SOIL
PASS-THRU WINDOW
SUPPLY & CONTROL
INSTRUMENT
LABOR DELIVERY SUPPORT BELOW
CLEAN
SCRUB
CHARTING
SCRUB

Geocentric plan, Harvard Affiliated Hospitals, Boston [fig. 9]

Bertrand Goldberg's diagrams, various rounded-plan hospitals [fig. 10]

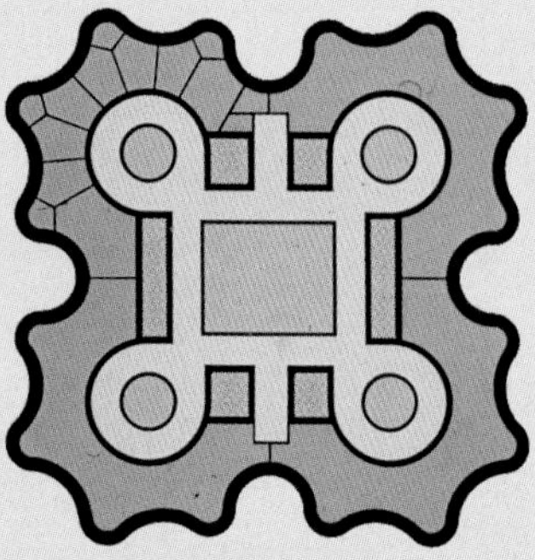

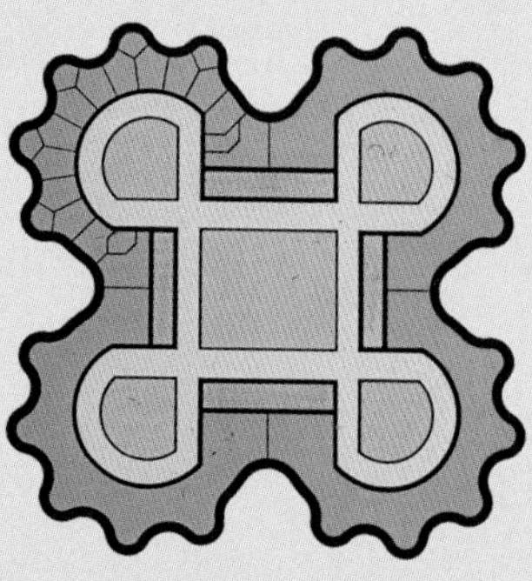

development and institutional agglomeration to protect exemplary historical projects from the wrecking ball.

But preservationist and architectural arguments, put to hospitals that require new space, can appear reactionary, stilted, cumbersome, and illogical if they do not take into account the functional requirements and public mission of the institutions. Northwestern Medicine, the company that ran Prentice, argued that lifesaving treatments would be hindered by the building's aged infrastructure, a contention that — whether accurate or not — positioned the architecture, regardless of its provenance or authorship, as merely stylistic and inessential (and in fact detrimental) to the mission of the institution. The architects rallying to save Prentice were battling the very powerful institution of modern health care, and, in defending the building's public value, they were also facing a moral question: should these forms be saved if they no longer functioned? The debate over Prentice took on a dramatic tenor, and the advocates for preservation lost.

Prentice offers an alternate architectural history. Behind the facades of the two contrasting forms was an admission that the functional requirements of a hospital necessitate two different formal responses. The top exemplifies the elemental ratio of nurse to patient; below is the control center of systems, operations, and technology. The architect Louis I. Kahn would have identified these spaces as the "servant" (the block) and the "served" (the clover). Both, however, are intimately implicated in the function of the hospital.

Historians and theoreticians of architecture generally ignore the hospital as a type or relegate it to a subvector of consideration. Hospitals are often, like Prentice, inelegant Frankensteins whose hints at the stylistic zeitgeist are often described through purer, less programmatically demanding examples. They are *too* functional. Their functional requirements are so demanding that the elegant architectural resolutions preservationists savor signal an exemplary project, inevitably compromised. However, if we read architecture through its purpose instead of its style, the hospital emerges as paradigmatic, essential, and even canonical. The history of hospitals is a Rosetta stone — a deciphering tool. It can unlock the elemental laws of architecture and thus the intractable human and social laws that architecture serves in each of our lives.

With his maxim "Form ever follows function," Louis Sullivan launched American modernism and with it the skyscraper and the distillation of architectural theory into natural law. In 1896, he wrote:

> Where function does not change, form does not change. The granite rocks, the ever-brooding hills, remain for ages; the lightning lives, comes into shape, and dies, in a twinkling. It is the pervading law of all things organic and inorganic, of all things physical and metaphysical, of all things human and all things superhuman, of all true manifestations of the head, of the heart, of the soul, that the life is recognizable in its expression, that form ever follows function. *This is the law.*[7]

Functionalism emerged in the early twentieth century as a description of the changing purpose of architecture, acknowledging its elemental

7 Louis Sullivan, "The Tall Office Building Artistically Considered," *Lippincott's Monthly Magazine* (March 1896): 403–9 (emphasis mine).

8 Charles Jencks, *The Language of Post-Modern Architecture*, rev. enlarged ed. (New York: Rizzoli, 1977), 9–10.

9 In 1970, sociologist Lee Rainwater claimed of Pruitt-Igoe that "no other public housing project in the country approaches it in terms of vacancies, tenant concerns and anxieties, or physical deterioration. Rather, Pruitt-Igoe condenses into one 57-acre tract all of the problems and difficulties that arise from race and poverty and all of the impotence, indifference, and hostility with which our society has so far dealt with these problems." See *Behind Ghetto Walls: Black Families in a Federal Slum* (Chicago: Aldine, 1970), 3.

reason for existence. Functionalist architecture prioritized a reading of the building as a change agent — in its use, not in its style — and inherently bound buildings to a social outcome.

If buildings can shape our lives and improve our health, can they also shape the broader social order? There is strong evidence of correlation between buildings and social or physiological outcomes. At least, this was the point of Nightingale's design for hospital wards: to inscribe in physical form a structure that would improve public health. And so the modern era's antecedents were born — not in the skyscraper, but in the hospital, where function is inseparable from form. This is the law.

In 1975, when Prentice opened its doors, architectural history and theory were in the process of transformation. By then branded as a failed social project, modernism had "died," Charles Jencks claimed, with the razing of the Pruitt-Igoe public housing project in St. Louis, Missouri, in 1972 (fig. 15).[8] Public good had not been achieved with the construction of Pruitt-Igoe; in fact, much the opposite. The modernist housing project, which had opened in 1954 to great fanfare, had become unlivable by 1970. The complex, designed by Minoru Yamasaki, was eventually dynamited in 1972, and sociologist Lee Rainwater argued that functionalist modernism deserved some of the blame for its failure.[9] In 1971, Adolfo Natalini of the Italian collective Superstudio declared that architecture was "one of the superstructures of power."[10] For Superstudio and other radical architects, modernism had become a tool of capitalism, alienating the masses and taking away their individuality and freedom.[11] "Post-functionalism," the architect Peter Eisenman theorized in 1976, would liberate architects from their social and behaviorist responsibilities.[12] In other words, form shouldn't follow function. Form should follow form.

And yet, there stood Prentice — proof that, despite the theories, post-functionalism could not be applied universally. Hospitals embody functionalism in two interrelated but distinct ways. One is the function that shapes behavior — *control*. The other is the function that shapes societal outcomes — *charity*. In the clover-shaped bed tower, nurses observed patients from a station designed equidistant from the patient rooms. Surveillance went both ways: it was designed to see and *be* seen. Both parties' experiences were shaped by a spatial configuration that eliminated blind corners, reduced staff needs, and increased responsiveness. The building worked to guide personal behavior and, therefore, personal health outcomes. This relationship of control, theorized by Michel Foucault as "biopower," links a building's design to its effectiveness at modifying human behavior.[13] In the hospital and the prison, this control is achieved through spatial planning. The hospital could not operate without it; nor could the medical system at large.

Through their second function — charity — hospitals create and serve a public they cannot fully know. At Prentice, the block building housed the hospital's services and technological systems, putting a rationalist plan to work to address the health of the masses. Like a factory floor, it was designed to maximize efficiency, reduce redundancy, and consolidate waste, air, and mechanical systems while also retaining enough flexibility to meet the indeterminate future needs of a changing system. Charity, in this context, conceives of the public as a whole, in

10 Adolfo Natalini, lecture at Architectural Association School of Architecture, London, March 3, 1971, quoted in *Superstudio: Life without Objects*, ed. Peter Lang and William Menking (Milan: Skira, 2003), 167.

11 See James Imam, "Architects Dreaming of a Future with No Buildings," *New York Times*, February 14, 2021.

12 Peter Eisenman, "Post-Functionalism," *Oppositions*, no. 6 (Fall 1976), repr. in *Architectural Theory since 1968*, ed. K. Michael Hays (Cambridge, MA: MIT Press, 1998), 234.

13 Michel Foucault, *The History of Sexuality*, vol. 1 (New York: Vintage, 1990), 140.

15

Floor plan, Marina City, Chicago [fig. 14]

Marina City, Chicago, designed by Bertrand Goldberg, 1968 [fig. 9]

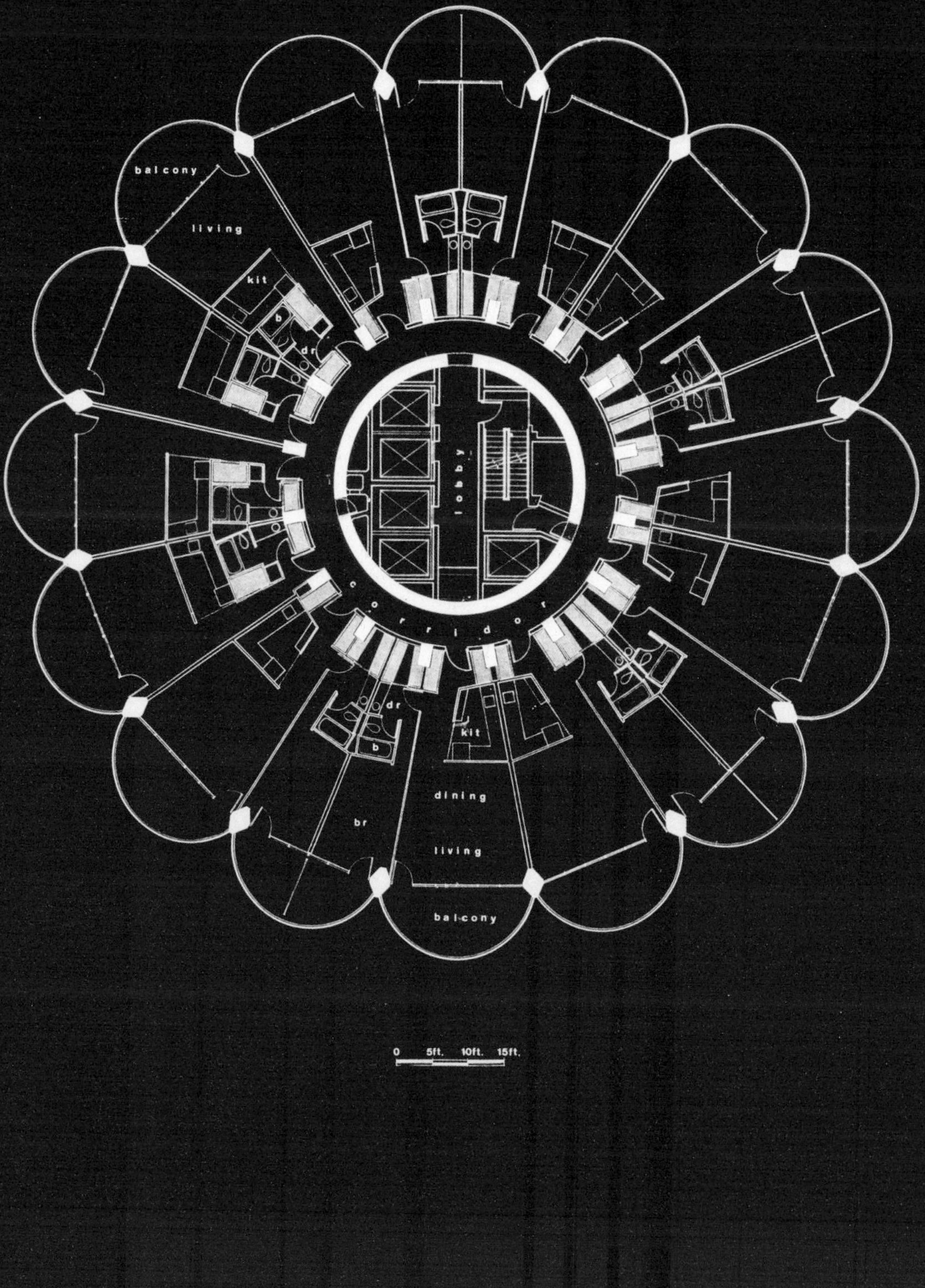

Transcendent architecture, like Marina City, communicates cultural meaning over time and records the social order of a place, its shared values, beliefs, and history.

14 Karl Marx, *Economic and Philosophic Manuscripts of 1844* (New York: International Publishers, 1964), 29.

need of service from the state. Public health is a function of a public and its access to, or injury from, environmental and social determinants of health. As Karl Marx theorized, concepts such as these can estrange individuals from their own humanity, alienating the individual as preference is given to the masses.[14] Hospital design, however, is predicated on population health data. And the hospital itself, as a public institution, originated from the charitable arms of the church, the state, and the elite. Without it, our collective rights — to health, for example — are impaired.

Success in the tower was measured in the patients' sense of being cared for and in their individual health outcomes. Success in the block, on the other hand, was tied to measurable improvements in public health. People's lives were unquestionably altered at Prentice, and it wouldn't have been possible without the assistance of the building itself. It is clear, therefore, that the medical system must be *designed*. In this system, two elemental architectural functions shape our personal and collective rights. These are charity and control. Inseparable from hospitals, they are imbricated in the very laws of the built environment.

Through the Contradictions

The 1970s critique of modernism should not be dismissed. Negligent utopias, alienating superblocks, dehumanizing megastructures, irreconcilable planning strategies, and the corporatist adoption of efficiency should all give architects pause. But in relation to the hospital, the aspiration to liberate architects from their social and behaviorist tendencies is a mere provocation, a hollow creed, impossible to square with the elemental functionality of the medical building. Architecture can be sculptural, beautiful, cultural, and inspiring — but also inessential and a luxury. In a hospital, however, architecture is essential. It impacts our rights as individuals.

All of this is likely why the hospital has been largely understudied in the history of architecture. Its complications are prevalent, its authorship multiheaded, its forms jumbled, incoherent, inelegant, and bipolar. And yet, at each moment of historical architectural change there is a hospital: a structure both of its time and following timeless laws of functionality.

Through the hospital, architecture emerges at various moments of history as elemental, rights based, and essential. The hospital also subverts a critique of architecture that labels it as either authoritarian or liberating, instead emerging as both — as a public service that must also serve the individual, as an instrument of both control and charity. How well does a building accommodate and enable those sometimes competing rights and functions? That is the premise of evaluation. As in medicine or law, it is possible to unlock and work through the contradictions between the individual and the collective. It is hard work, but it is *the* work.

Built projects that fail to achieve balance and elegance should be critiqued for their inability to resolve the dual functionality of all buildings. Those that do resolve it stand timeless, exemplary, iconic, and instructive. They are transcendent and should be preserved. The rise and fall of Prentice is a story about the design and life of hospitals — how they are born and evolve, the forces that give them shape, and the powers that conspire to render them inadequate (fig. 16). It is also a window into the reasons hospital architecture matters. It is not because we should care about buildings for buildings' sake, but because without those buildings and their functionality, our social fabric would tear. The hospital proves that architecture is a human right.

16

Demolition of Prentice
Women's Hospital, Chicago,
2014 [fig. 16]

Typologies
a Taxonomy
of Type

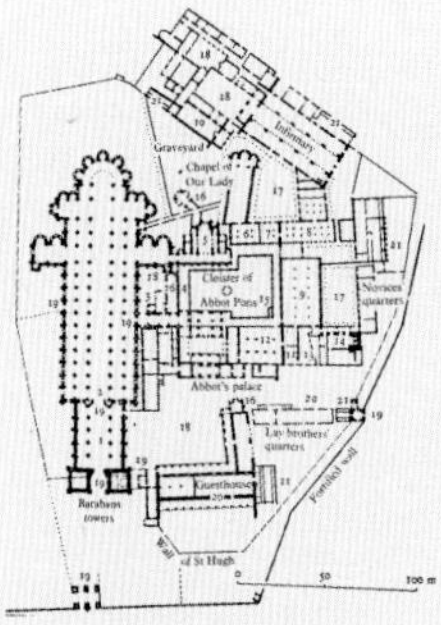

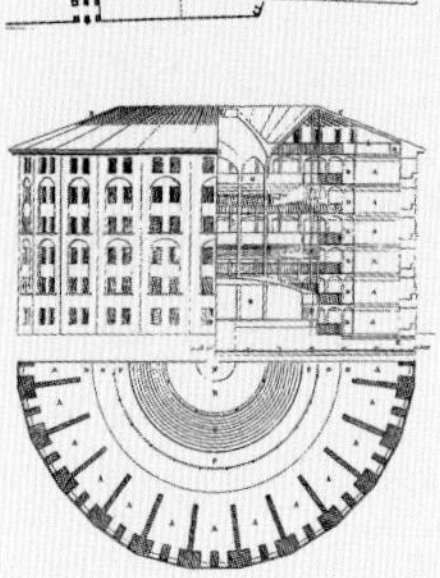

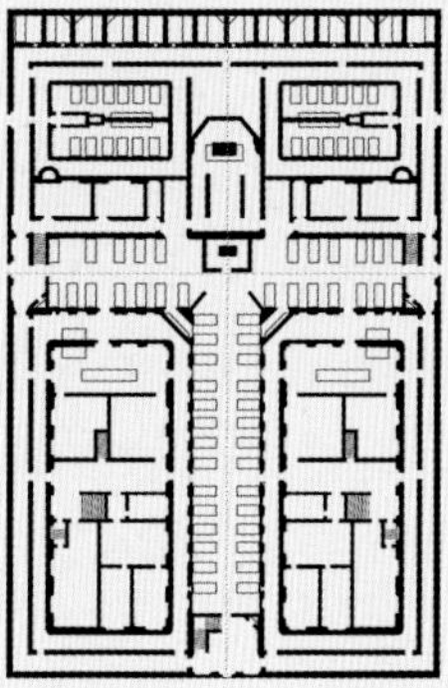

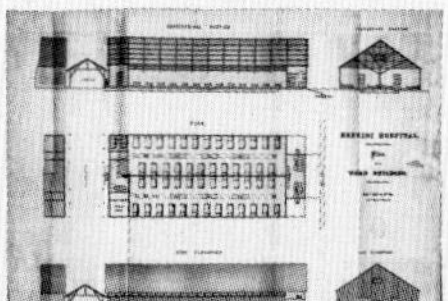

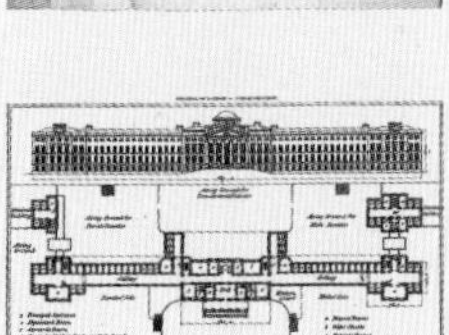

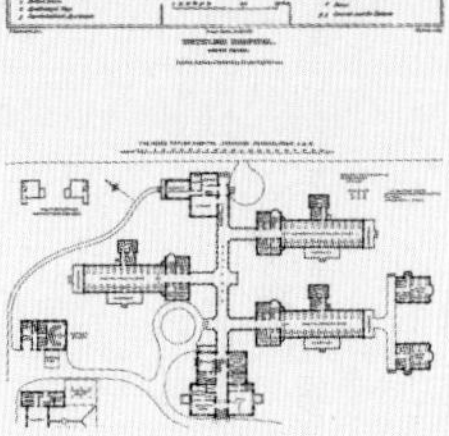

Each historical era created its own unique hospital type that responded to the practice of health care and medicine in that period. An analysis of these hospital types reveals how their designers conceptualized care and the role architecture could play in delivering it. Beginning with the basilica and the cross ward (the first "designed" hospital in Europe) and moving through subsequent types, a history of the hospital — one of architecture's most confounding and evolving typologies — provides us with a conceptual framework in which to imagine future hospitals and, perhaps, reimagine assumptions about architecture itself.

Basilica (c. 900–1800)

Monastery of Cluny, France, 909–1131

In antiquity, the basilica was a large, open public meeting hall used to transact business or host large audiences. As Christianity rose in status, the pagan temples of the Roman Empire fell out of favor, and basilicas were adopted as religious buildings. During the Middle Ages, they were used as churches and cathedrals. As a growing number of people sought care and refuge, the basilica and the hospital merged in the monasteries of St. Gall, Switzerland (c. 747), and Cluny, France (c. 910), where the sick and wounded were given shelter. The basilica hospital — generally a large, open ward with an altar at one end — reached a crisis in Paris's Hôtel-Dieu in the late eighteenth century, when a swelling patient population undermined its ability to provide efficient care.

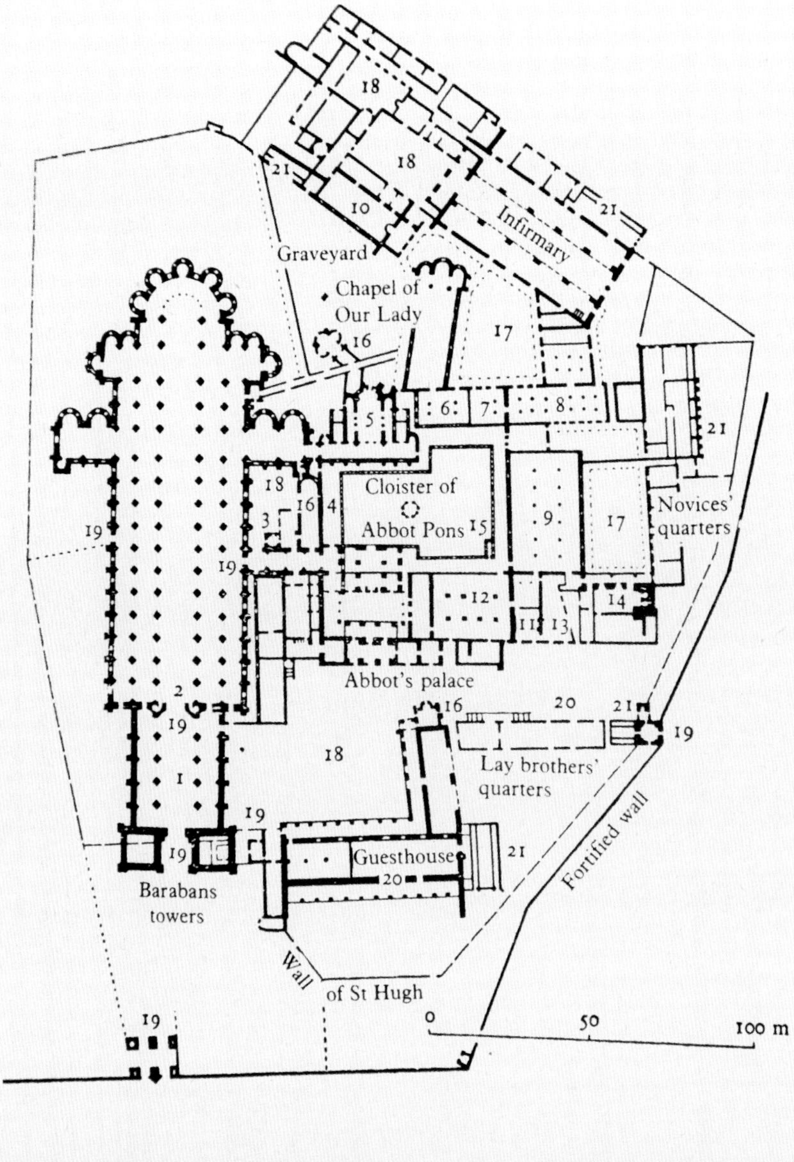

Cross ward (c. 1400–1700)

The cross-ward hospital emerged during the Renaissance as a solution for ward expansion. Previously, the typical expansion strategy was to lengthen the wards (width being limited by the vaulting methods of the time), but this had the disadvantage of positioning some patients — those at the end of the ward — too far from the altar to hear Mass. The cross-ward hospital solved this problem by creating four open wards at ninety degrees to each other with an altar at the center, thus quadrupling the hospital's capacity without compromising any patient's access to prayer. The most famous architect of the cross ward was the Italian Antonio di Pietro Averlino, known as Filarete, who published his plans for the Ospedale Maggiore in Milan in his *Treatise on Architecture* in 1465. That hospital, influential across Europe, featured two crossed wards, one each for male and female patients, and eight courtyards between them.

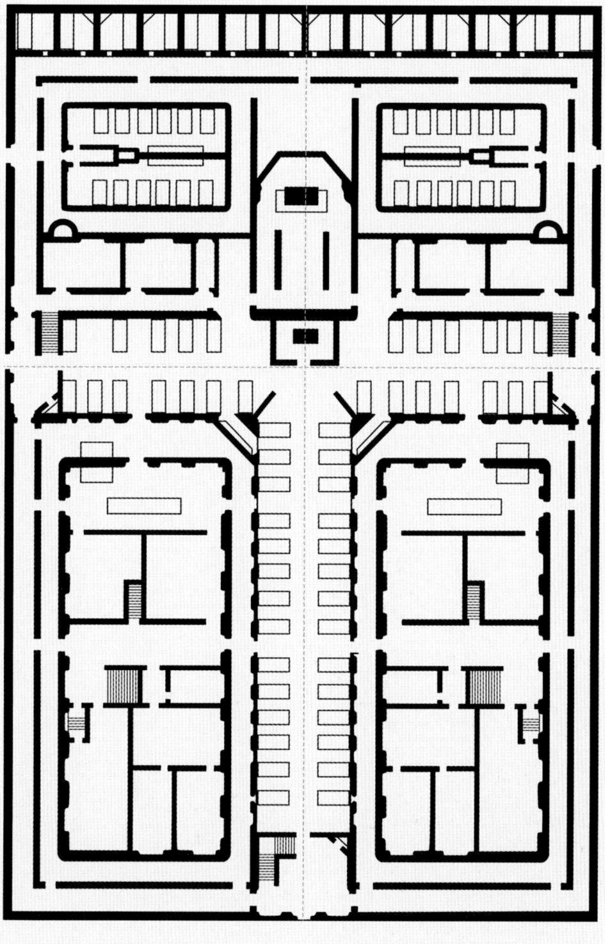

Hospital in the form of a Roman cross, designed by Joseph Furttenbach, 1655 (redrawn by MASS Design Group)

Panoptic (c. 1800–1900, 1960–70)

The panopticon prison, designed by Jeremy Bentham with Willey Reveley, 1791

In panoptic hospitals, influenced by Jeremy Bentham's eighteenth-century panopticon prison design, ward configurations maximize sight lines from nurses' stations to patient beds. Panopticism has been a recurring theme in hospital design, dating back to the cross-ward hospital, a radial design in which pavilion wards converged at a central core. This configuration provided for outdoor space between the wards while connecting each to the administrative center of the institution, improving the supervision of patients. Due to the enhanced level of surveillance it enabled, the radial design was adopted in several asylums, military hospitals, and prisons, including the Glasgow Lunatic Asylum (c. 1814) and the Eastern State Penitentiary in Pennsylvania (c. 1829). In the mid-twentieth century, panoptic designs reemerged, featuring the nurses' station at the center and patient beds ringing the exterior wall.

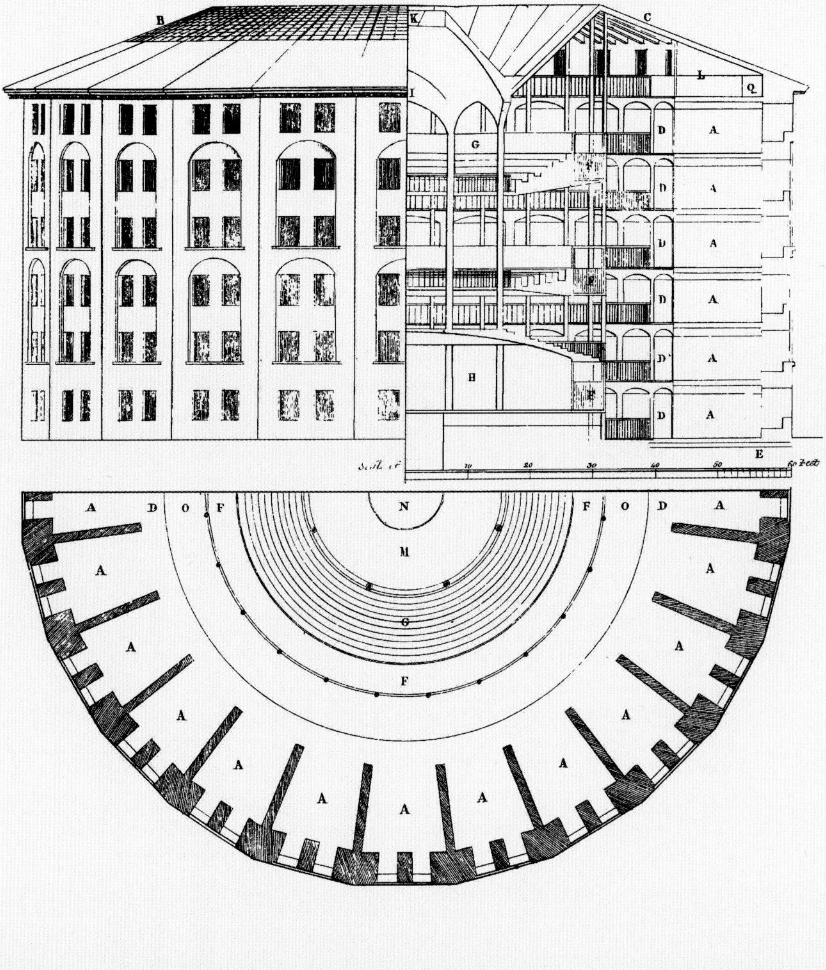

Manor (c. 1600–1800)

The Reformation led to the destruction of many of Britain's religious hospitals, which largely served the poor. In the aftermath, a committee of wealthy patrons banded together to rebuild the country's charity hospitals. They chose a form familiar to them: the manor house. Manor houses were generally classical in style, with an exacting symmetry that lent itself to a gender-segregated ward plan. The grandeur of the style, however, required aligned doors, creating a configuration in which rooms at the end of a floor could be accessed only by walking through the other wards, and privacy was minimal. The manor was exported beyond Britain: Philadelphia's Pennsylvania Hospital, the first hospital in what would become the United States, was completed in 1755 in the manor style, with male and female patients each allocated a wing and administration offices and an apothecary located in the central structure.

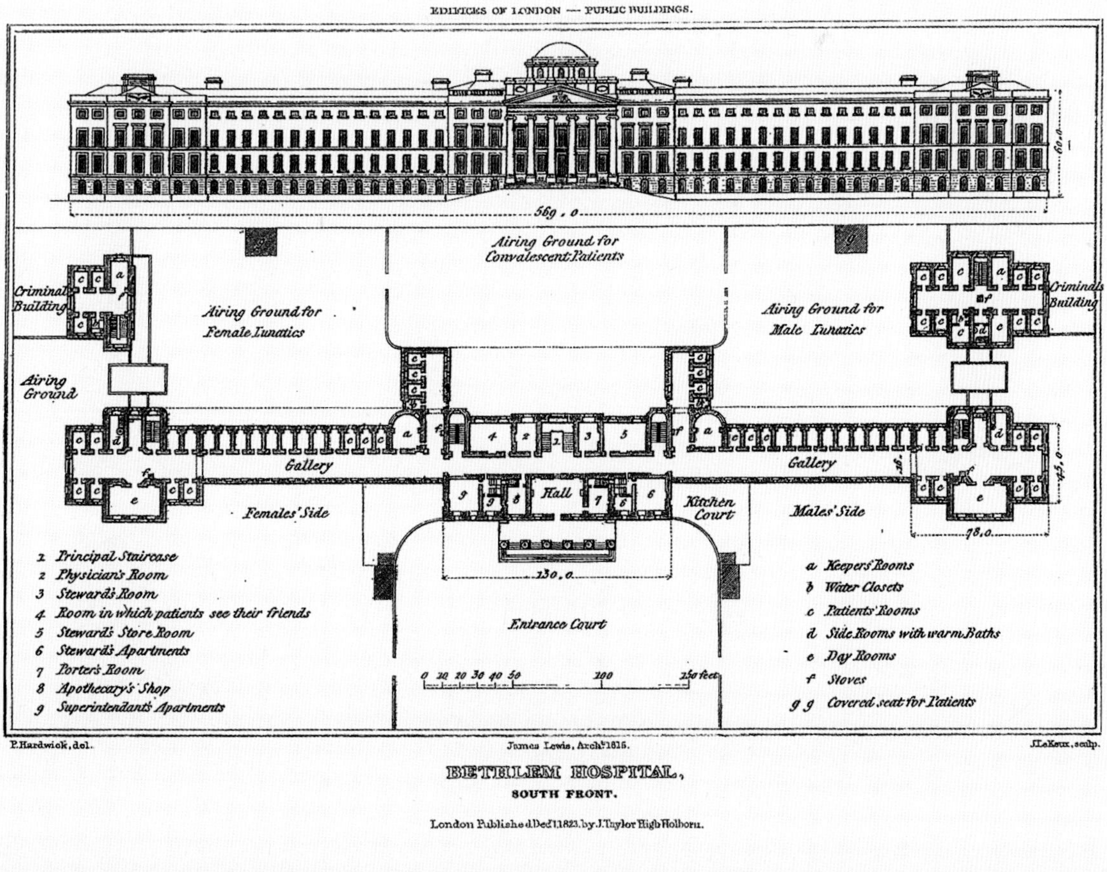

Bethlehem Royal Hospital, London, designed by James Lewis, 1815

Field Hospital / Barracks (c. 1800–)

Quick to deploy and easy to assemble and expand, the barracks hospital is often used when a new facility is urgently needed, as in times of war or natural disaster. Like the temporary soldiers' lodgings they evolved from, these hospitals are frequently conceived as kits of parts and prefabricated off-site or constructed with simple, cheap, and readily available materials. With their compromised ventilation, airflow, and construction, they are not necessarily designed for optimal patient comfort and safety. However, in some cases, such as the Chris Hani Baragwanath Hospital in Johannesburg and the tent hospitals set up in Haiti after the 2010 earthquake, barracks hospitals continue to serve a sizable population well past their intended life span.

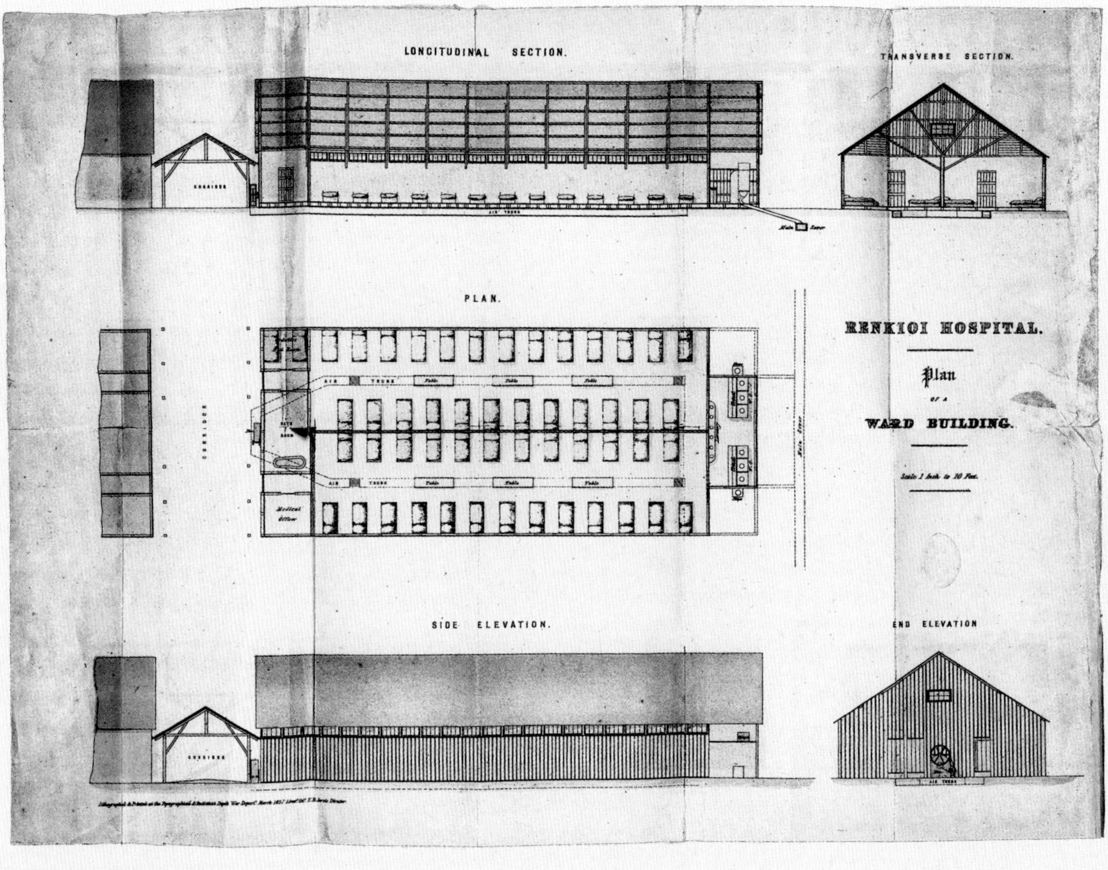

Renkioi Hospital, single-ward drawings by Isambard Kingdom Brunel, 1857

Pavilion (c. 1800–1900)

In the late eighteenth century, a scientific model of hospital design was developed with the goal of maximizing the quality and efficiency of care. The pavilion plan, popularized by Florence Nightingale in her 1859 book *Notes on Hospitals*, called for open wards of limited length and width, naturally ventilated with windows along the long walls, with doors along the short walls, and joined to a circulation spine that connected the wards and provided storage and service space. The pavilion was remarkable for maximizing airflow: Peter Bent Brigham Hospital in Boston (1913) achieved five air changes per hour through a ventilation strategy that combined ordinary wall windows, windows in the roof, heating coils in stacks, and inlet and outlet fans. Patients also spent significant time outdoors in the wards' pergolas, sunrooms, and verandas.

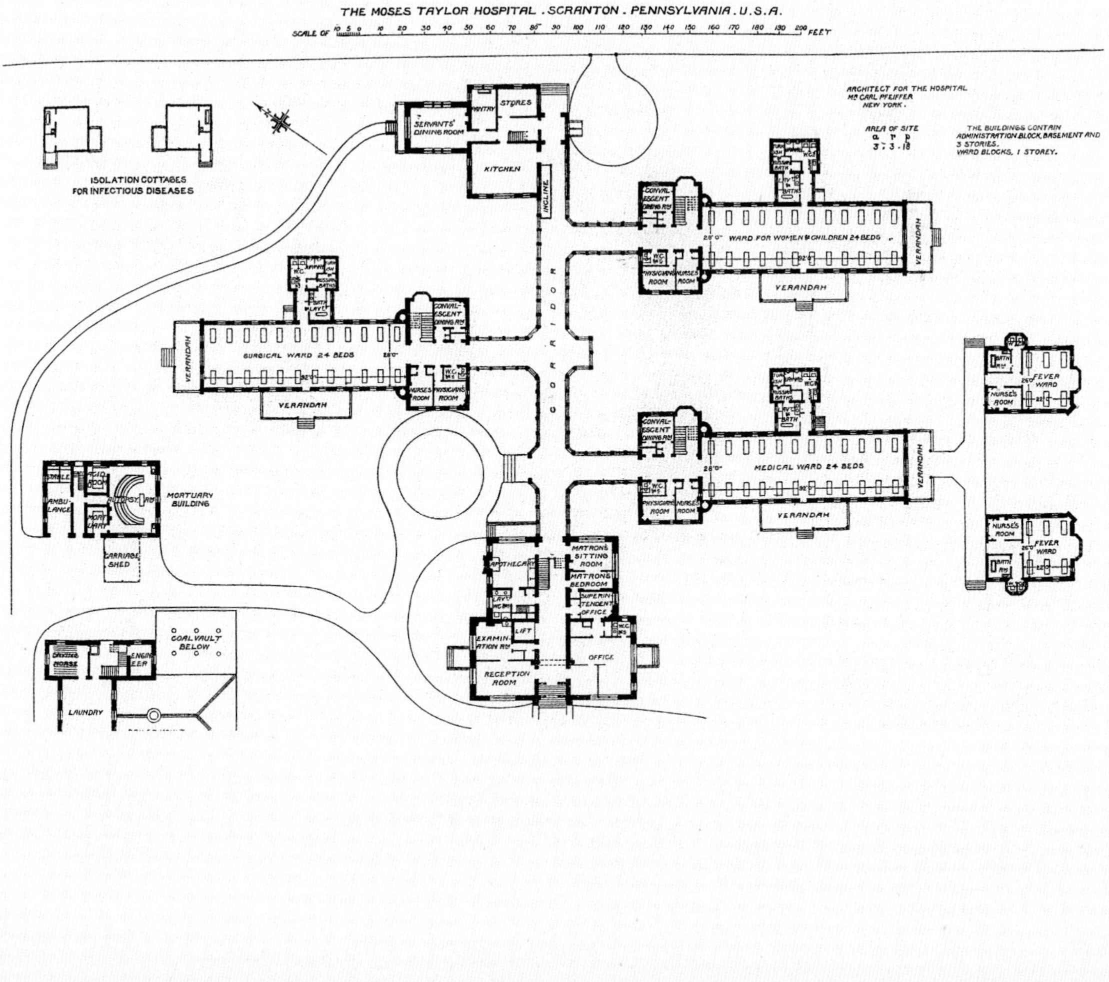

Moses Taylor Hospital, Scranton, Pennsylvania, designed by Carl Pfeiffer, 1892

Bar (c. 1900–40)

Old Main Hospital, Ann Arbor, Michigan, designed by Albert Kahn, 1925

In the early twentieth century, improvements in sanitary practices and the invention of new medical technology drew middle- and upper-class patients to the hospital for the first time. The resulting architecture type, the bar hospital, was an amalgam of old open wards for the poor and new private rooms for the wealthy, all with attention to optimal lighting, ventilation, and airflow. This era also saw the rise of more complex planning strategies to improve efficiency and supervision and accommodate an expanding technical apparatus and increasing medical specialization. For example, Albert Kahn designed the Old Main Hospital in Ann Arbor, Michigan (1925), using concepts of scientific management and productivity he had used in his design of the Ford Motor Company's Highland Park plant in Detroit (1910).

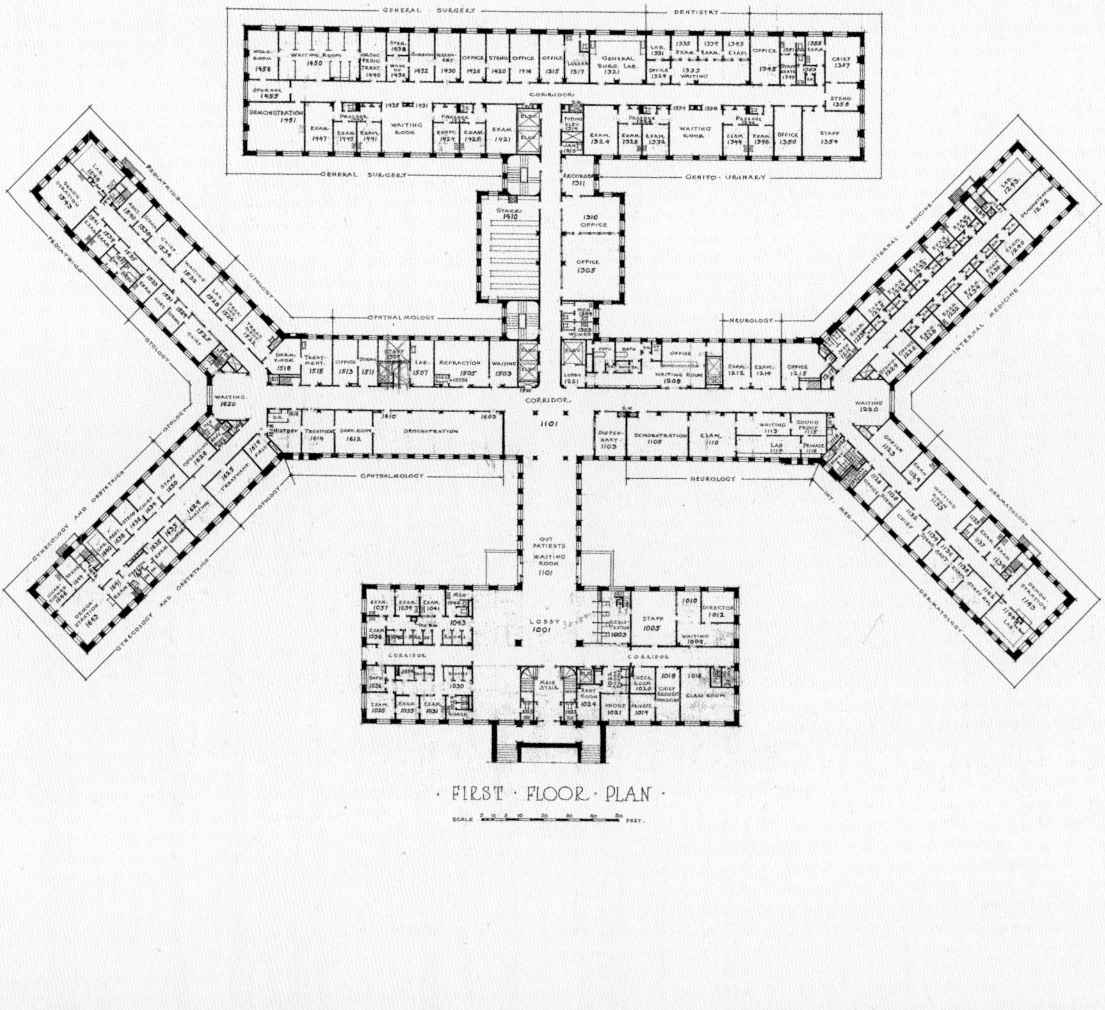

Block (c. 1950–)

The block was the dominant hospital style of the mid-twentieth century. It was born in the era of "machine medicine," amid the proliferation of new health care technologies and the growing cultural perception of medicine as an almost miraculous science capable of curing previously intractable health problems. The block hospital is characterized by a minimal modernist style, specialized zones for different services, a monolithic form, and reliance on long-span structural and HVAC systems. Above all, the design prioritizes space for technology and planning for staff performance. In block hospitals such as New York's Bellevue New Building (1973), vast areas of the interior lack windows or other natural lighting, and existing windows are sealed so that the indoor environment can be mechanically controlled.

Bellevue Hospital "New Building," New York, designed by Pomerance and Breines in association with Katz, Waisman, Weber, Strauss, and Blumenkranz, 1973 (redrawn by MASS Design Group)

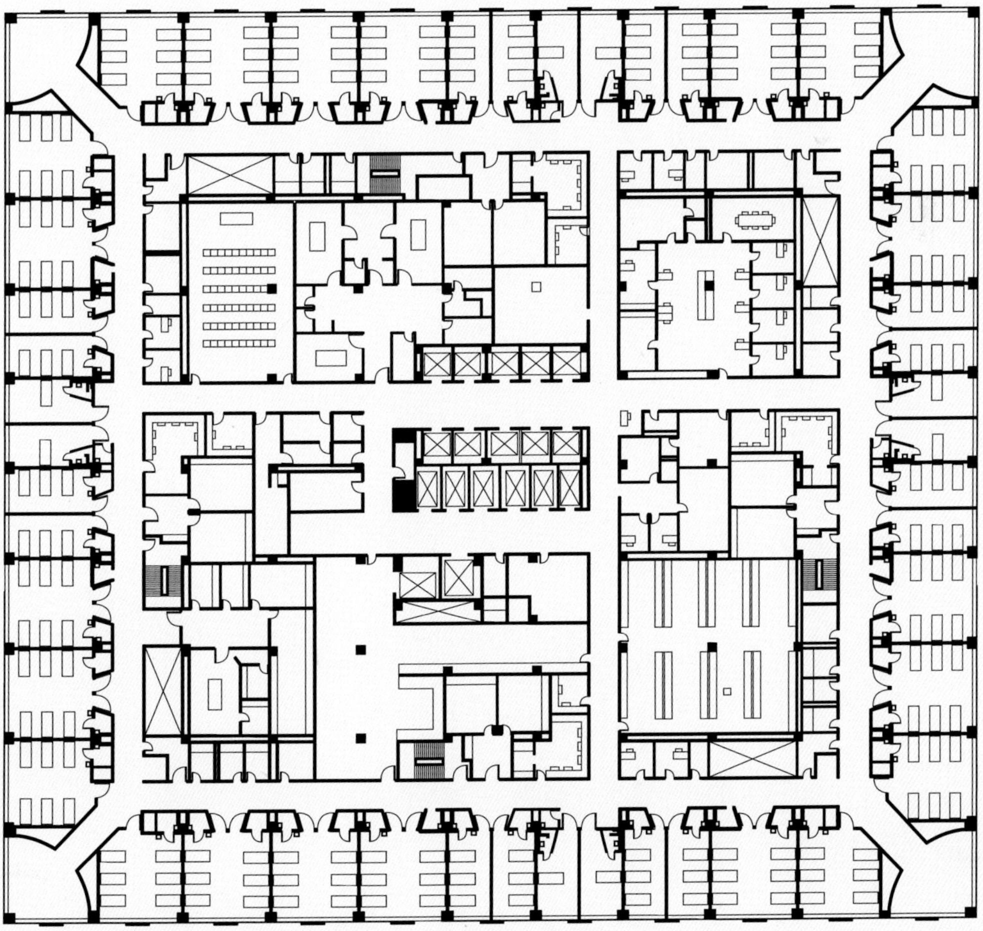

Utopian (c. 1960–70)

Concept section of Marine Hospital, E. Todd Wheeler, 1971

In the mid-twentieth century, the block type was ubiquitous in hospital design. There were, however, a few exceptions, and these can accurately be characterized as utopian. Utopian designs had little in common beyond an aspiration to defy the logic of the block (at least superficially). Most historical examples in the United States come from E. Todd Wheeler, a partner at health care giant Perkins and Will from 1936 to 1972. Wheeler presented a number of radical concepts for hospitals of the future, attempting to address the biggest challenges in hospital design at the time: controlling the environment (in underwater and tent hospital designs) and facilitating flexibility and expansion (in designs for tree and tent hospitals). Other sketches incorporate cultural tropes such as drive-in theaters and atria.

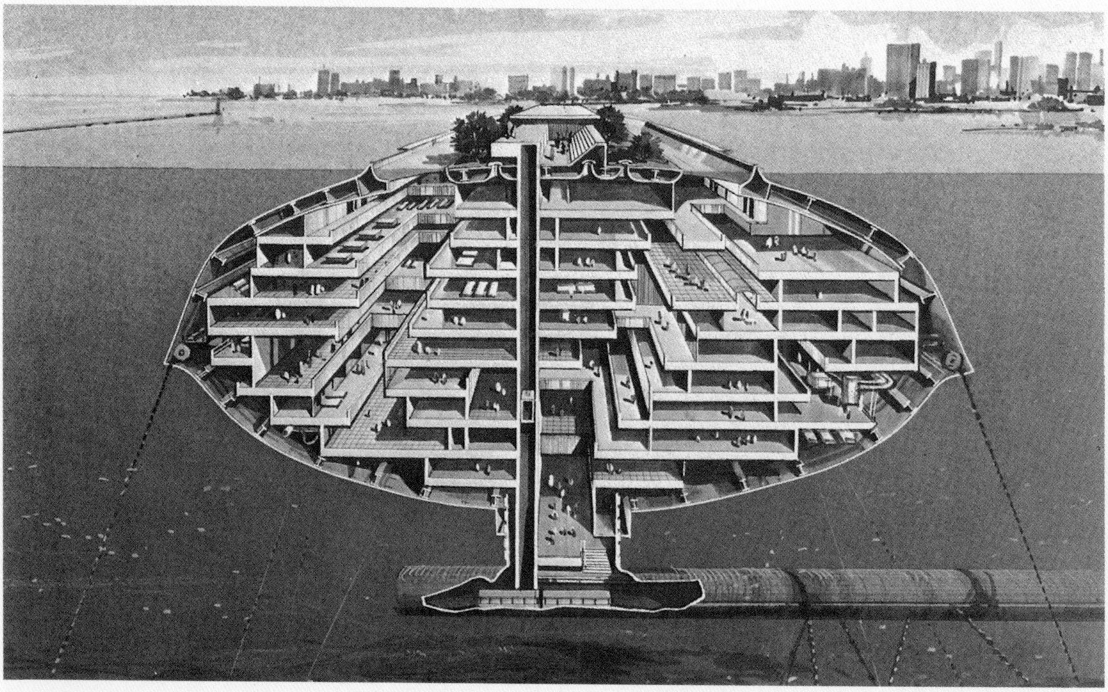

Mega-Hospital (c. 1960–80)

The mega-hospital arose as a response to the ever-increasing needs of the medical machine and the public sector. Speculative and seldom built, these megastructures decentered form in favor of the function and demands of a system, and were intended to change and resist obsolescence over time. One of the most dynamic mega-hospitals ever built is the McMaster University Health Sciences Center in Hamilton, Ontario (1972), a massive city-scale superstructure to which floors, bays, modules, and districts can be added when necessary. McMaster is also an interstitial hospital, a form of mega-hospital that is characterized by alternating spaces: one floor for the undefined and evolving, and the next for the controlled and precise. At McMaster, for example, every second floor is dedicated solely to medical and building technology.

McMaster University Health Sciences Center, Hamilton, Ontario, designed by Craig, Zeidler and Strong, 1972

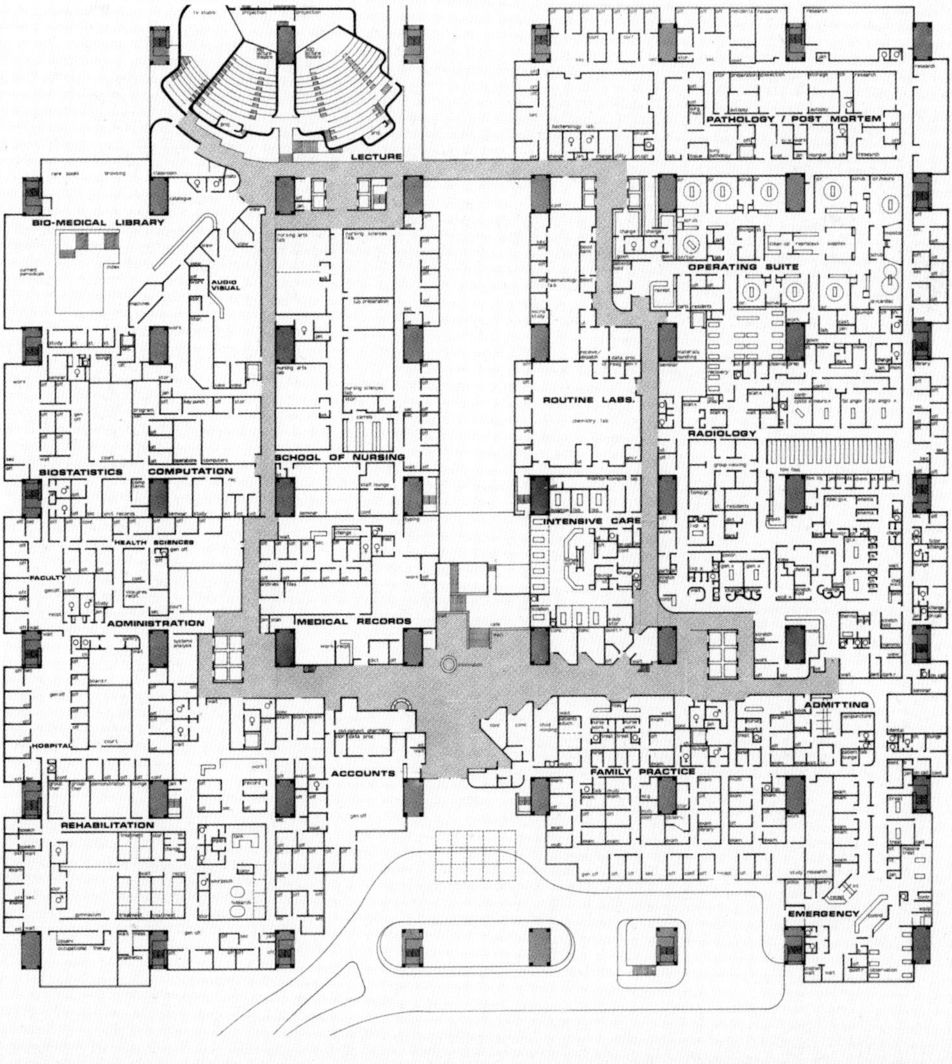

Mat (c. 1960–90)

Wexham Park Hospital, Slough, England, designed by Powell and Moya with Llewelyn-Davies, Weeks, and Partners, 1965

Mat buildings became popular across sectors in the late 1950s and early 1960s owing to the work of the architecture group Team X, particularly Alison Smithson, Peter Smithson, and Aldo van Eyck. The mat type — which consists of a nonformal, horizontal series of spaces and courtyards — is rare, however, in health care, perhaps because it entails significant walking distances for staff. The first and most famous mat hospital, designed in the 1960s (though never built), is Le Corbusier's Venice (Italy) Hospital. Another mat hospital of the era is Wexham Park Hospital in Slough, England (1965), designed by Powell and Moya. There, hospital administration is housed in a large central tower surrounded by single-story patient wards.

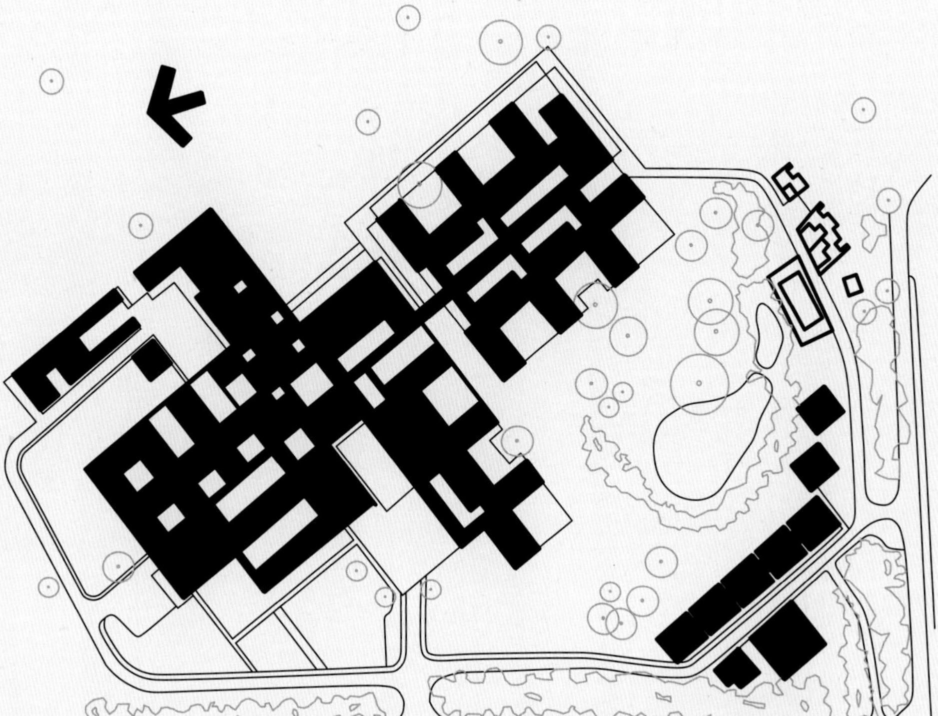

Labyrinth (c. 1960–)

Most hospitals eventually, through expansion and amalgamation, unintentionally become labyrinths: spaces difficult and confusing to navigate. But some designers in the late mid-twentieth century sought to harness the labyrinth to fight the sense of institutionalization that health care settings perpetuated. They introduced labyrinthine elements to create an experience of discovery and delight and to counter the hegemony of modernist design. Boston's Erich Lindemann Mental Health Center (1971), designed by Paul Rudolph, is a prime example. The amalgam hospital, another labyrinth form, is the result of the expansion of a single hospital through successive eras of care; this is the hospital as campus. For example, Massachusetts General Hospital (1811) and Brigham and Women's Hospital (1913), both in Boston, are sprawling campuses of buildings expanded on an ad hoc basis as they grew, added specializations, or reached functional obsolescence.

Erich Lindemann Mental Health Center, Boston, designed by Paul Rudolph, 1971

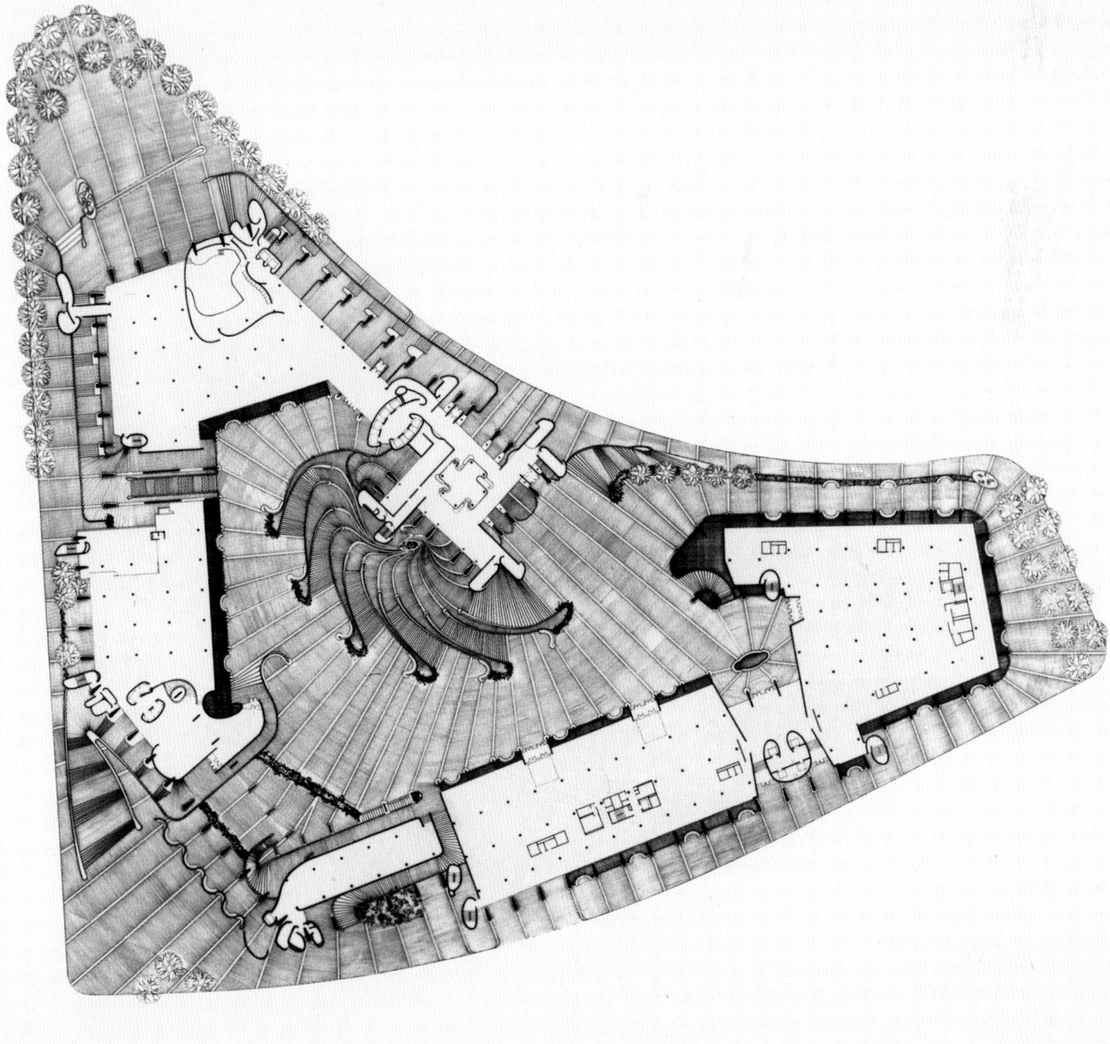

Chapter 1
Charity and Control: The Birth of the Hospital

Ospedale Maggiore, Milan

The history and theory of hospital architecture has been understudied and relegated to subspecialty. Of the few texts that trace the architectural historiography of the hospital, John D. Thompson and Grace Goldin's foundational 1975 book, *The Hospital: A Social and Architectural History*, stands out as an essential primer.[1] In it Thompson and Goldin explain that from antiquity to the Renaissance, medical spaces in Europe were generally inherited structures, such as chapels or basilicas, retrofitted with beds. By the mid-fifteenth century, however, with the growth of city-states such as Milan and Florence, purpose-built health care institutions were not only possible but necessary. The most prominent and influential of these was the Ospedale Maggiore in Milan, designed by Antonio di Pietro Averlino (c. 1400–1469), known as Filarete.[2]

In the mid-1440s, Duke Francesco Sforza summoned the young sculptor to Milan. At that point, Filarete (meaning "lover of virtue") had spent the last decade creating a single bronze door for Pope Eugenius IV. The duke was impressed by Filarete's craftsmanship and (we must assume) his patience, and he commissioned him to design a new hospital "for sick men and women, and the innocent children born of wedlock."[3] The result, a campus of multiple buildings organized orthogonally, would influence the design of hospitals around the world for centuries to come. Ordered and symmetrical, it was, Thompson and Goldin observed, not derived from the contours of the land but rather designed on the page, siteless and idealized.

The Ospedale Maggiore, designed around 1456 and finally completed more than three centuries later, was a massive, almost fortress-like structure. Beyond its exterior wall, the campus was organized in two identical squares — one for men and one for women — each made up of long buildings (patient wards) joined together in a cross formation, creating eight open courtyards (fig. 1). Between the two squares, in the center of the plan, was a rectangular yard with a chapel (fig. 2).[4] The Ospedale Maggiore's most significant break with the past was its scale, but it also implied a change in the conception of the public, signaling the importance bestowed by the Milanese aristocracy on controlling public health.

1

2

Architecture's DNA

Filarete's design signaled the emergence of the hospital as a public institution. The new establishment communicated the charitable largesse of the city-state and its responsibilities to its subjects: the sick would no longer be isolated into leprosaria outside the city walls or coddled until their deaths in converted rural basilicas. The scope and purpose of the hospital was crystallized in the four distinct architectural features in Filarete's drawings: the bed, the altar, the window, and the privy — the institution's DNA.

The Bed

The bed is a key unit in the scale of a hospital. Compared to a fifty-bed facility, a three-hundred-bed hospital demands much more of what Dr. Paul Farmer has called "space, stuff, systems, and staff."[5] The bed is an index for the patient. The hospital, as it developed, gave a location to clinical medicine and became a laboratory in which the patient is, Michel Foucault argued, "transform[ed] into an object of clinical observation."[6] In the Ospedale Maggiore, the public was newly visible and observable, and it could, in turn, envision the authority of salvation in the figure of the attending professional. Healing and cure became spatial, and a contract of power emerged between the professional and the public.

The Altar

Before the Renaissance, the hospital ward was a large open space with high ceilings, large windows, and an apse at one end for an altar **(figs. 3, 4)**. As with the basilicas that wards were often derived from, the space was configured to amplify the priest's prayers from the altar, where Mass was delivered throughout the day — as the word of God was thought to be curative. As the number of patients grew and the wards expanded, they ran up against the spatial limits of audible speech. To address this, in the Ospedale Maggiore Filarete placed the altar at the center of a cross formation, where four open wards met, making prayer audible to four times as many patients. This is the cross-ward hospital, an innovation that quadrupled the individuals served and made possible a larger, more centralized medical institution.

The nurses' station, eventually replacing the altar as the sensory locus of the hospital ward, determines the relationship between staff and patient. For hospitals to function, staff members must be able to observe the patients and communicate with them. The bed and the nurses' station are defined in relationship to each other. This is the essential ratio of the hospital, for it influences the experience of both patients and staff, in effect making behavioral control spatially determinable. The relationship among the beds constructs the public, deindividualizing the patients and eliding their unique experiences and needs.

The Window

As a feature that can be opened and closed, the window provides patients with agency in relation to their personal needs. The window modulates the environmental and physiological impacts of airflow, filtering the climatic conditions of the world outside into the interior. Before

1 For a thorough summary of historical studies on hospital architecture, see Jeanne Kisacky, "Bibliographic Essay," in *Rise of the Modern Hospital: An Architectural History of Health and Healing, 1870–1940* (Pittsburgh, PA: University of Pittsburgh Press, 2017), 407–26.

2 John D. Thompson and Grace Goldin, *The Hospital: A Social and Architectural History* (New Haven, CT: Yale University Press, 1975), 31.

3 Giorgio Vasari, *Lives of the Most Eminent Painters, Sculptors, and Architects*, vol. 3, *Filarete and Simone to Mantegna*, trans. Gaston du C. de Vere (London: Macmillan and Medici Society, 1912–14), 4.

4 Thompson and Goldin, *The Hospital*, 31–35.

5 Paul Farmer, *Fevers, Feuds, and Diamonds: Ebola and the Ravages of History* (New York: Farrar, Straus and Giroux, 2020), 42.

6 Michel Foucault, *The Birth of the Clinic: An Archaeology of Medical Perception* (London: Tavistock, 1973), 83.

3

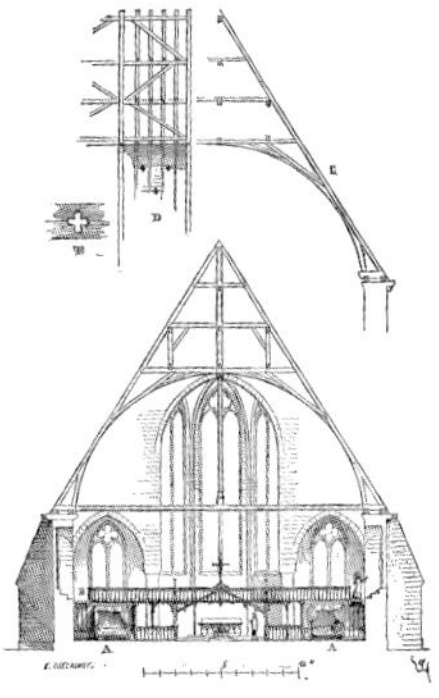

4

Plan of the Ospedale Maggiore, Milan [fig. 1]

Ward at the Ospedale Maggiore, Milan, designed by Filarete (Antonio di Pietro Averlino), 1456 [fig. 4]

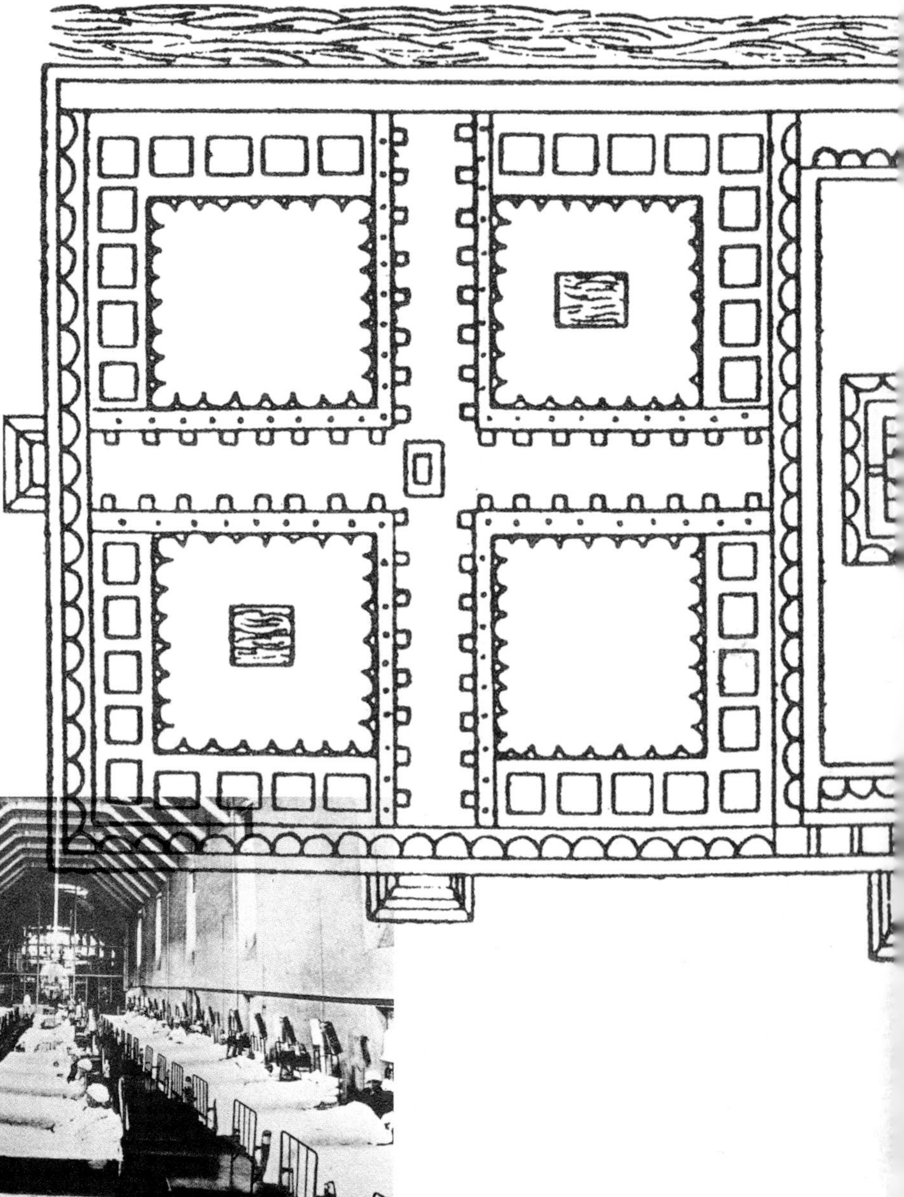

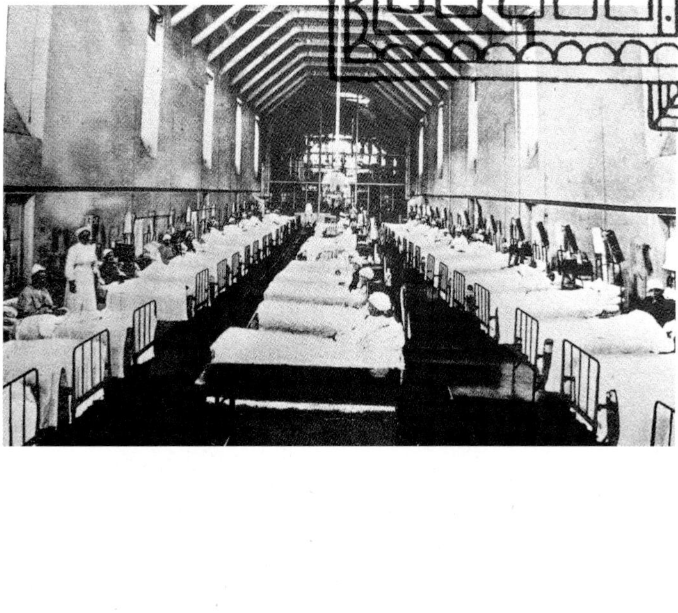

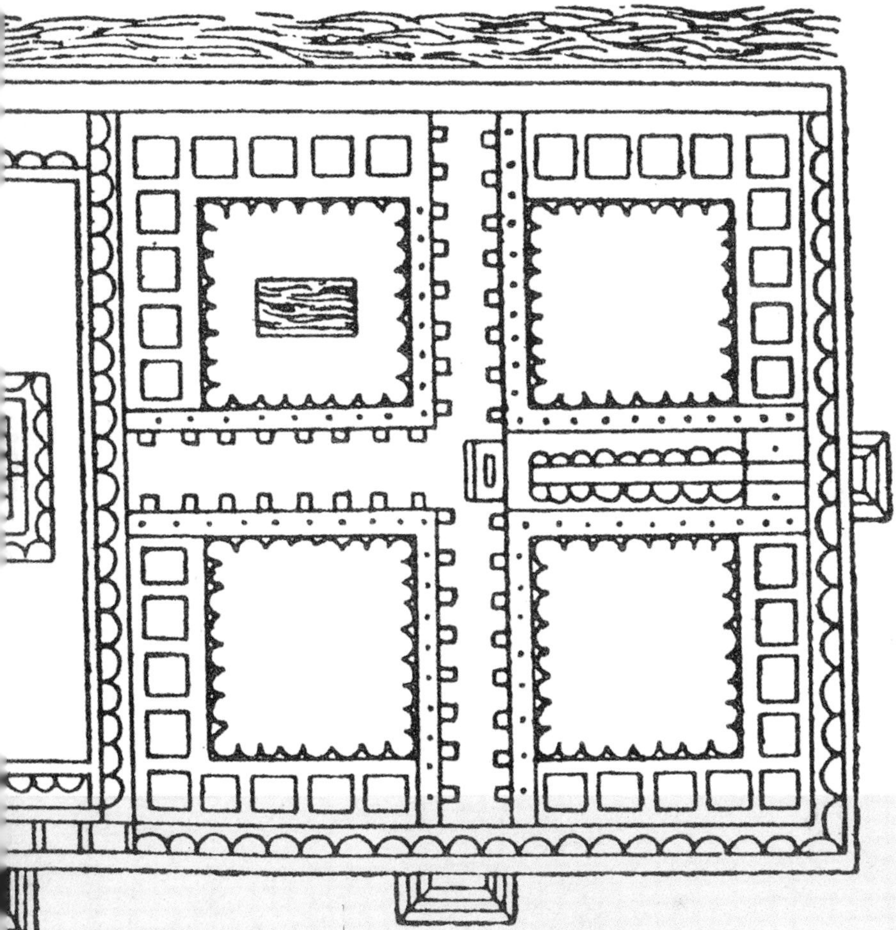

The rectangular courtyard at the Ospedale Maggiore, Milan [fig. 2]

germ theory, noxious smells were considered harbingers of disease, and ventilation needs drove fenestration design. Filarete's design for the Ospedale Maggiore included a vertical spiracle vent from the privy channel to the roof every twenty-two inches (fifty-six centimeters), although, despite this, the hospital was criticized for its foul odor (fig. 5).[7] Later facilities, such as the Hôtel-Dieu of Lyon (1622–31; fig. 6), employed architectural strategies including domes designed to accelerate ventilation, and the Nightingale wards of the nineteenth century featured prescribed window locations and sizes to facilitate the movement of air.

Windows also functioned to illuminate the secular and spiritual mission of these spaces. "Sick and very human beings, feeding and eliminating and being bandaged and vomiting and screaming with pain, were at the same time potential candidates for salvation, on their way to heaven," Thompson and Goldin explain.[8] Stained-glass windows offered a visual opportunity to reinforce narratives of salvation and morality for an illiterate (and captive) audience (fig. 7). These narratives also functioned politically, intertwining indications of the charitable largesse of sponsoring institutions and patrons with stories of the saints.

While knowledge of the causes of disease was not well advanced in this period, the movement of air through buildings was an effective method for the reduction of airborne disease transmission. The design of windows is one of the most direct ways in which spatial strategies can be tied to public health. Windows also have been used to illuminate (both literally and figuratively) existential questions of the individual and the relationship of individuals to the public and the spiritual worlds around them.

The Privy

In section drawings of the Ospedale Maggiore, it is clear that managing the vast amount of human waste generated by such a large institution was a primary design challenge, and Filarete's solution represented a dramatic leap forward (fig. 8). Because of the scale of service and the number of beds, waste collection by bedpan was not sufficient. Filarete instead designed a sewer system with an individual access point for each patient — a secondary arched corridor, running the length of either side of each ward, in which human waste could be deposited. Between every two beds was a door to the corridor, the floor of which was fitted with drains for wastewater. This water was funneled into a catacomb-like basement, where sluices moved it through the building and into a moat adjacent to the hospital complex.[9] In essence, Filarete wrapped the hospital in a sewer system.

This hospital-as-wastewater-management-system exemplifies functionalism as a theory in design: the building is defined by and predicated on its functional performance. While future hospitals would eventually channel waste through vertical chases hidden inside walls, indoor plumbing would not be fully adopted in most buildings until the early twentieth century. In fifteenth-century Italy, it was innovated, notably, through the design of a hospital.

Filarete's section drawings signal a reconsideration of waste, and thus health, as a state problem, and they imagine the hospital as

7 Salvatore Spinelli, *La Ca' Granda 1456–1956* (Milan: Consiglio degli istituti ospitalieri, 1956), 248–51, cited in Thompson and Goldin, 22.

8 Thompson and Goldin, 22.

9 Thompson and Goldin, 25.

5

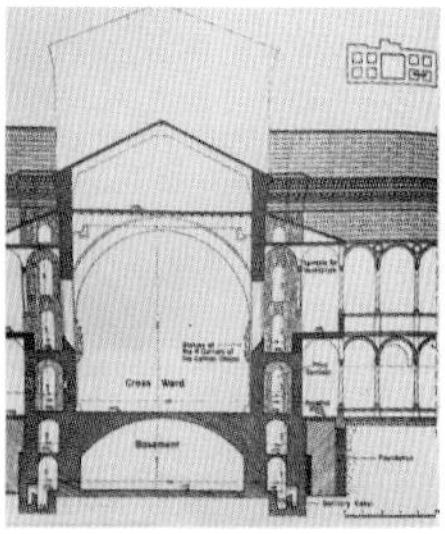

6

7

8

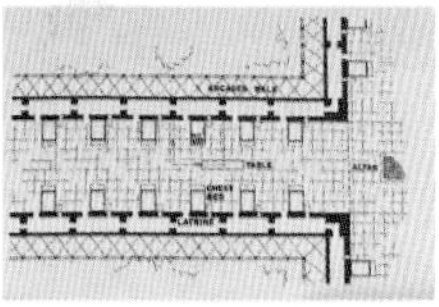

a working, living system. The performative, occupiable, and structural secondary corridor makes visible the physical resources necessary to serve this volume of waste and also suggests the volume of staff required. It signals the emergence of the public institution as a type of civic infrastructure necessary to the performance of social functions.[10]

The Ospedale Maggiore is evidence that the hospital as a built form has been integral to the management of illness for centuries. It also demonstrates that medical architecture has advanced innovations in the built environment more broadly. After the Ospedale Maggiore, the hospital continued to grow in reach and influence, increasingly funded through new classes of charitable wealth and spread through emerging consolidations of institutional, religious, and monarchical power across Europe.

Austerity and Ornament: The Manor Hospital

In the eighteenth century, class and public consciousness shifted along with religious membership and practice, and new forms of representative government shared responsibility for the poor with religious institutions. The hospital was a key messenger of evolving narratives of altruism and influence, and it was implicated in debates about architectural beauty and who deserved it. In 1753, the priest and architectural theorist Marc-Antoine Laugier argued that such institutions should be austere and unadorned:

> Hospitals should be built solidly but plainly. There is no edifice wherein sumptuousness is more contrary to decency. Houses designed to lodge poor people, ought to taste something of it.... So much magnificence declares either much superfluity in the foundation, or very little economy in the administration: it is therefore a magnificence very ill placed.... The poor should be lodged as poor, much propriety and convenience, but not pomp.[11]

Laugier's position, that "the poor should be lodged as poor," expresses an unsubtle paternalism. In this model, hospital architecture was a communication device, expressive of the patronage body's conception of the needy and what they deserved. Beauty repels charity, it claimed, and — in relation to function — it is inessential.

Not everyone agreed, however. In the manor hospital, exported throughout the globe, the ornate and well-constructed home of Europe's privileged classes was adapted to conceal behind its facade the wards, beds, and services of the medical facility. The manor hospital spoke to the street, projecting the adornments and permanence of an enlightened elite as moral goals and guideposts for self-improvement for the less fortunate. In this model of charity, members of the benevolent class communicated their values through well-adorned and well-fabricated public institutions, harnessing beauty to communicate their ideals.

10 Carla Yanni has charted the architectural emergence of the public-benefit institution alongside emerging notions of "treatment" — not of waste, but of mental health — as a state function. See *The Architecture of Madness: Insane Asylums in the United States* (Minneapolis: University of Minnesota Press, 2007).

11 Marc-Antoine Laugier, *An Essay on Architecture*, 2nd ed. (London: T. Osbourne and Shipton, 1755), 191.

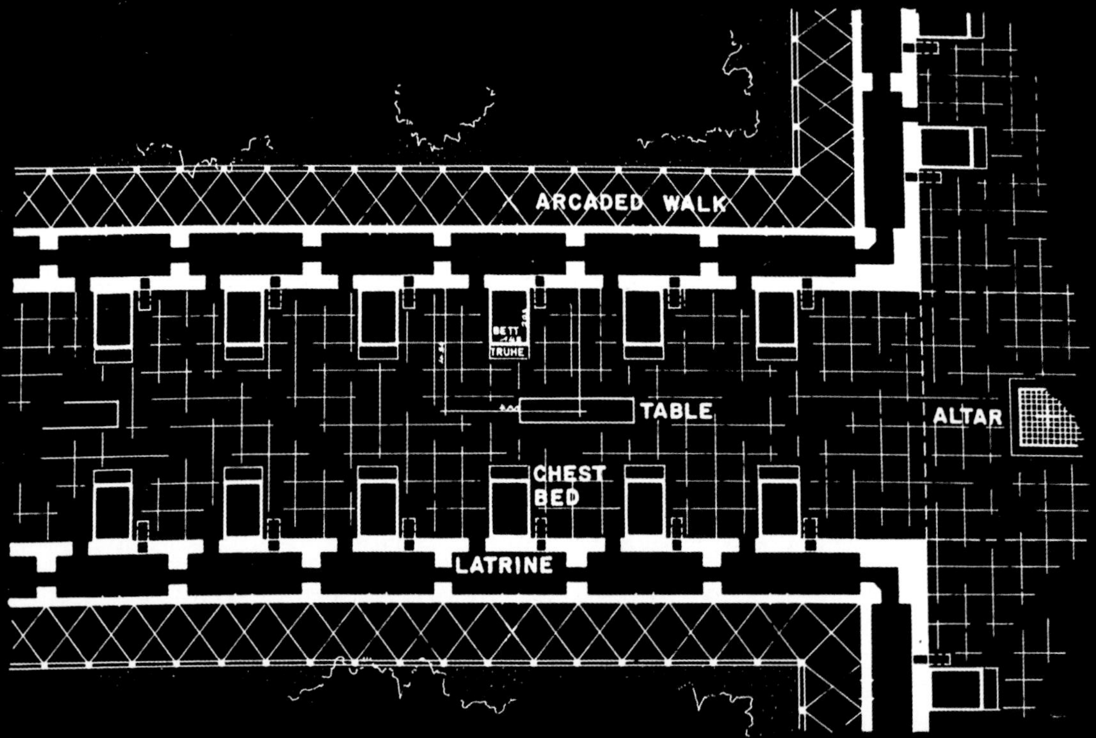

Filarete's section drawings signal a reconsideration of waste, and thus health, as a state problem, and they imagine the hospital as a living, working system.

Plan of a ward, Ospedale Maggiore, Milan [fig. 8]

Section drawing showing vertical ventilation design, Ospedale Maggiore, Milan. Drawing by Liliana Grassi [fig. 5]

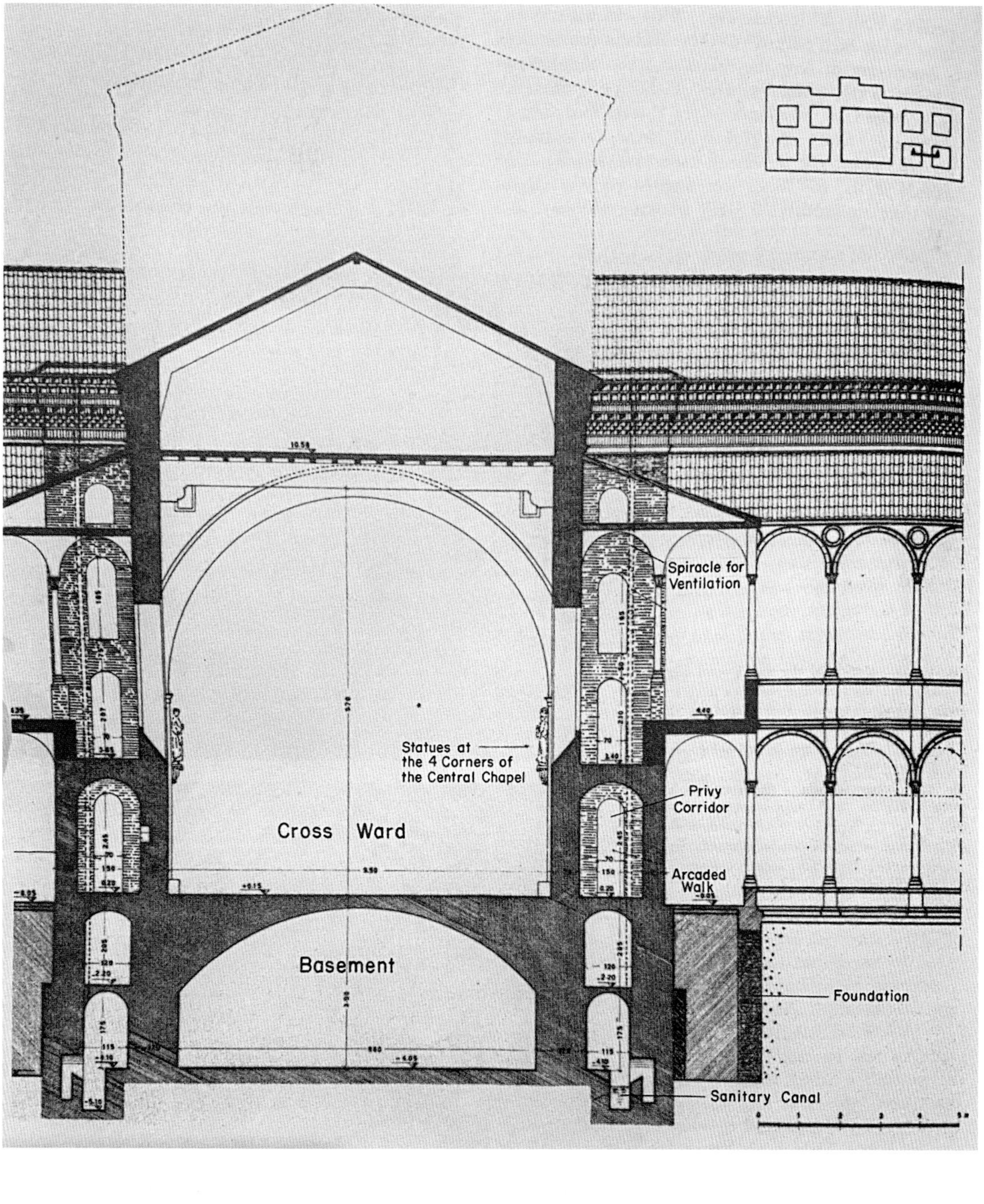

12 John William Reps, *The Making of Urban America: A History of City Planning in the United States* (Princeton, NJ: Princeton University Press, 1965), 317.

13 Thompson and Goldin, 122.

Exportation and Colonial Influence

Throughout the nineteenth century, the manor was deployed as a tool of Western colonial influence. The form proliferated globally, packaged along with exported conceptions of status, dismissive of localized symbols, and justified as neoclassical. In early colonial settlements in Europe, Southeast Asia, the Middle East, the Americas, and Africa, the manor took on a civilizing mission of charity.

The Pennsylvania Hospital, one of the first public manor hospitals, was built in Philadelphia in 1751 **(fig. 9)**. Seen from the street, the edifice, designed by Samuel Rhoads (1711–1784), did not resemble an institution of last resort or an austere poorhouse but seemed, rather, to be a stately domicile, like the others lining Philadelphia's Spruce Street — its appearance belying the wards and cells, the kitchens and privies, and the poor and the infirm who sought refuge behind its many windows.

It is perhaps no accident that American institutional architecture was born in Pennsylvania, the site of William Penn's colonial "Holy Experiment." One of the earliest planned cities in what would become the United States, Philadelphia was conceived around Quaker ideals of civic engagement and designed in part to prevent outbreaks of the plague.[12] The city was laid out in a rectangular grid of evenly spaced lots and divided into quadrants, each of which contained a public square surrounded by cultural and civic institutions **(fig. 10)**. Both this city plan and the manor hospital were symbolic extensions of Quaker ideals of social reform, but they were also imported ideals, transplanted, as an experiment, to stolen land.

9

10

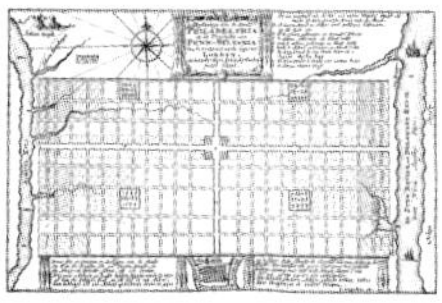

11

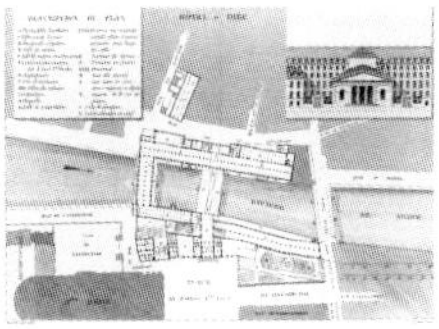

12

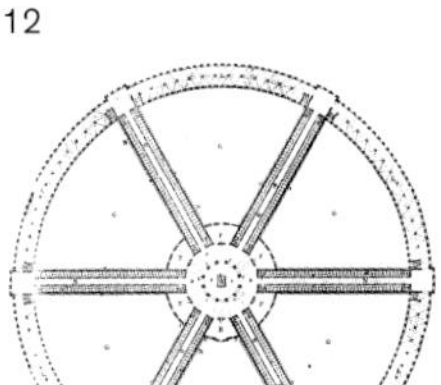

13

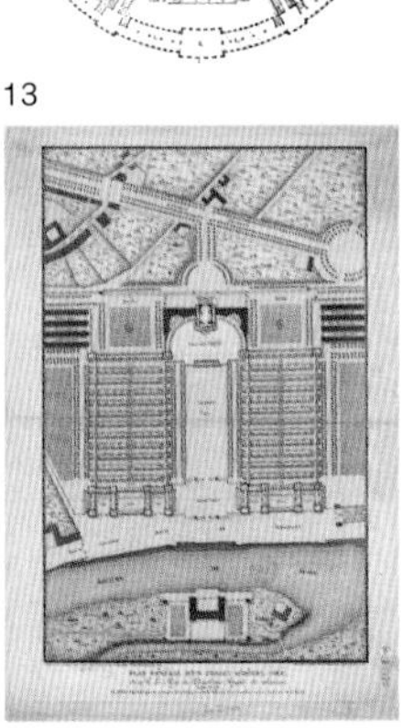

The manor form, pervasive and adaptable, was used for a variety of emerging colonial institutions: colleges, asylums, schools, and government buildings throughout Africa, Asia, and the Americas all began to resemble manor homes. Was domesticity itself considered a civilizing influence? Or were the benefits of narrative projection more essential to the colonial project than the functional performance of the institution? All institutions are not alike, however, and the functional needs of the hospital soon began to put pressure on the manor's facade. By the end of the eighteenth century, those needs would manifest in facilities so large that the manor house could no longer disguise them.

The Hôtel-Dieu, Paris: Sickness and Scale

Straddling the Seine, one wing resting on the Île de la Cité and the other clinging to the Left Bank, the Hôtel-Dieu was for centuries Paris's largest medical institution **(fig. 11)**. Built in the Middle Ages, by the late 1700s it had been subject to a series of ad hoc additions and renovations, expansions that created a health and safety disaster. Poor planning and insufficient space had led to overcrowding: many patients, for example, were kept in *grands lits* (big beds for three or more people), and during a pestilence yet more patients climbed atop the canopy of the bed.[13] In addition to its various spatial issues, the Hôtel-Dieu suffered a spate of fires throughout the eighteenth century, including conflagrations in 1718, 1737, 1742, and 1772.

These tragedies led to a climate of public outrage centered on the negligence of the political officials who had created a dangerous environment for Paris's poor — a failure of the hospital's charitable intent. If one was committed to the Hôtel-Dieu, death was assumed. In response, in the 1770s King Louis XVI appointed a commission from the Académie Royale des Sciences to solve the problem of the Hôtel-Dieu. The commission was tasked with designing a plan for a safe, hygienic, thousand-bed hospital. One of the earliest of these plans, a radial cross-ward design conceived by Antoine Petit (1722–1794) in 1774, resembled a wheel, each spoke containing four stories of wards with patient beds arranged along the perimeter walls: the first iteration of the pavilion hospital. Its six huge wings were organized around a central church, in the cupola of which noxious air, as well as exhaust from the neighboring kitchen, laundry, apothecary, and bakery, was meant to collect before being siphoned to the exterior **(fig. 12)**.

At this time, it was known that air circulation was an important aspect of disease prevention. The British army physician John Pringle, for example, had observed its efficacy in the 1740s in Germany, during a British campaign. Astonished by the fact that sick and wounded soldiers lodged in hospitals died while those who were housed in barns recovered, Pringle concluded:

> The sick should not be sent to one common hospital. . . . Barns, granaries, and the like places, will allow the steam to disperse. . . . It is common to look out for close and warm houses, and therefore to prefer a peasant's house to his barn; but experience has convinced us, that air more than warmth is requisite.[14]

A 1773 proposal by Julien-David Le Roy (1724–1803) and Charles-François Viel (1745–1819) contained twenty-two long wards with fifty-four beds each **(fig. 13)**. For ventilation, this design capitalized on a free draft (or wind tunnel) from one end of each narrow ward to the other. Domes placed at regular intervals were capped with "flag-shaped extensions that would turn with the wind **(fig. 14)**."[15]

In 1785, Bernard Poyet (1742–1824) published a plan for a radial Hôtel-Dieu surrounded by an "isolation space" and a man-made canal **(fig. 15)**. Poyet's hospital would contain an unprecedented 5,200 beds on sixteen three-floor buildings arranged like spokes of a wheel, with eighty-four beds per ward.[16] For hygiene, it included a sewer running under the building and a canal separating the hospital from the mainland **(fig. 16)**. Airflow, however, was not prioritized: the circular "rim" of the wheel would have prevented effective cross-ventilation between the wards and courtyards.

In 1787, members of the Hôtel-Dieu commission traveled to Plymouth, England, to examine the Royal Naval Hospital, which was reputed to be the "most up to date in Europe, if not in the world **(fig. 17)**."[17] With a capacity of 1,250 patients, it was considered an ideal precedent for the thousand-bed Hôtel-Dieu.[18] The Royal Naval Hospital was scaled to facilitate ventilation, single-patient beds, and patient supervision, with its ten three-story ward buildings, each of which contained two twenty-five-bed wards per floor. It was designed like a series of

14 John Pringle, *Observations on the Diseases of the Army*, 1st US ed. (Philadelphia: Edward Earle, 1810), 91.

15 Thompson and Goldin, 132.

16 Thompson and Goldin, 127.

17 Christopher Lloyd and Jack L. S. Coulter, *Medicine and the Navy* (Edinburgh: Livingstone, 1961), 275, quoted in Thompson and Goldin, 142.

18 Thompson and Goldin, 142.

14

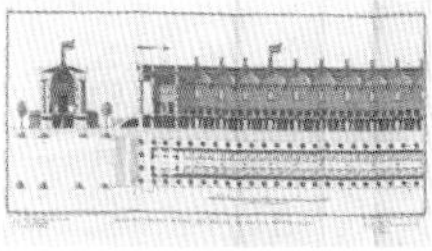

15

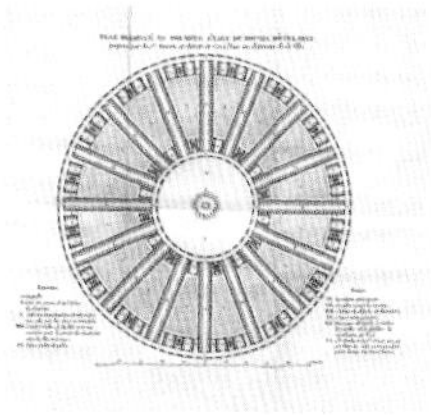

16

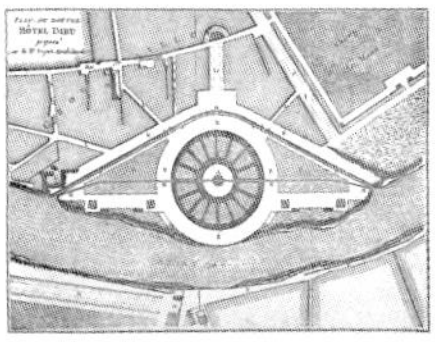

17

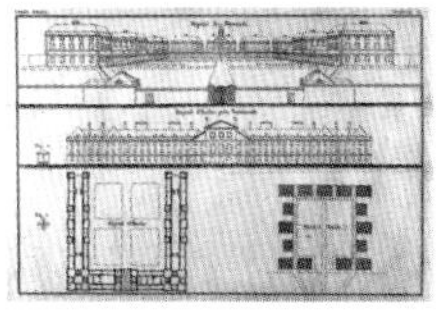

Site plan for the Hôtel-Dieu, Paris, designed by Jacques Thierry, 1808 [fig. 11]

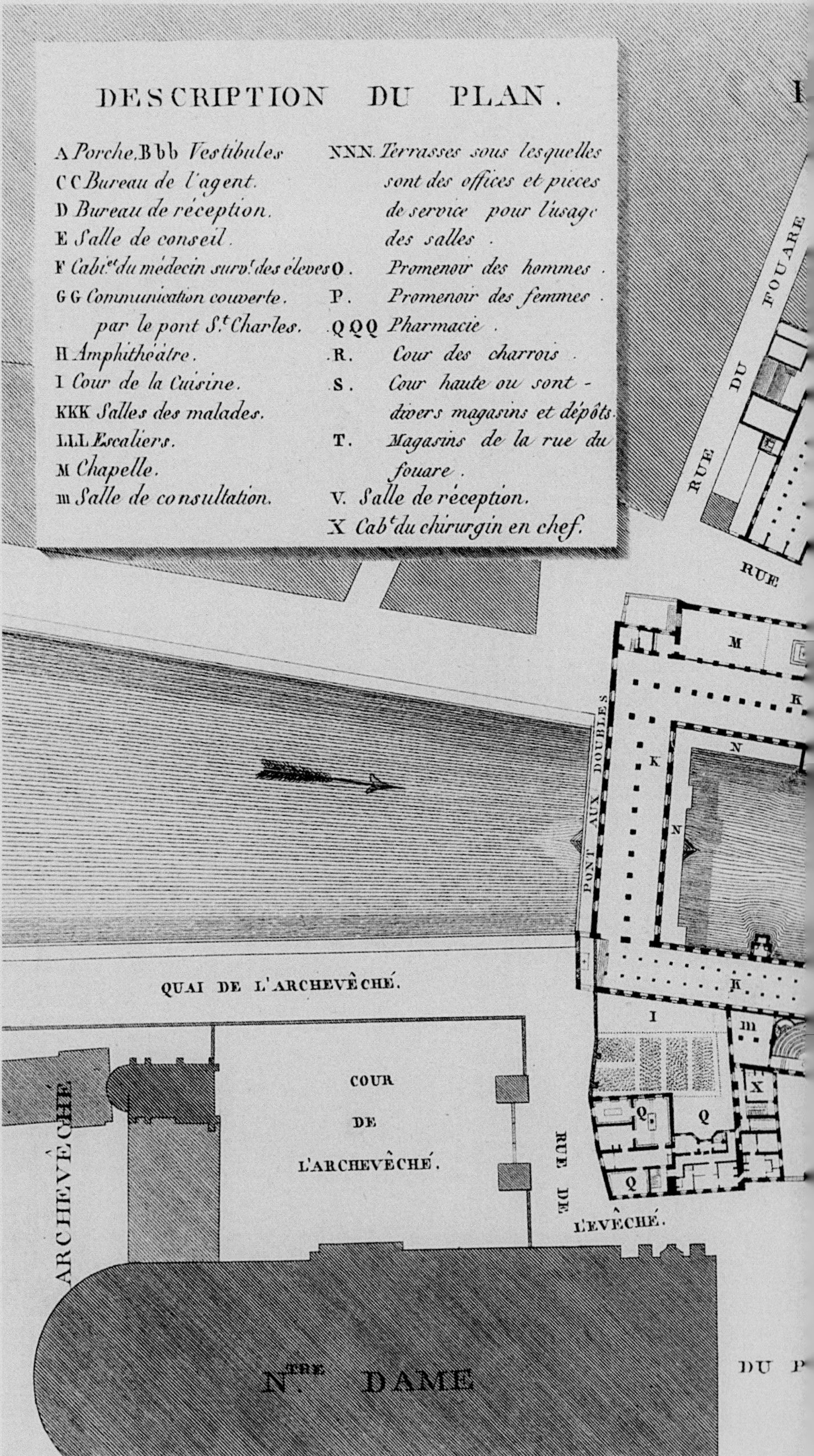

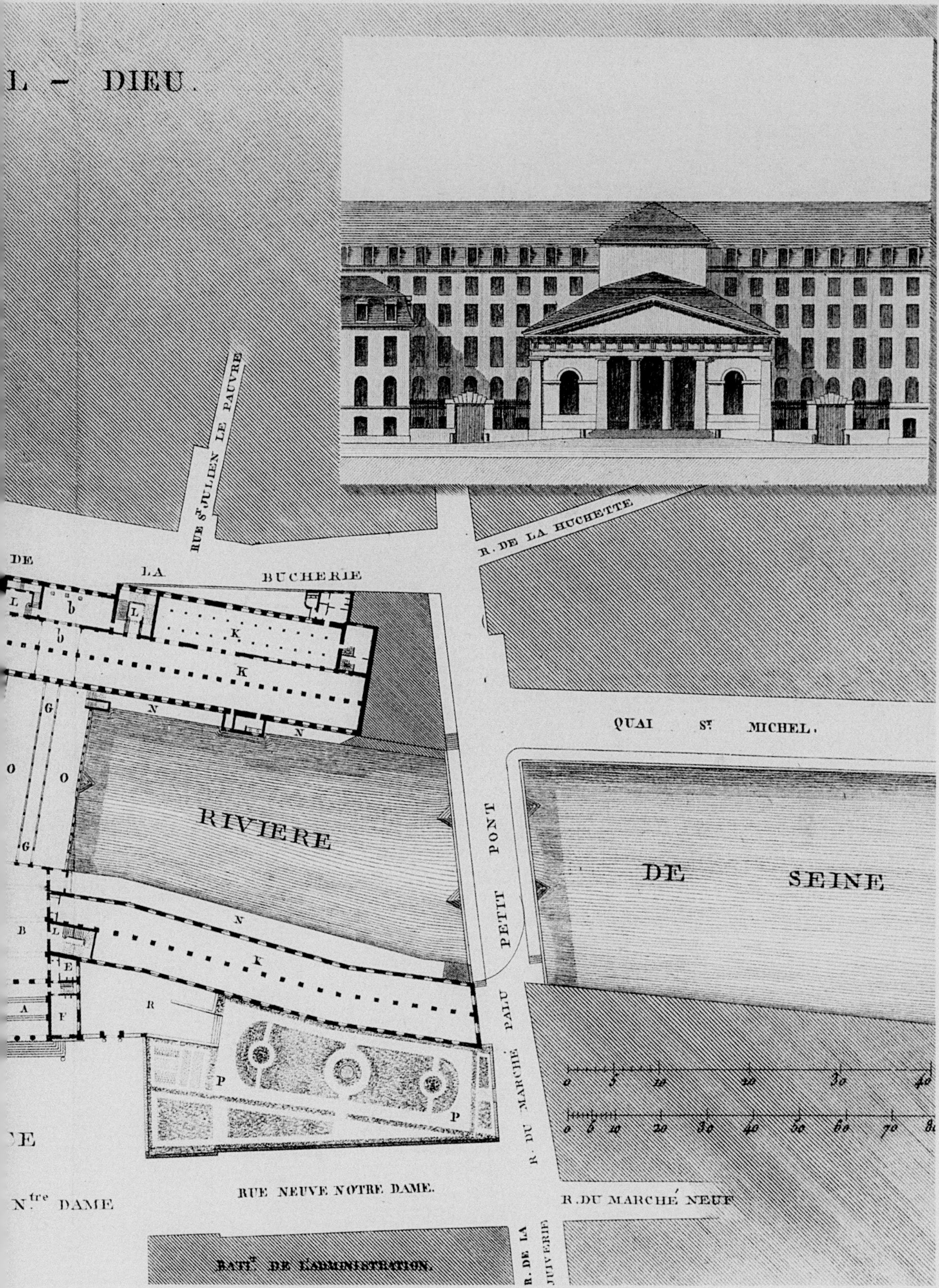
L – DIEU.
RUE St JULIEN LE PAUVRE
R. DE LA HUCHETTE
DE LA BUCHERIE
QUAI St MICHEL.
RIVIERE DE SEINE
PETIT PONT
R. DU MARCHÉ PALU
RUE NEUVE NOTRE DAME.
R. DU MARCHÉ NEUF
N.tre DAME
R. DE LA JUIVERIE
BATIt DE L'ADMINISTRATION.

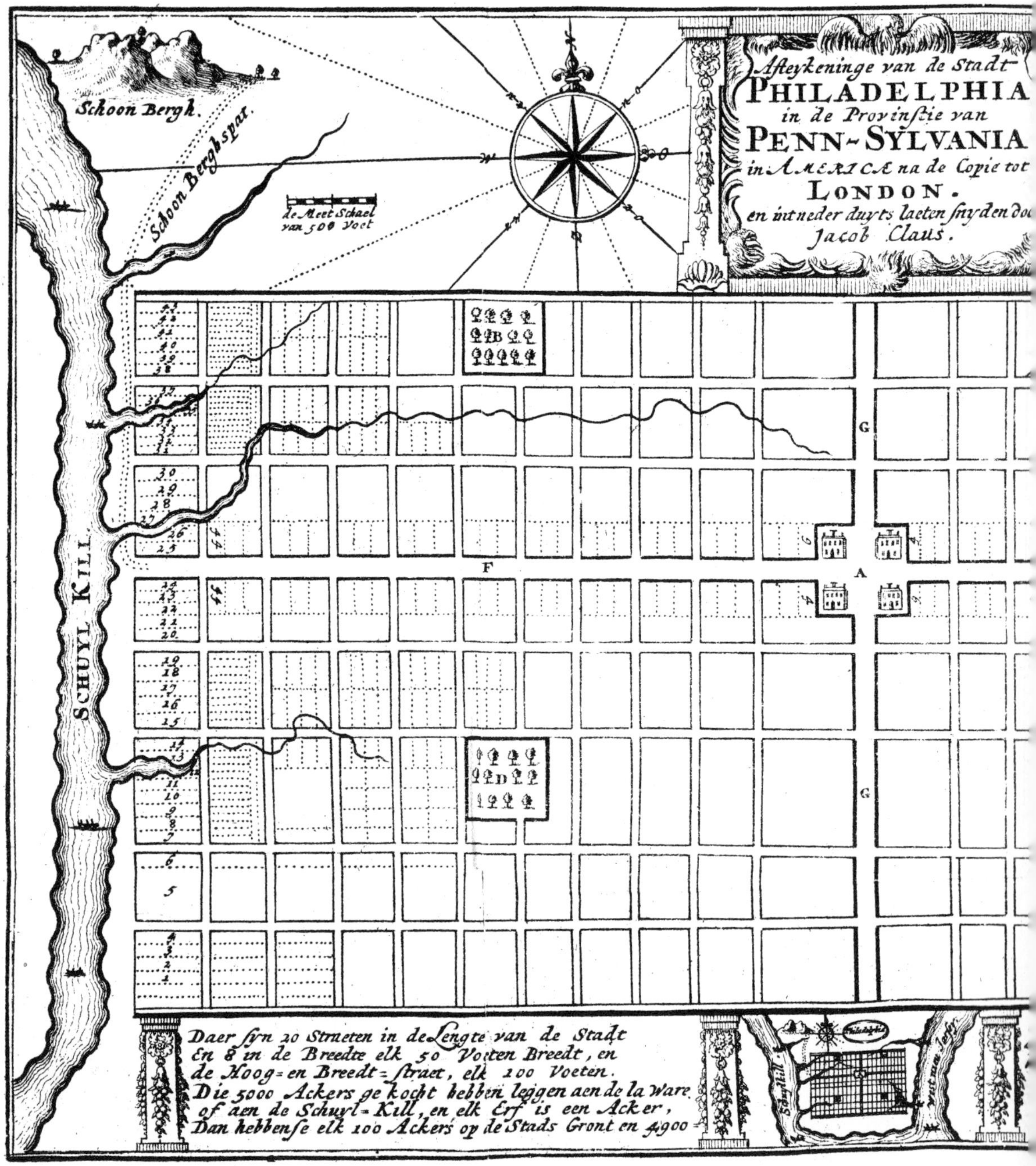

Philadelphia's rectangular street grid, designed by William Penn, 1682 [fig. 10]

North elevation, Pennsylvania Hospital, designed by William Strickland, 1751 [fig. 9]

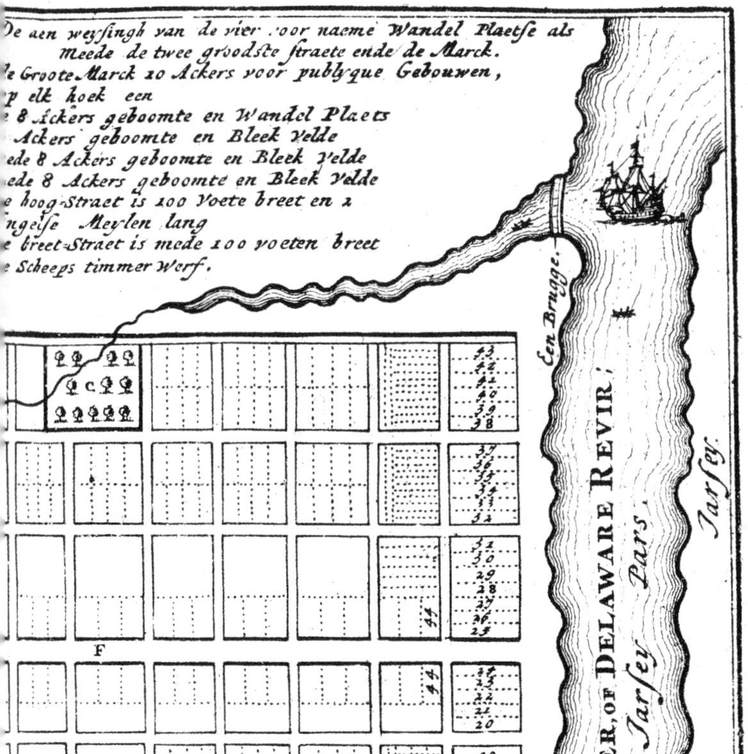
De aen weysingh van de vier voor naeme Wandel Plaetse als
meede de twee groodste straete ende de Marck.
e Groote Marck 20 Ackers voor publyque Gebouwen,
p elk hoek een
8 Ackers geboomte en Wandel Plaets
Ackers geboomte en Bleek Velde
ede 8 Ackers geboomte en Bleek Velde
ede 8 Ackers geboomte en Bleek Velde
e hoog-Straet is 100 Voete breet en 2
ngelse Meylen lang
e breet-Straet is mede 100 voeten breet
e Scheeps timmer Werf.
Een Brugge.
DE ZUYD REVIER, OF DELAWARE REVIR.
West Nieu Jarsey Pars.
Jarsey.
Nieu
Een Brugge.
Sulx schenkt de Gouverneur elk een Acker in de
minder als 5000. (tot 1000 toe) gekocht
nen haer Lott in de Hoogh Straet, van
f tot 94 toe aen weerseyden.
r als 1000 Ackers gekocht hebben, hebben
sen in de andere Straten.
G. Drogenham, fec.

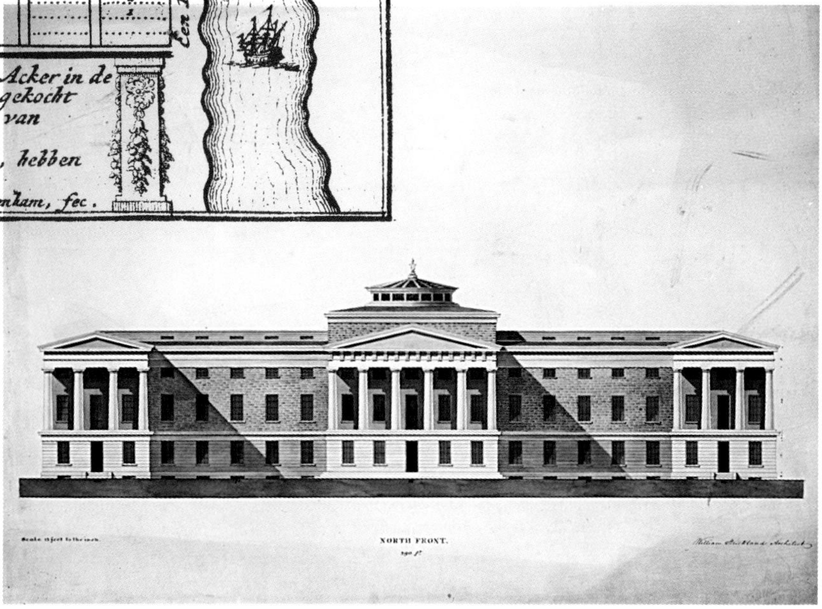
NORTH FRONT

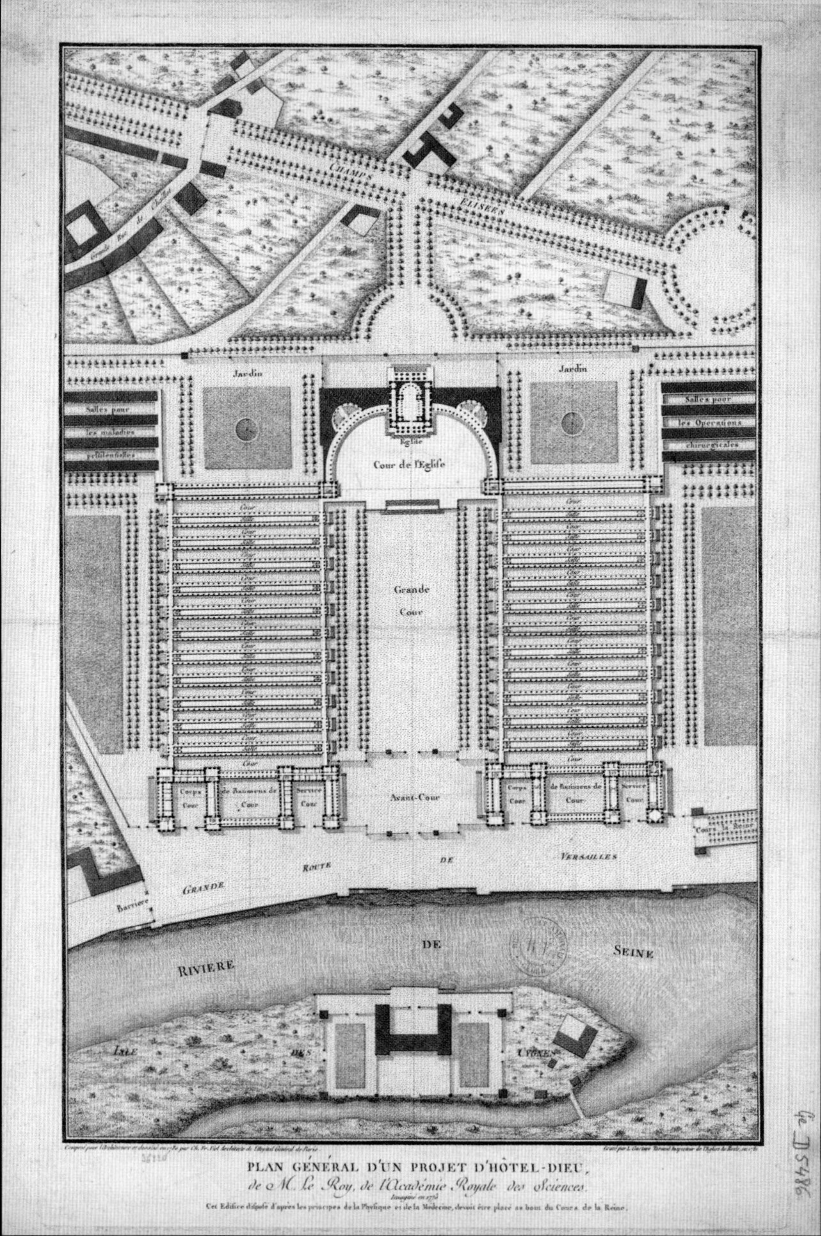

Plan view of Julien-David Le Roy and Charles-François Viel's design for the Hôtel-Dieu, Paris, showing wards with beds, 1787 [fig. 13]

Views of the Royal Naval Hospital, Plymouth, England, designed by Alexander Rowehead, 1765 [fig. 17]

The original Hôtel-Dieu, a place to recover from disease, was also a place where disease spread.

independent homes, framed around a square courtyard with a covered colonnade. In the final, approved plan for the Hôtel-Dieu — submitted by Jacques-René Tenon (1724–1816) and Poyet in 1788 — the influence of the symmetrical English plan was evident. However, unlike the Royal Naval Hospital (which served only seamen), the Hôtel-Dieu design would accommodate both men and women in separate spaces and also provide for maternity care **(fig. 18)**.[19]

The Hôtel-Dieu as conceived by Tenon was never relocated or rebuilt. Land was cleared, but construction halted in 1789, at the outbreak of the French Revolution, and never restarted. In the two decades of design and research for the project, however, we see the emergence of empirical evidence as a guide for design, and of new concepts regarding society's role in managing public health. New data showed that certain buildings were correlated with better health outcomes, although there was not enough evidence to explain why. The original Hôtel-Dieu, a place to recover from disease, was also a place where disease spread, and the new designs, with their expanded configurations of the bed, the altar, the window, and the privy, would not have adequately solved that problem. However, the attempts — both heroic and ghastly — paved the way for Isambard Brunel's engineered pavilion design of 1855, a project driven by more specific and measured scientific knowledge regarding the role of the building in controlling infection and in delivering care to the patient.

19 Thompson and Goldin, 146.

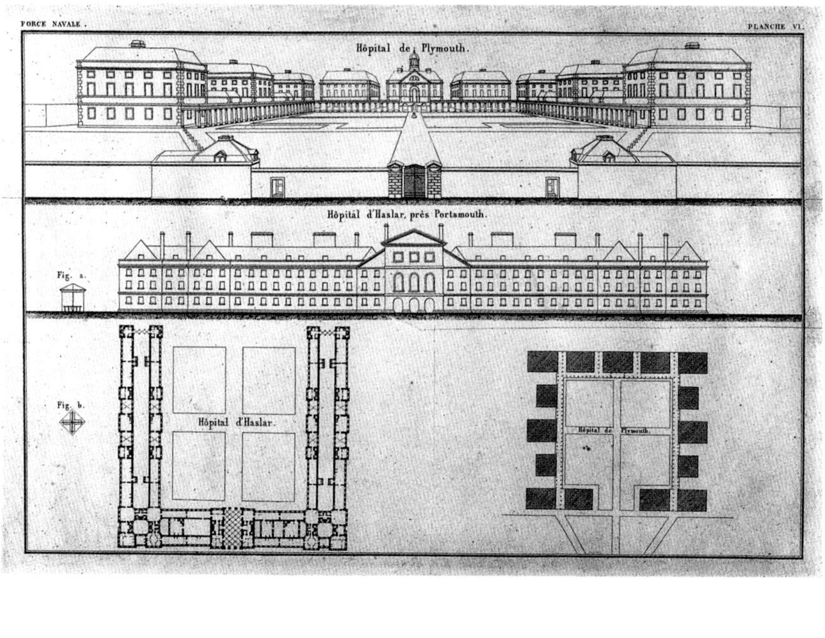

18

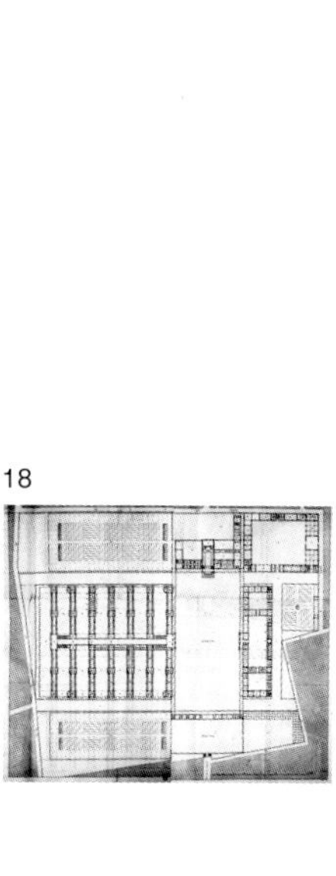

A radial cross-ward design conceived by Antoine Petit resembled a wheel, each spoke containing four stories of wards with patient beds arranged along the perimeter walls: the first iteration of the pavilion hospital.

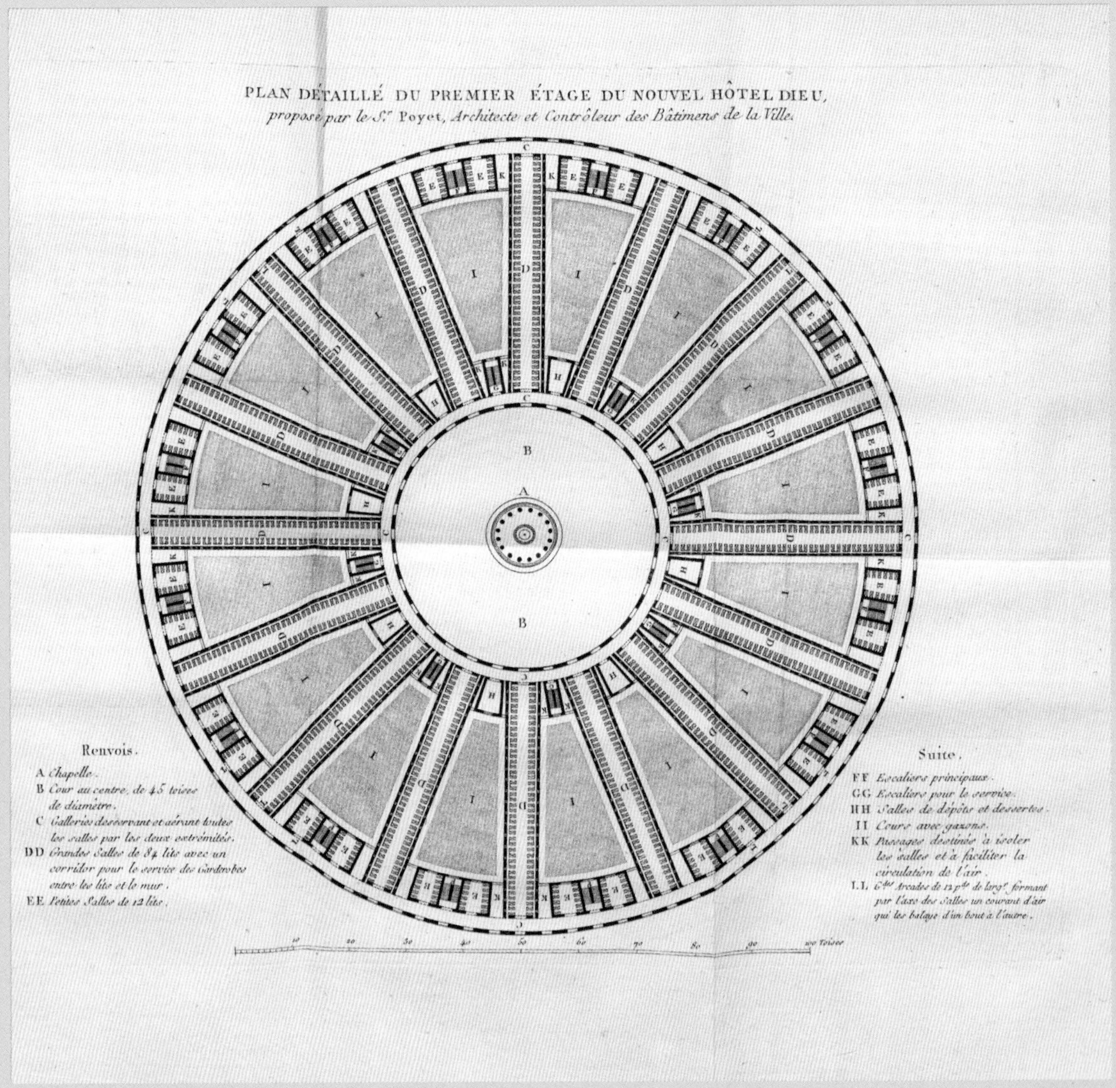

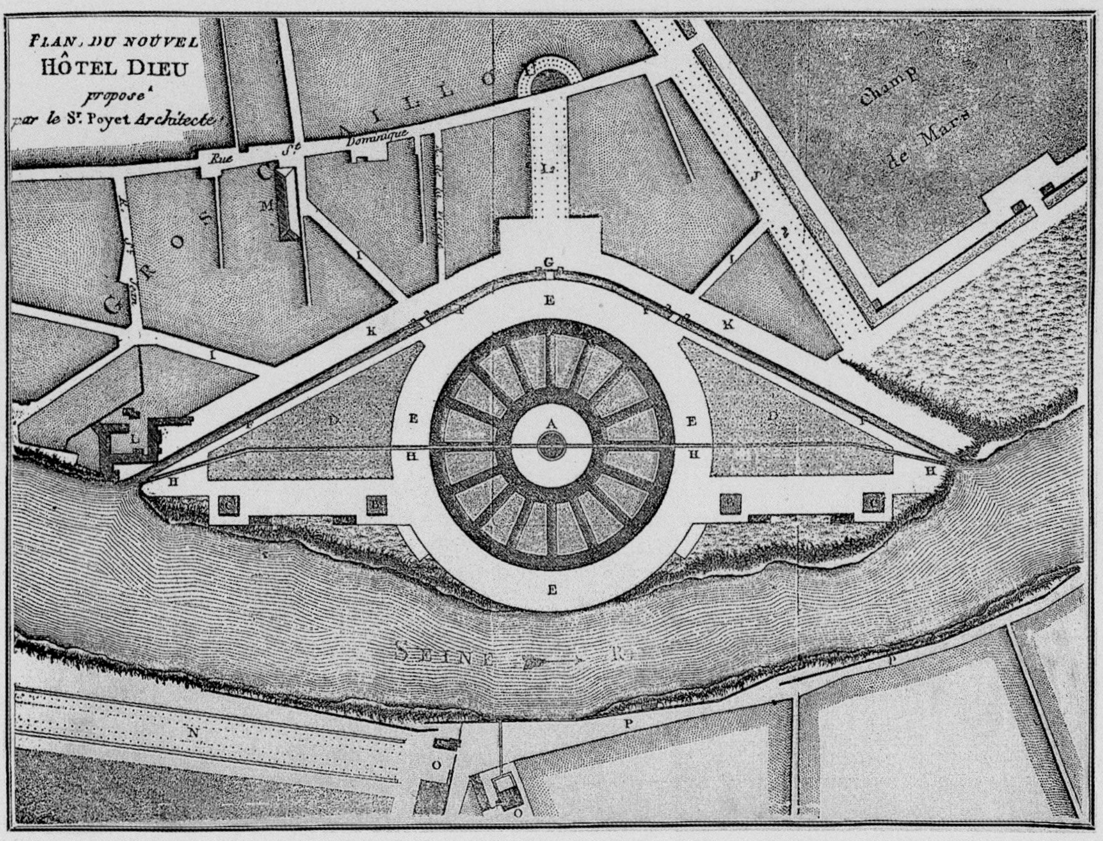

Plan view of Bernard Poyet's design for the Hôtel-Dieu, Paris, 1785 [fig. 15]

Site plan for Bernard Poyet's design for the Hôtel-Dieu, Paris, 1785 [fig. 16]

Plan view of Antoine Petit's design for the Hôtel-Dieu, Paris, 1774 [fig. 12]

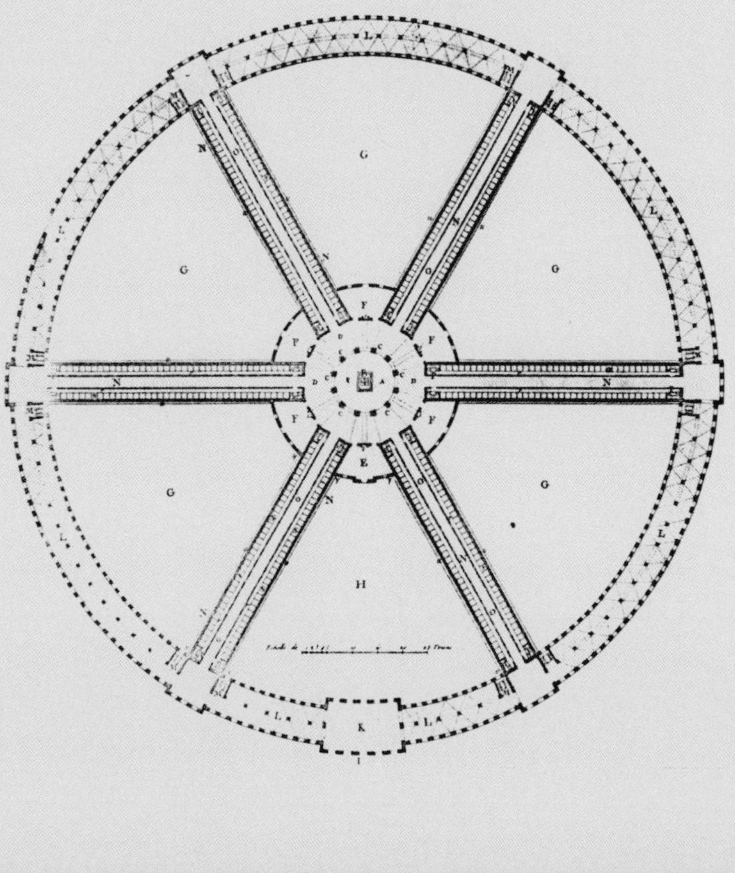

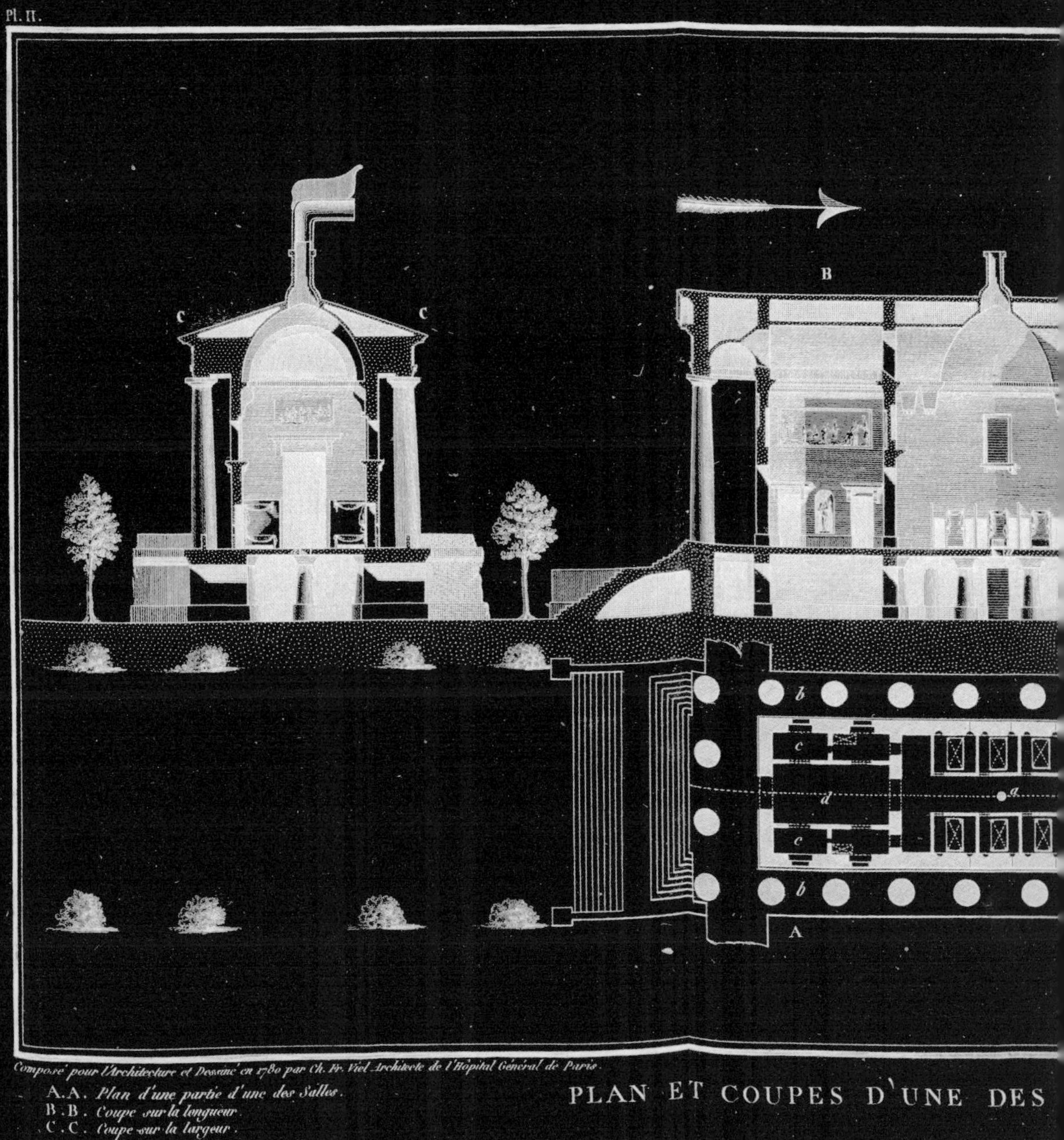

Plan and section drawings of one ward at the proposed Hôtel Dieu, designed by Julien-David Le Roy and Charles-François Viel, 1773 [fig. 14]

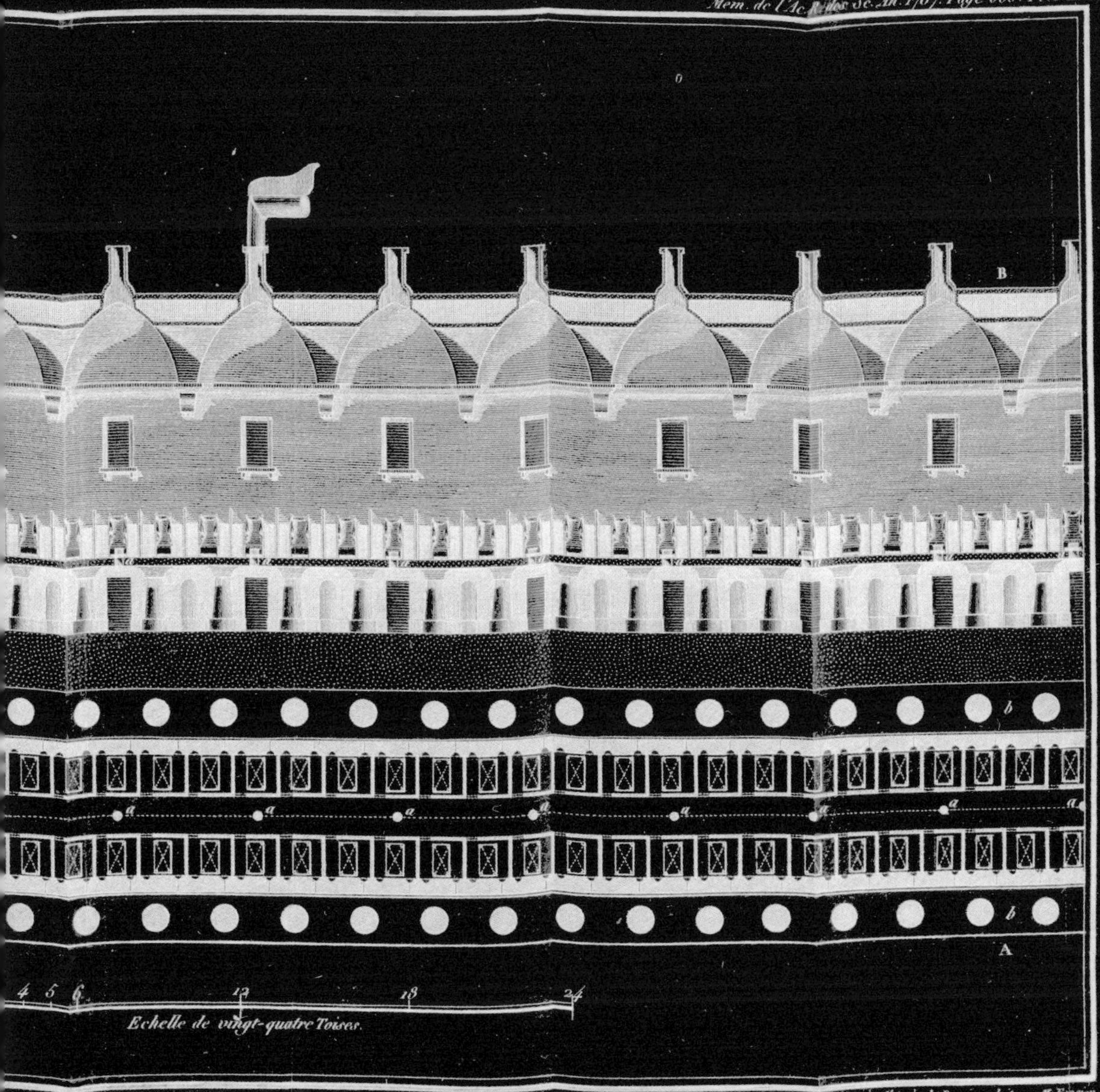

Gravé par P. Le Gouaz d'après le Dessin reduit par M. Poyet.

ES DU NOUVEL HÔTEL-DIEU.

a. a. a. a. Puits à Air.
b. b. b. b. Galerie pour desservir les Salles.
c. c. Office.
d. Vestibule.

Chapter 2
Sanitation and Experimentation

Brunel in Crimea

In 1855, Isambard Kingdom Brunel (1806–1859) was called into the British War Office to investigate a crisis. At that time, Brunel (fig. 1) was one of England's most famous engineers: He had designed and built the Thames Tunnel, the first to be constructed underneath a navigable river (1840). He was responsible for the SS *Great Britain*, the first iron steamship to cross the Atlantic. He had built numerous long-span steel bridges, including the Royal Albert Bridge in Plymouth. And he was the engineer for England's Great Western Railway, designing Bristol Temple Meads station (1840) as well as London's Paddington station (1854; fig. 2), which features a 102-foot (thirty-one-meter) span as well two other spans of sixty-eight and seventy feet (around twenty-one meters).

It was the height of the Crimean War (a proxy war with Russia for territorial influence on the Continent) and innumerable British soldiers were dying — from bullet or bayonet wounds but also from infectious diseases such as cholera, malaria, and typhoid, which spread unchecked through overcrowded barracks hospitals and tents. The tents then in use were notoriously poor spaces in which to recover. Called bell tents because their shape resembled the top of a dinner bell, these canvas huts had limited ventilation and were placed directly on the ground without any infrastructure to separate waste and water (fig. 3). A report from the British War Office testified, "The bell-tents ... are peculiarly ill adapted for hospital purposes. They are not always wind or water-tight, and they do not admit more than three or four stretchers."[1] A nurse named Florence Nightingale (1820–1910) was deployed to the front line to help wounded soldiers in the hospital in Scutari (today Üsküdar; fig. 4). Hers was one of the voices that brought the poor conditions to the attention of the British public, which responded with outrage. Brunel was invited to devise a solution: a prefabricated field hospital that could be made in England, shipped by rail to Turkey, and assembled by soldiers on-site — a deployable medical infrastructure designed to save soldiers' lives and help them win the war (fig. 5).

The Sanitary Era and Cholera

This concept — a hospital helping to win a war — would have been a pipe dream even a few decades earlier. But recent advancements in medical science had led to new conclusions about diseases and contagion. In the Crimean theater, the hospital was transformed from a space of care into an instrument of medicine.

Before the advent of germ theory — elucidated in 1883 by Louis Pasteur and Robert Koch, among others — scientists were confounded by the cholera pandemics that had scourged the globe beginning in the early nineteenth century. This new plague — "the wasting death," "the midnight raid" — turned bustling cities into ghost towns overnight. It crossed the oceans on the east-west trade routes fueled by the growth of colonialism and global trade, creating pandemics of increasing ferocity.[2] The number of deaths was staggering. The first pandemic, which began in Calcutta in 1817, killed hundreds of thousands by the time it ended, in 1824. The second pandemic emerged in 1826 and spread to Great Britain, where it killed some twenty thousand people in less than two years.[3] By 1854, another eighty thousand people had died in two subsequent outbreaks.[4] The world was besieged, and few understood why. The theory of the time, later disproven, was that diseases like cholera and the bubonic plague spread through miasmas, noxious clouds of "bad air" that made people sick. This thinking was represented in the Scottish cartographer Alexander Keith Johnston's 1856 Health & Disease map, which assigned broad-ranging "miasmic" zones of naturally occurring disease transmission aligned with isotherms **(fig. 6)**. The same year, Adolph Mühry, a German medical geographer, also traced the presence of cholera along isotherms, but by noting specific areas of outbreak, Mühry applied miasmic theory with greater attention to geographical and botanical detail, hypothesizing that miasmas were related to local botanical features. In 1873, the New York physician John C. Peters rejected the notion that cholera was naturally occurring along isotherms, instead tracing a direct link between colonialism and the spread of the disease **(fig. 7)**.[5]

1 Arthur Cumming, Peter Benson Maxwell, and Patrick Sinclair Laing, *Report upon the State of the Hospitals of the British Army in the Crimea and Scutari* (London: Eyre and Spottiswoode, 1855), 10.

2 Steven Shapin, "Sick City," *New Yorker*, October 30, 2006.

3 E. Ashworth Underwood, "The History of Cholera in Great Britain," *Section of Epidemiology and State Medicine: Proceedings of the Royal Society of Medicine* 41 (November 3, 1947), 173.

4 J. N. Hays, *Epidemics and Pandemics: Their Impacts on Human History* (Denver, CO: ABC CLIO, 2005), 230.

5 Shapin, "Sick City."

1

2

3

4

5

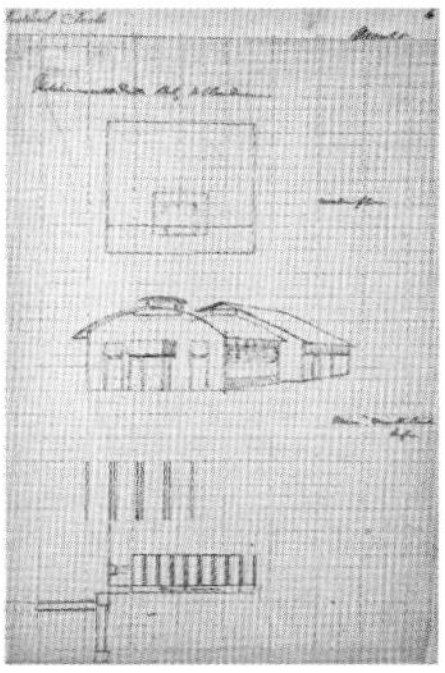

6

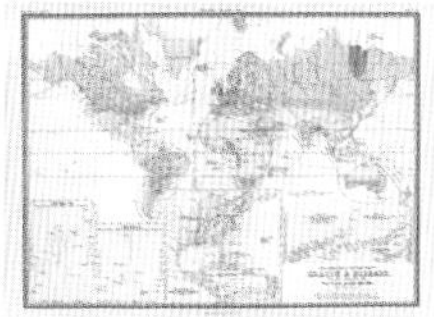

7

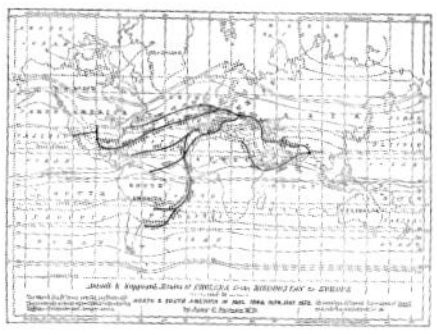

Map showing the geographical distribution of diseases, by Alexander Keith Johnston, 1856 [fig. 6]

Map showing direct links between the spread of cholera and trade routes, by John C. Peters, 1873 [fig. 7]

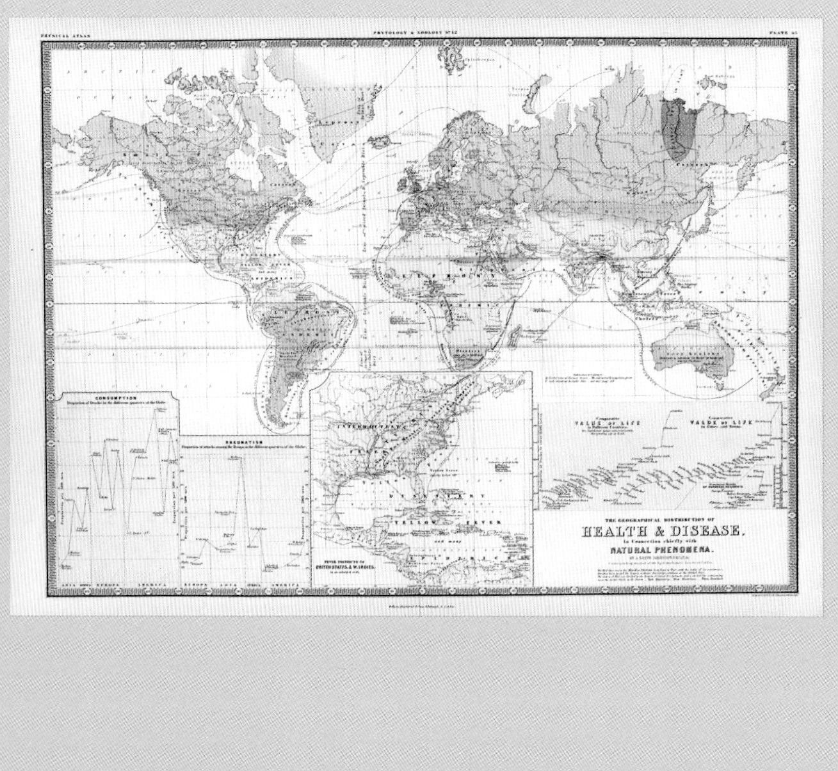

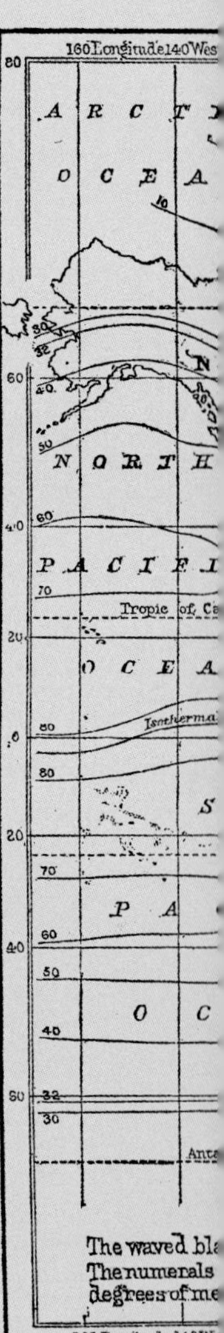

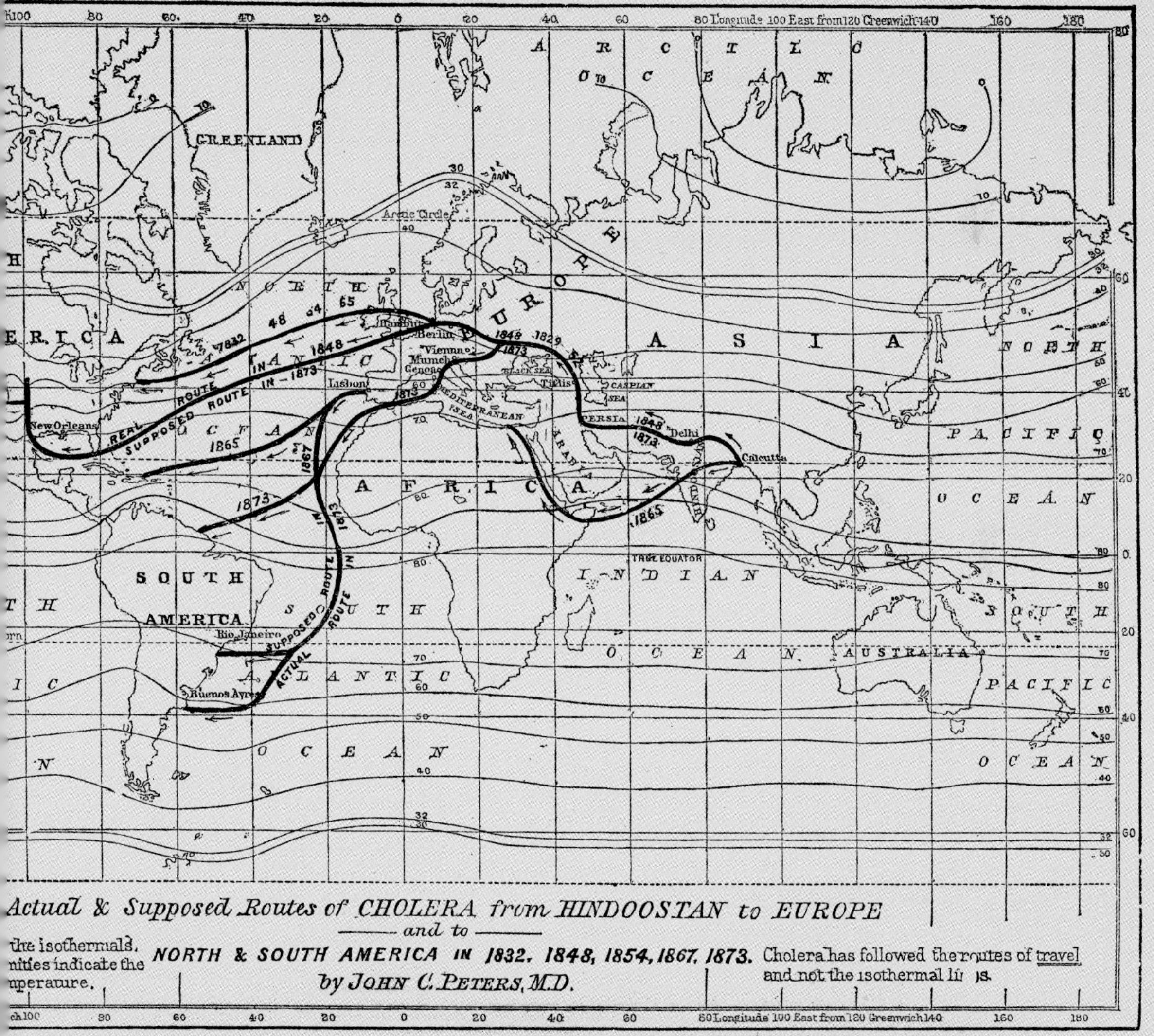
Actual & Supposed Routes of CHOLERA from HINDOOSTAN to EUROPE
and to
NORTH & SOUTH AMERICA IN 1832. 1848, 1854, 1867, 1873.
by JOHN C. PETERS, M.D.
Cholera has followed the routes of travel and not the isothermal lines.
the isothermals.
nities indicate the
nperature.
80 Longitude 100 East from 120 Greenwich 140
ARCTIC OCEAN
GREENLAND
Arctic Circle
EUROPE
ASIA
AFRICA
SOUTH AMERICA
NORTH ATLANTIC OCEAN
SOUTH ATLANTIC OCEAN
INDIAN OCEAN
PACIFIC OCEAN
NORTH PACIFIC
SOUTH PACIFIC OCEAN
AUSTRALIA
New Orleans
Lisbon
Berlin
Vienna
Munich
Genoa
BLACK SEA
CASPIAN SEA
MEDITERRANEAN SEA
PERSIA
ARABIA
Tiflis
Delhi
Calcutta
Rio Janeiro
Buenos Ayres
TRUE EQUATOR
REAL ROUTE IN 1873
SUPPOSED ROUTE IN 1873
ACTUAL ROUTE
SUPPOSED ROUTE

Interior of Paddington
station, London, 1930s.
Designed by Isambard
Kingdom Brunel, 1854
[fig. 2]

Florence Nightingale in the military hospital at Scutari, 1855. Lithograph by Joseph-Austin Benwell [fig. 4]

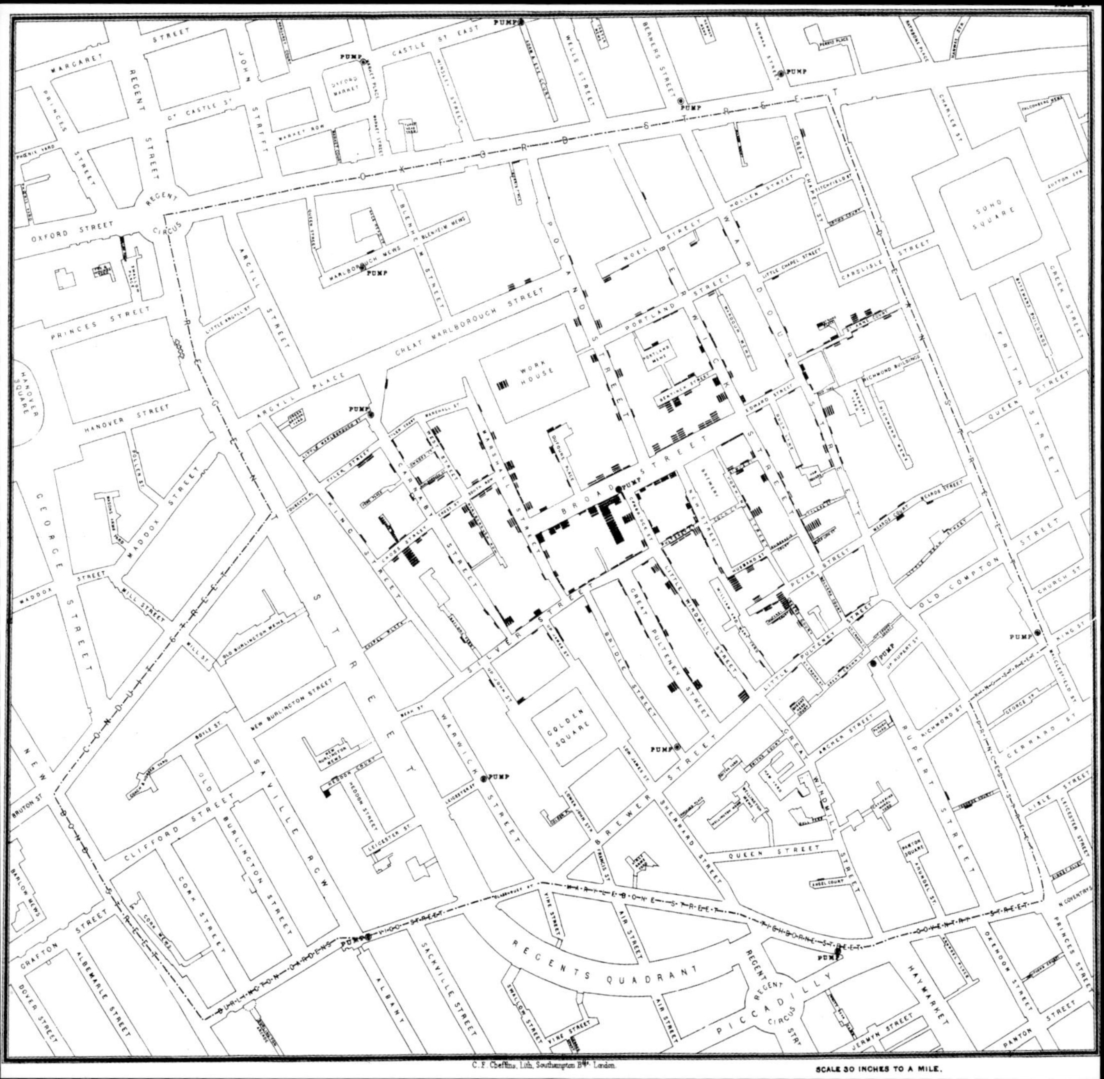

Map showing distribution of cholera cases in Soho, London, during the 1854 cholera outbreak, from John Snow, *On the Mode of Communication of Cholera*, 2nd ed. (London: John Churchill, 1855) [fig. 8]

Cholera seemed to afflict the poor most severely, especially those living in overcrowded tenements. Epidemics such as cholera and, later, HIV/AIDS have often been used to reinforce puritanical prejudices and the moral superiority of the wealthy classes. In the nineteenth century, "medical opinion was unanimous in agreeing that the intemperate, the imprudent, the filthy were particularly vulnerable," Charles E. Rosenberg has written.[6] But as moral theories fester, they also breed skepticism. One young London doctor, John Snow (1813–1858), sought a scientific explanation for rampant disease in the newly minted capitals of industrial wealth.

In the 1850s, London's Soho neighborhood was a thick layer cake of tenements separated only by narrow footpaths, a prime breeding ground, it turned out, for the 1854 cholera outbreak. Snow's approach to extrapolation was novel. Instead of emptying the city, as had been done in prior outbreaks, he placed a mark on a map of Soho where each cholera case had emerged (fig. 8). At the largest cluster of markings — a clear nucleus — Snow isolated a water pump where a broken sewer pipe was dumping human waste into the drinking water. He had the handle of the pump removed, and the outbreak in the area declined. Snow's research proved that cholera was not morally borne; it was *water*borne.[7] The roads and alleyways, the buildings built among them, and the pipes laid beneath them — mixing and pooling human waste — enabled the disease to spread. He also proved that biological survival is spatially reliant.

Snow's simple mapping method is a foundational document in the study of disease and of the design of cities. Cited as a founding father of epidemiology and urban design alike, he demonstrated that poor (or nonexistent) spatial planning puts public health at grave risk. He also revealed a structural solution that was (at least empirically) blind to class, linking the working-class neighborhood of Soho and the workers' health to the health of the public at large. The moralizing constraints placed upon the public shifted, dislodged by the foundational tenets of the modern era: data, empirical evidence, and the scientific method. A redesign of piped city substructure (fig. 9), increased zoning and regulatory superstructure, and the decongestion of dense tenement housing in industrial capitals such as London and New York followed in the latter part of the nineteenth century — all under the rubric of health, sanitation, and hygiene. The sanitary era (as it became known) was not immune to moralizing, however, and while scientific evidence increasingly led to significant population health outcomes, it was also deployed to defend and support missions of imperial and colonial aggression, such as the war in Crimea and the scramble for Africa.[8]

Renkioi, Turkey

These new theories of contagion were circulating among health care professionals in the 1850s, when Brunel was tasked with designing a demountable military clinic for Crimea. His design accordingly homed in on the essentials: controlled access to light and fresh air, the separation and removal of waste, and the prevention of overcrowding.

6 Charles E. Rosenberg, *The Cholera Years: The United States in 1832, 1849, and 1866* (Chicago: University of Chicago Press, 1987), 40.

7 K. S. McLeod, "Our Sense of Snow: The Myth of John Snow in Medical Geography," *Social Science Medicine* 50, nos. 7–8 (April 2000): 923–35. Snow's discovery contributed to a growing body of evidence that challenged miasma theory, but the latter would continue to dominate medical planning for another half-century.

8 Jason Corburn, "Reconnecting with Our Roots: American Urban Planning and Public Health in the Twenty-First Century," *Urban Affairs Review* 42, no. 5 (2007), and Sara Jensen Carr, *The Topography of Wellness: Health and the American Urban Landscape* (Charlottesville, VA: University of Virginia Press, 2021).

8

9

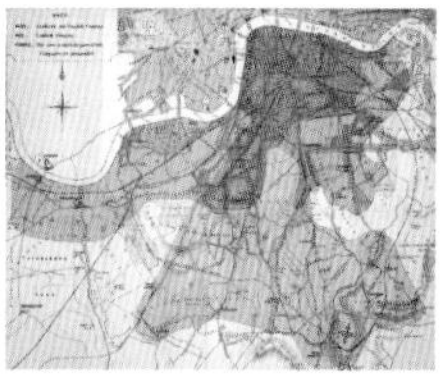

10

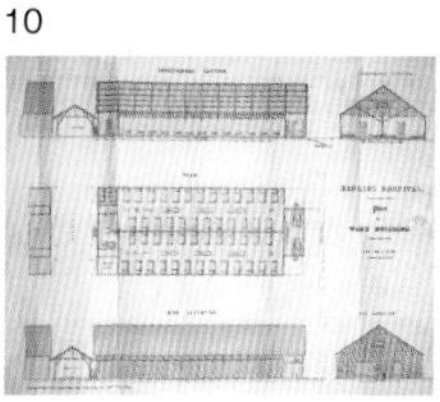

Brunel delivered a never-before-seen structure: a flat-packed, prefabricated emergency field hospital. His replicable unit — a single ward **(fig. 10)** — was lightweight, made of wood, and covered in a thin layer of tin that acted as insulation. It was extremely well ventilated, with a series of openings running under the eaves, two long rows of narrow windows designed to let in air even when shuttered, and a rotary air pump at one end of the structure for hand-crank ventilation when needed **(fig. 11)**. As the arrival of individual units would be staggered, each ward was designed to be self-sufficient, containing its own lavatory, nurses' room, storage facility, and surgical theater. Before the hospital was deployed to Turkey, a prototype was erected in Paddington station.

Construction of Brunel's field hospital began on May 21, 1855, in the Turkish town of Renkioi. Less than two months later, on July 12, it was ready to treat three hundred soldiers. By August 11 it housed five hundred patients, by December 4 one thousand, and by the end of March 1856 **(fig. 12)**, when the war ended (less than a year after construction started), the hospital had expanded its capacity to 2,200 beds **(fig. 13)**.[9] Prefabricated and incremental construction meant that the hospital could be rescaled as demand waxed and waned.

The industrialization of England influenced warfare and occupation abroad. The prefabrication of prototypes is an industrialized building method; scale, replicability, and speed are the priorities, not craftsmanship. For Brunel's design, context, culture, and site mattered little: the goal was a temporary structure that could be erected quickly and function more effectively. And in Renkioi, the goal of treatment was not a reduction in suffering so much as the protection of military assets, the prolonging of British soldiers' lives so that they might more decisively shorten the lives of the enemy. In this way, health care was also industrialized.

By the end of the war, the mortality rate at the Renkioi hospital was around 3 percent; in Scutari, at the barracks hospital where Nightingale worked, the mortality rate was 42.7 percent.[10] This 40 percent difference was evidence of the profound impact of simple architectural and spatial methods — methods that, when fully understood and replicated, would go on to prolong untold nonmilitary lives. The hospital, no longer a hall of the dead, was now a mechanism of science and its architecture a humanitarian conduit to a longer life.

The Nightingale Era

The Renkioi hospital's enduring influence is due not to Brunel but to Nightingale, who had an opportunity to observe it while nursing in the nearby Scutari barracks hospital. In her book *Notes on Hospitals* (1859; **fig. 14**), she described the components of the pavilion hospital and praised its logic and scientific rigor. The ideas Nightingale set forth are generally considered the first treatise on modern hospital planning and quickly became foundational references for hospital design. Nightingale presented an extensive list of standards: for example, wards should be no more than two stories high, beds should be at least three and a half feet apart, and all woodwork should be finished in such a way as to allow

9 John D. Thompson and Grace Goldin, *The Hospital: A Social and Architectural History* (New Haven, CT: Yale University Press, 1975), 153.

10 Florence Nightingale, *Notes on Hospitals, with Evidence Given to the Royal Commissioners on the State of the Army in 1857*, 2nd ed. (London: Parker and Son, 1859), 25–28.

11

12

13

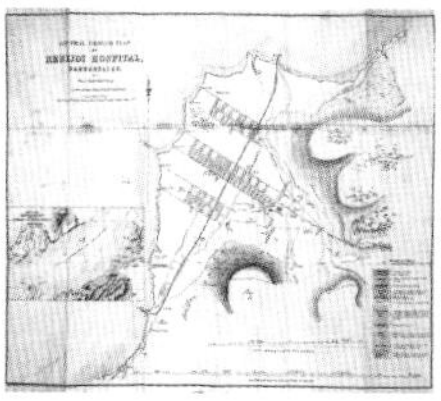

14

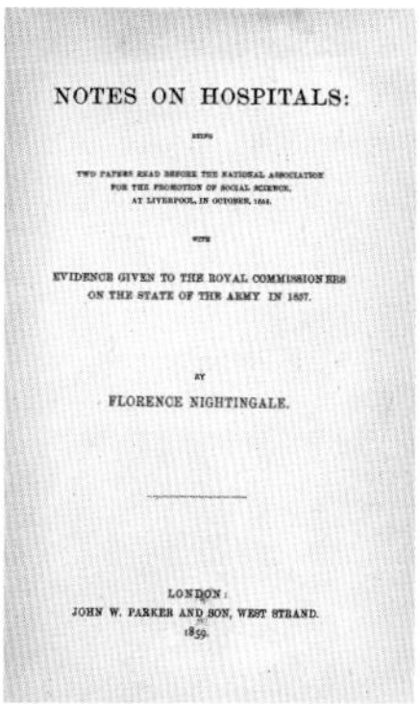

NOTES ON HOSPITALS:

EVIDENCE GIVEN TO THE ROYAL COMMISSIONERS ON THE STATE OF THE ARMY IN 1857.

FLORENCE NIGHTINGALE.

LONDON:
JOHN W. PARKER AND SON, WEST STRAND.
1859.

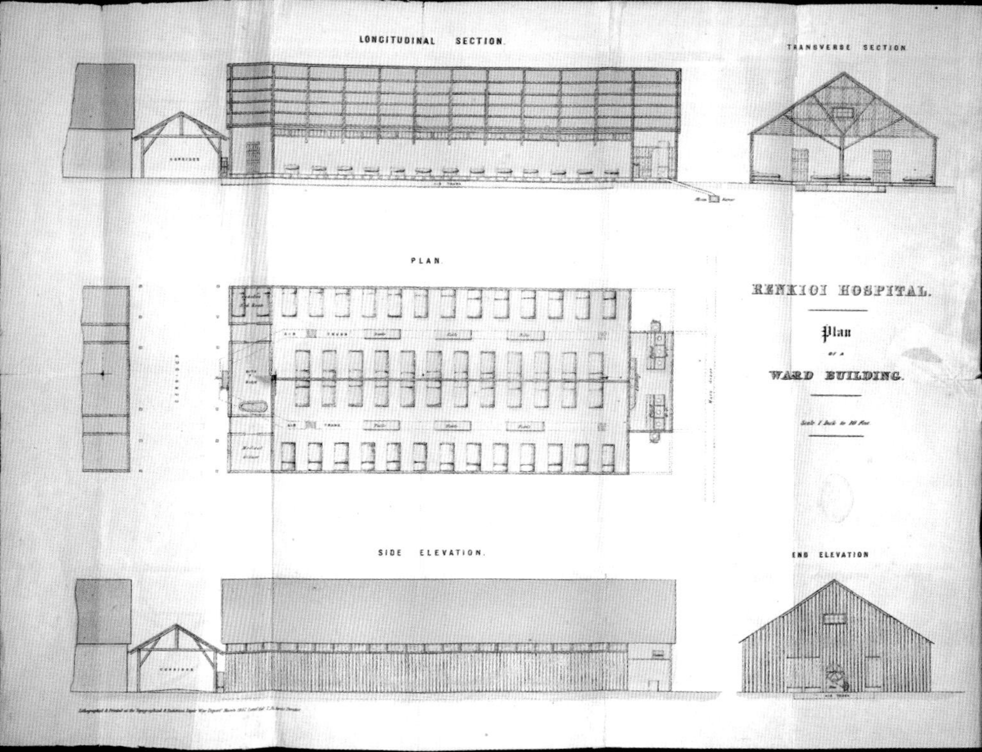

Brunel designed a prefabricated field hospital that could be made in England, shipped by rail to Turkey, and assembled by soldiers on-site — a deployable medical infrastructure designed to save soldiers' lives and help them win the war.

Views of ward building for Renkioi Hospital, designed by Isambard Kingdom Brunel, 1857 [fig. 10]

Sketches of prefabricated field hospital by Isambard Kingdom Brunel, 1855 [fig. 5]

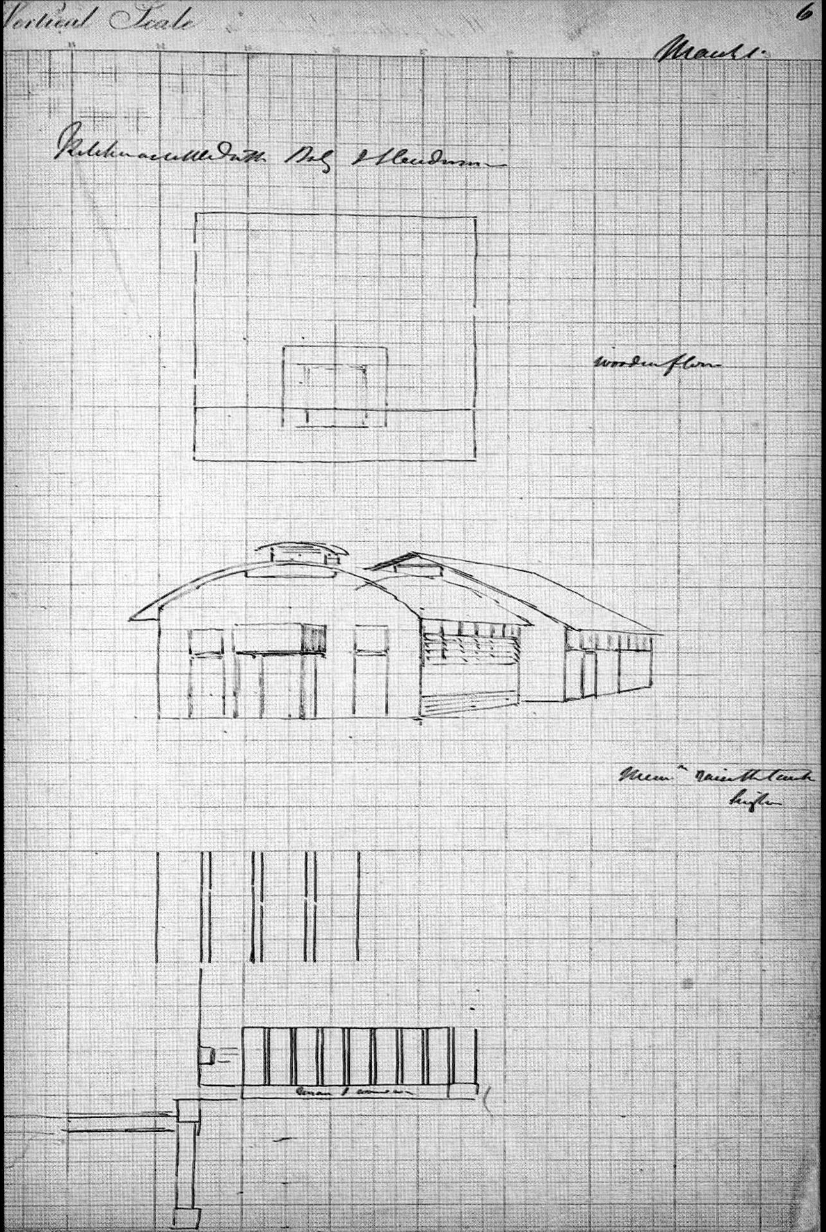

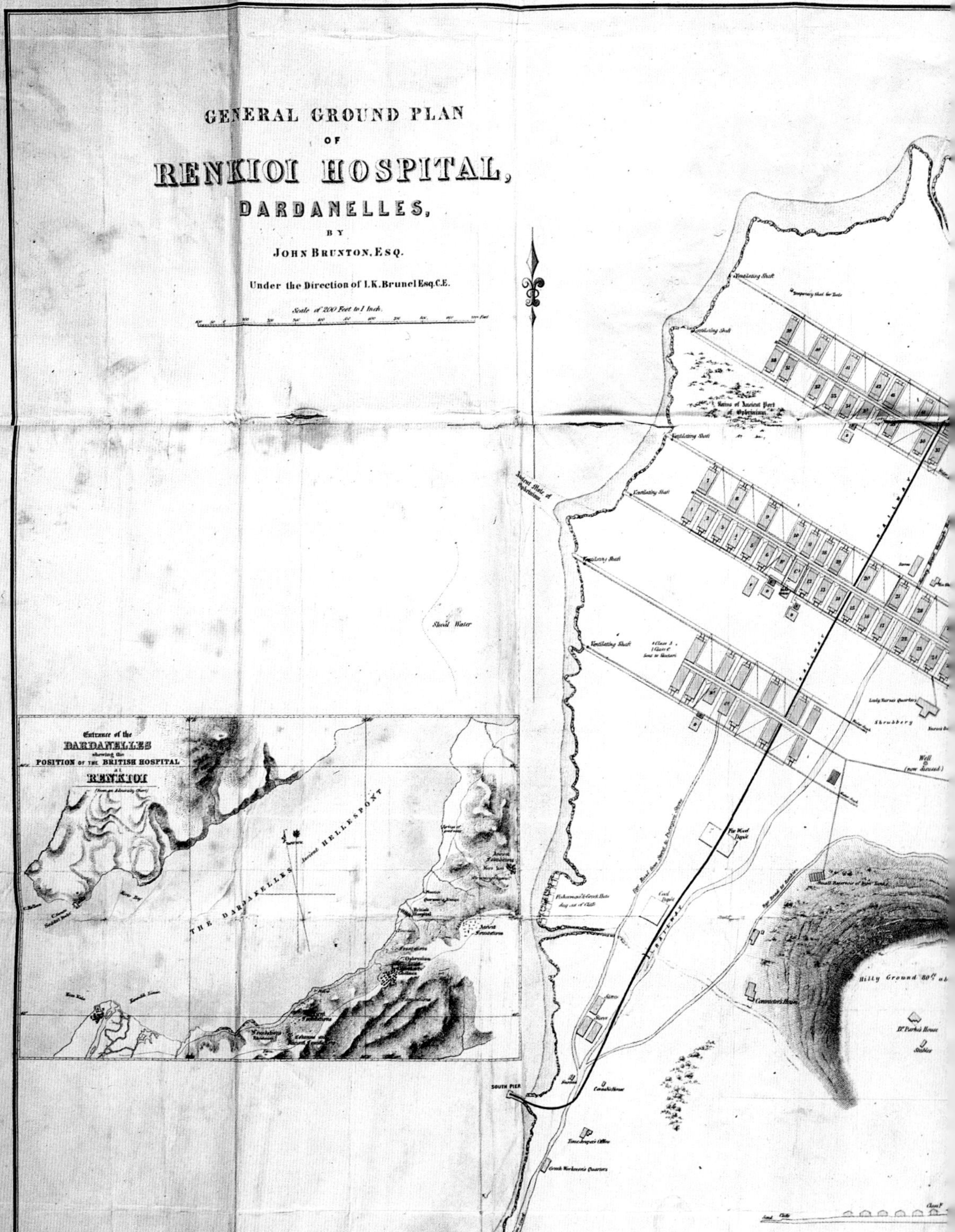
GENERAL GROUND PLAN
OF
RENKIOI HOSPITAL,
DARDANELLES,
BY
JOHN BRUNTON, ESQ.
Under the Direction of I.K. Brunel Esq. C.E.
Scale of 200 Feet to 1 Inch.
Entrance of the
DARDANELLES
shewing the
POSITION OF THE BRITISH HOSPITAL
at
RENKIOI
THE DARDANELLES Ancient HELLESPONT
Ventilating Shaft
Ruins of Ancient Port of Ophrinium
Shoal Water
Lady Nurses Quarters
Shrubbery
Well (now disused)
Fir Wood Depot
Coal Depot
Small Reservoir or Water Tanks
Hilly Ground
Contractor's House
Dr. Parkes House
Stables
SOUTH PIER
Timekeeper's Office
Greek Workmen's Quarters
Springs
Fountain
Road
Bridge
Coal Depot
Fire Wood Depot
RAILWAY

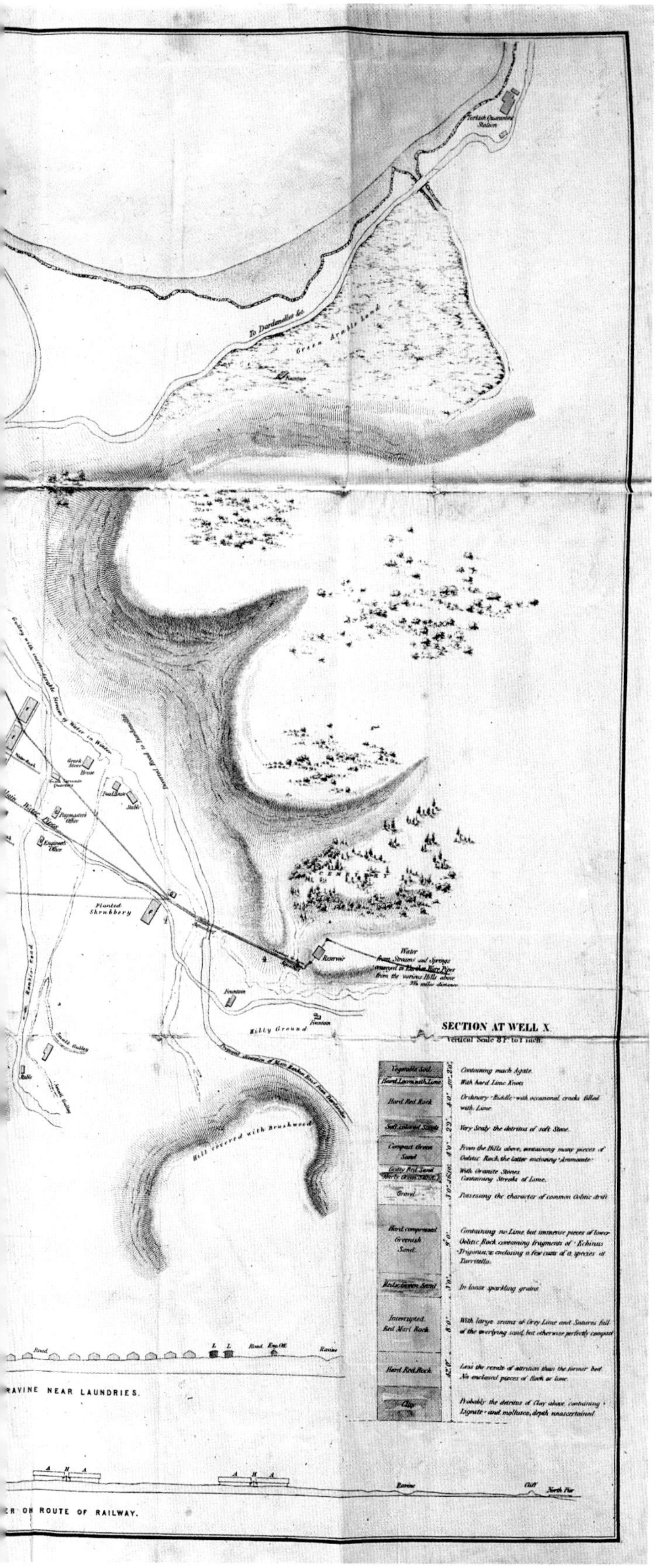

Site plan, Renkioi Hospital.
Drawing by John Brunton
[fig. 13]

11 Nightingale, *Notes on Hospitals*, 90, 152.

12 Florence Nightingale, *Notes on Nursing* (London: Harrison, 1859), 9.

13 Thompson and Goldin, *The Hospital*, 118.

for quick washing and drying (fig. 15).[11] In all her writings, she stressed the importance of clean air above all:

> The very first canon of nursing ... is this: to keep the air [the patient] breathes as pure as the external air, without chilling him.... In admitting air into the patient's room or ward, few people ever think, where that air comes from. It may come from a corridor into which other wards are ventilated, from a hall, always unaired, always full of the fumes of gas, dinner, of various kinds of mustiness; from an underground kitchen, sink, washhouse, water-closet, ... and with this the patient's room or ward is aired, as it is called — poisoned, it should rather be said.... It is quite ripe to breed small-pox, scarlet-fever, diphtheria, or anything else you please.[12]

Nightingale's various publications — she also wrote *Notes on Matters Affecting the Health, Efficiency, and Hospital Administration of the British Army* (1858) and *Notes on Nursing* (1859) — contained detailed records and pioneering visual graphics. The rose chart (fig. 16), or coxcomb diagram, is attributed to Nightingale, who used it to quantify and compare the prevalence of preventable wartime deaths. *Notes on Hospitals* also contained architectural drawings, which described the benefits, dimensions, and parameters of the ideal hospital ward. By the late 1800s, Nightingale's design — the pavilion ward — was deployed around the world, another colonial beachhead in the sanitation era. This standardized, replicable model (known also as the Nightingale ward) transformed hospitals from buildings full of beds into vital instruments of health. "The pavilion plan," Thompson and Goldin wrote, "was a sanitary code embodied in a building."[13] Hospitals, and their design, would become as influential to healing as the physicians within them.

Form Follows Facts

The pavilion ward, as disseminated by Nightingale, was early evidence that the form of a building could lead to measurably improved outcomes. At its core, it unveiled a foundational conflict within architecture. If used as designed, the pavilion ward was a medical instrument that could shape human behavior and quantifiably improve people's health. However, if used *not* as intended, the outcomes would be uncertain or, worse, harmful. The proper use of architecture and its optimal functionality emerged, therefore, as a key parameter in the evaluation of a built structure over time.

Form, we might say, followed facts. Nightingale and other reformers of her time led a movement to replicate the pavilion model and, overall, to promote the design of built spaces and landscapes as strategies for improving public health. The sanitary era shaped communities the world over, and it had a particularly strong impact on industrializing cities, where parks, open spaces, housing regulations, and piped wastewater systems all came to be acknowledged as necessary investments. Also considered imperative in this era of industrialization were imperial occupation and colonial extraction (sources of cheap labor and

15

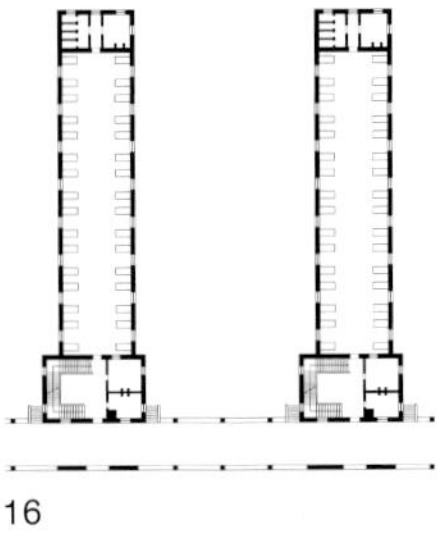

16

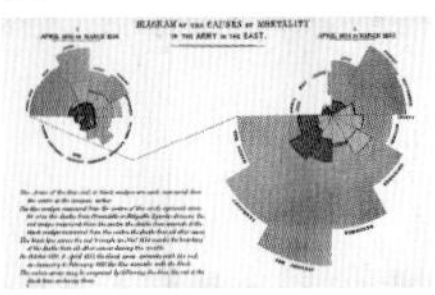

raw materials), and concepts of hygiene and sanitation were used to defend racial and social segregation in colonial outposts, reinforcing systemic racism. By the end of the century, waterborne diseases such as cholera and typhoid were no longer of major concern. The same could not be said for airborne and mosquito-borne diseases, however, and tuberculosis and malaria would have a profound influence on the conceptual and moral frameworks of modern architecture.[14]

The creation of the pavilion hospital and its spread across Europe, the Americas, and later the globe is one of the great untold stories of architectural revolution. Like Snow's cholera map, Nightingale's *Notes on Hospitals* drew connections between health, sanitation, and infrastructure, transforming the discipline of architecture by bringing it in contact with a body of scientific knowledge. Some architects became masters of this knowledge; it was a disciplinary birthing. The miasma theory advocated by Nightingale and her contemporaries, though mistaken, led to an increased awareness of the importance of ventilation and a sanitary environment to patient well-being and recovery. This move toward spatializing medicine introduced smarter, healthier designs into hospital architecture.

In outlining the design logic of the pavilion hospital, Nightingale created sanitary codes that were later expanded into a full-fledged legal code, with the British Public Health Acts of 1874 and 1875. These acts, which included specific infrastructure, planning, and residential provisions, held architects to an unprecedented fiduciary standard that continues to be central to the profession.

14 Beatriz Colomina, *X-Ray Architecture* (Zurich: Lars Müller, 2020), 10–11.

Craft and Dignity Construction

The *fin de siècle* ushered in new architectural styles and theories in hospital design. Radical developments in scientific knowledge — notably the advancement of germ theory and anesthesia — led to significant leaps in surgical medicine and new lifesaving treatments. Attention to germ theory necessitated that surgeries happen in hygienic conditions; no longer could the well-off have medical treatment in the comfort of their homes. Hospitals, until then primarily charitable providers for the poor, suddenly became essential institutions for the wealthy, and hospital campuses expanded to accommodate this growing need.

Hospital de la Santa Creu i Sant Pau, Barcelona

In the late nineteenth century, Barcelona was a capital of shipping and commerce. Pau Gil i Serra, a wealthy Catalan banker living in Paris, commissioned a new hospital based on French theories of sanitation to replace Barcelona's medieval Hospital de la Santa Creu **(fig. 17)**. Lluís Domènech i Montaner (1850–1923) — who would also design Barcelona's Palau de la Música Catalana (1908) — won the commission. As well as an architect, Montaner was a well-known activist, politician, visionary, and ardent nationalist. With the Hospital de la Santa Creu i Sant Pau (renamed in honor of its patron), he sought to design a new national beacon of Catalan identity, craft, and prominence.

17

NOTE.
BLUE,- Southwark and Vauxhall Company.
RED,- Lambeth Company.
PURPLE,- The area in which the pipes of both Companies are intermingled.
HYDE PARK
THE SERPENTINE
GREEN PARK
ST. JAMES'S PARK
BROMPTON
CHELSEA
BATTERSEA PARK
BATTERSEA
BATTERSEA NEW TOWN
FULHAM
PUTNEY
PUTNEY DISTRICT
WANDSWORTH
WANDSWORTH DISTRICT
RIVER WANDLE
WIMBLEDON PARK
WIMBLEDON
Wimbledon Common
Putney Heath
CLAPHAM
Clapham Common
Clapham Park
Wandsworth Common
BATTERSEA DISTRICT
STOCKWELL
KENNINGTON
BRIXTON
BRIXTON DISTRICT
Radius of 4 Miles from Charing Cross
UPPER TOOTING
TOOTING
Tooting Common
STREATHAM
STREATHAM DISTRICT
Streatham Common
LOWER NORWOOD
NORWOOD DISTRICT
DULWICH
WALWORTH
SOUTHWARK
NEWINGTON BUTTS
WEST END AND CRYSTAL PALACE RAILWAY

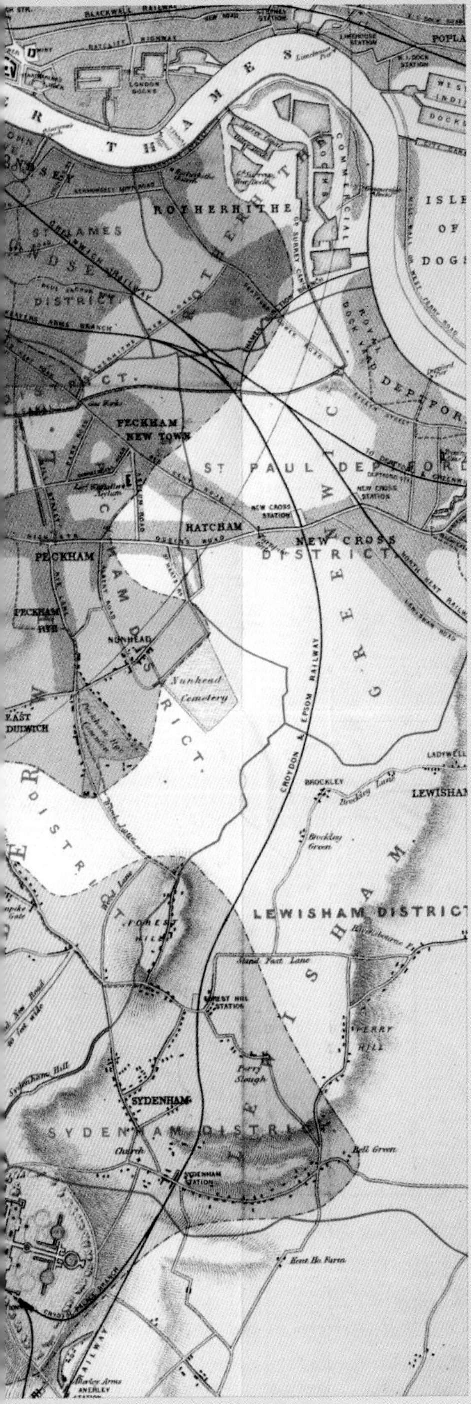

Map showing water supply of the Lambeth and Southwark and Vauxhall Companies, London, by John Snow, 1855 [fig. 9]

The north ward at Renkioi Hospital [fig. 11]

15 Miriam Giordano, "Santa Creu i Sant Pau Hospital: The Splendor of Catalonian Modernism," www.world-architects.com/en/architecture-news/headlines/santa-creu-i-sant-pau-hospital-the-splendor-of-catalonian-modernism, September 24, 2015.

16 In the modern era, the Belgian architect Henry van de Velde (1863–1967) popularized this concept as core to the emergence of modernity.

17 William Morris, *The Collected Works of William Morris: With Introductions by His Daughter May Morris* (Cambridge, UK: Cambridge University Press, 2012), 205.

Begun in 1902 and completed in 1930, Montaner's hospital attests to the integral role that open space and natural light played in treatment programs at the time. Like Nightingale, he emphasized ventilation and natural lighting, but he combined the principles of the pavilion with Catalan craftsmanship to create a space as focused on beauty as it was on care (figs. 18–21).

To capitalize on sea breezes for ventilation, Montaner oriented the hospital's pavilions at a forty-five-degree angle to the city grid (figs. 22, 23). He limited cross-contamination by including separate sanitary and waste services for each of the eight pavilion structures, which were distanced from one another. Each building had two open wards, each designed to house twenty-eight patients, with a few single rooms reserved for wealthy patients (figs. 24, 25).[15] Underground tunnels linked each pavilion to utilities and served as the main distribution route for all hospital services and for the sick.

The attributes of the built space — the relationships among bed, altar, window, and privy: the hospital's DNA — came together in a functioning, dynamic system. Nature was integrated into the complex throughout; each pavilion had two gardens planted with carefully selected medicinal flora (fig. 26). Patient rooms looked onto these open spaces, which helped to move air through the buildings, while large trees shaded the wards. The ventilation system, including vaulted ceilings and operable windows, positioned the building as not only a place of care but also a component of care. Montaner's hospital also linked both beauty and nationalist political values to medicine's social mission: wrapped in symbolic friezes containing religious and cultural iconography and executed by Catalan artisans in a stylistic bricolage of Moorish, Spanish, and Mediterranean tile work, the hospital exemplified the Wagnerian concept of *Gesamtkunstwerk* — it was a total work of art.[16]

The Politics of Beauty

Montaner, like Nightingale and Brunel before him, was a multidisciplinarian. He coined the word *modernismé* in his theoretical writings and instructed a generation of students in rethinking the role of design. More than simply the architect of a hospital, as an elected official and Catalan nationalist he was also the architect of a cultural and political movement. For him, architecture was an investment in place and in people. His projects are statements of Catalan identity and assertions of the role architecture can play in shaping political economy.

In England, William Morris (1834–1896; fig. 27) also saw architecture as a political project. A founder the Arts and Crafts Movement (*modernismé*'s analogue), Morris demonstrated that a total work of art, as an investment in craftsmanship, could be a form of resistance to the industrial era's diminishment of labor and its fetishization of the worker. "Nothing should be made by man's labour which is not worth making, or which must be made by labour degrading to the makers," he declared.[17] In response to the subjugation of industrial workers, the abuse of the masses — the same objectification that institutions like hospitals enabled — Morris, Montaner, and members of other international movements that emphasized craft found liberation through artistry and beauty. In 1753 Marc-Antoine Laugier made the case that "the poor should be lodged as poor" — in austere and unadorned surroundings — and that beauty was counterproductive to charity (see chapter 1). Architects around the turn of the twentieth century, on the other hand, made the opposite argument: Beauty, they declared, should play a key role in the provision of public welfare. Beauty was a conduit to charity. In this model, architecture was no longer a messenger of opulence or political power but rather an investment in the individual, in the public good, and in national as well as collective identity. In this way, the argument suggested, architecture can constitute dignity.[18]

Who deserves care, and who is worth caring for? The difference between an individual's worth and an individual's rights has to do with dignity. People deemed *worth* caring for are an investment for the state: more bodies for more labor. It is an economic argument, not a moral one. That some *deserve* care is a moral argument, focusing on individuals' rights as human beings, their dignity, their humanity. The proponents of the Arts and Crafts Movement linked beauty to satisfying labor, but beauty in public amenities produces something else as well: a belief in the value of the individual. It is a demonstration not of power deployed but of power shared, distributed, and used for social construction. Montaner's hospital, with its lush gardens, its ornament, its seeming excess, met a fundamental need: the nourishment of the whole being.

18 William Morris, "Art and Industry in the Fourteenth Century" (1890), in *Morris on History*, ed. Nicholas Salmon (Sheffield, UK: Sheffield Academic Press, 1996), 90–105.

18

19

20

21
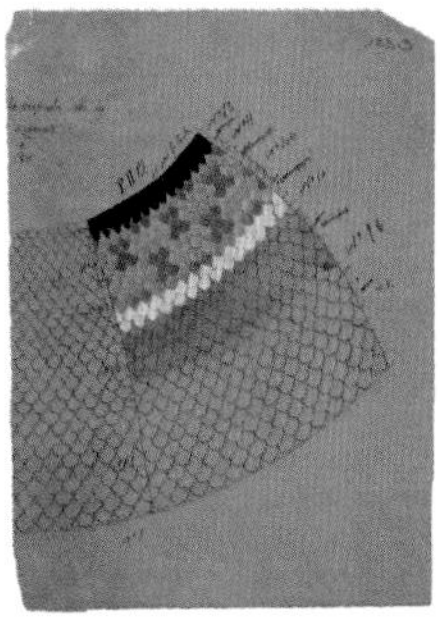
22

23
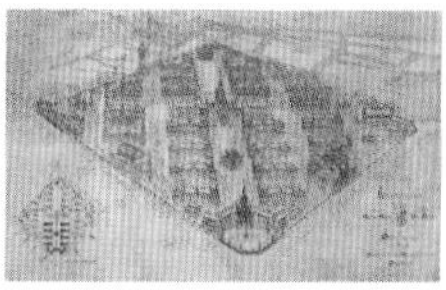
24
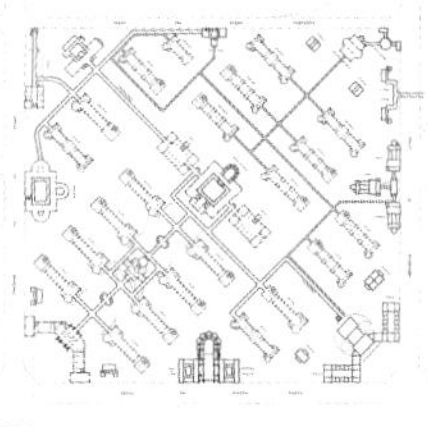
25
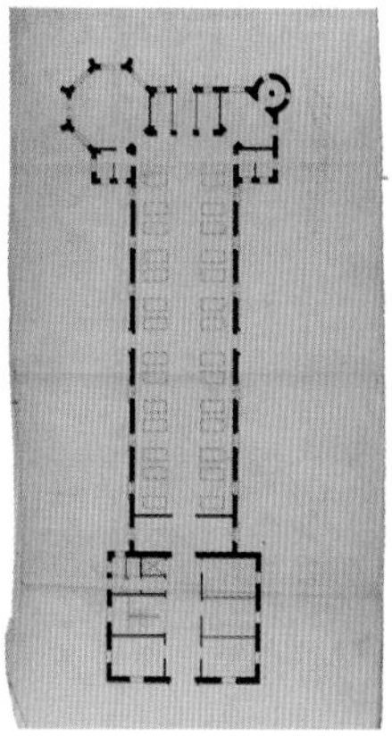
26

27

Montaner's hospital also linked both beauty and nationalist political values to medicine's social mission: wrapped in symbolic friezes containing religious and cultural iconography and executed by Catalan artisans in a stylistic bricolage of Moorish, Spanish, and Mediterranean tile work, the hospital exemplified the Wagnerian concept of *Gesamtkunstwerk* — it was a total work of art.

Ward in the women's infirmary pavilion at the Hospital de la Santa Creu i Sant Pau, Barcelona, designed by Lluís Domènech i Montaner, 1930 [fig. 18]

2015 aerial photograph of the Hospital de la Santa Creu i Sant Pau [fig. 22]

Roofs, domes, and water towers of the hospital's infirmary pavilions [fig. 19]

Birds'-eye axonometric drawing of the Hospital de la Santa Creu i Sant Pau, Barcelona, designed by Lluís Domènech i Montaner, c. 1901–03 [fig. 23]

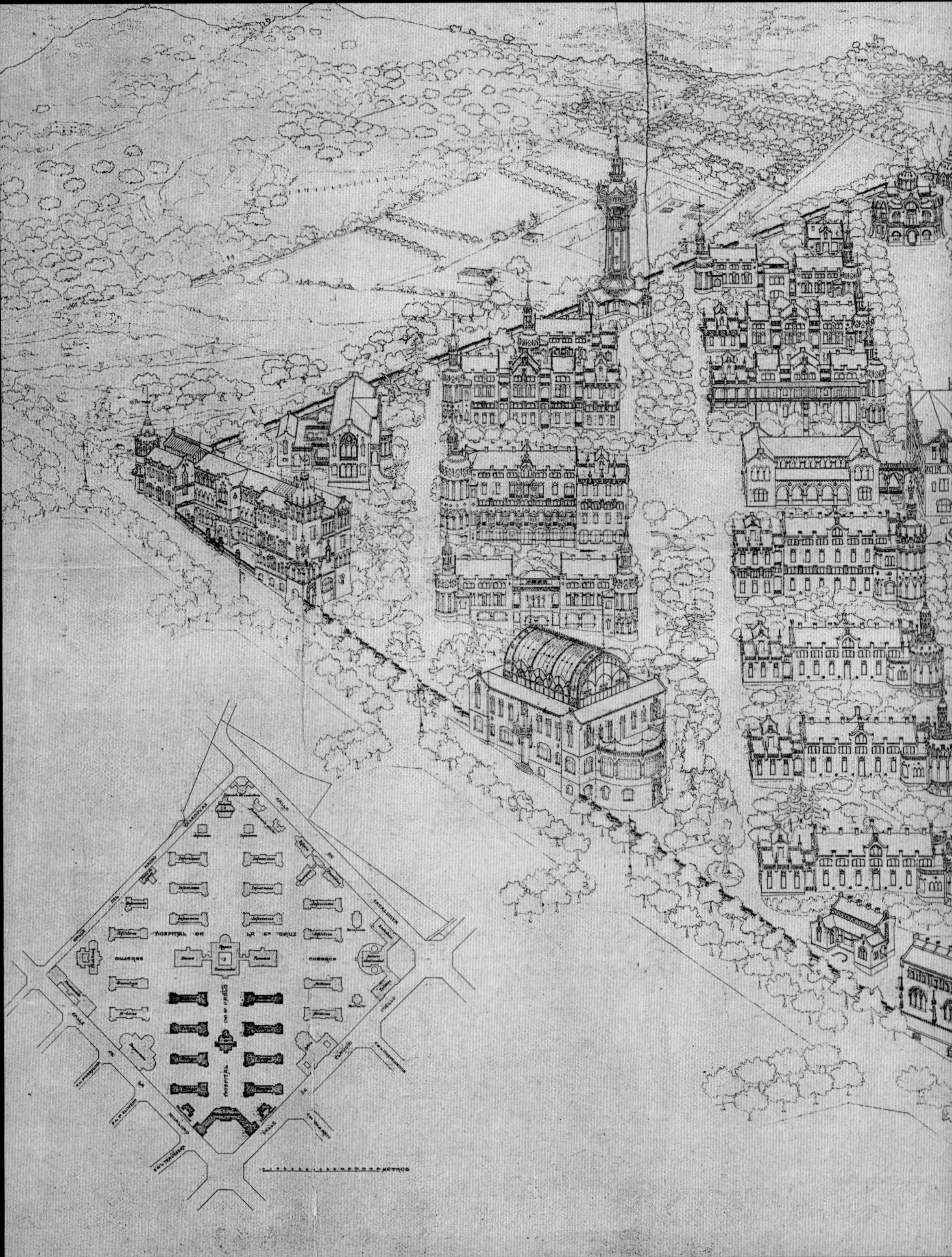

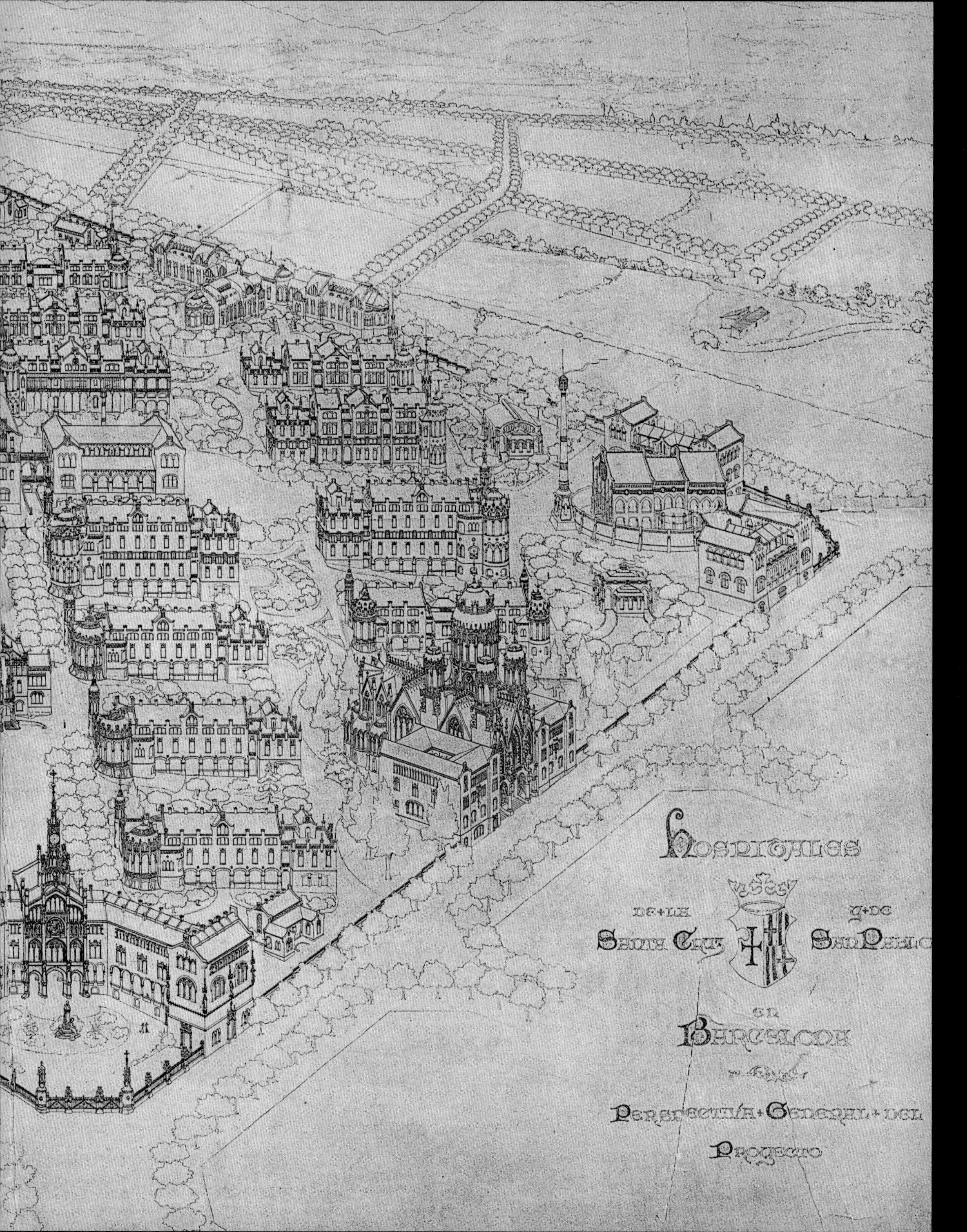
Hospitales
de la
Santa Cruz
y de
San Pabl
en
Barcelona
Perspectiva General del
Proyecto

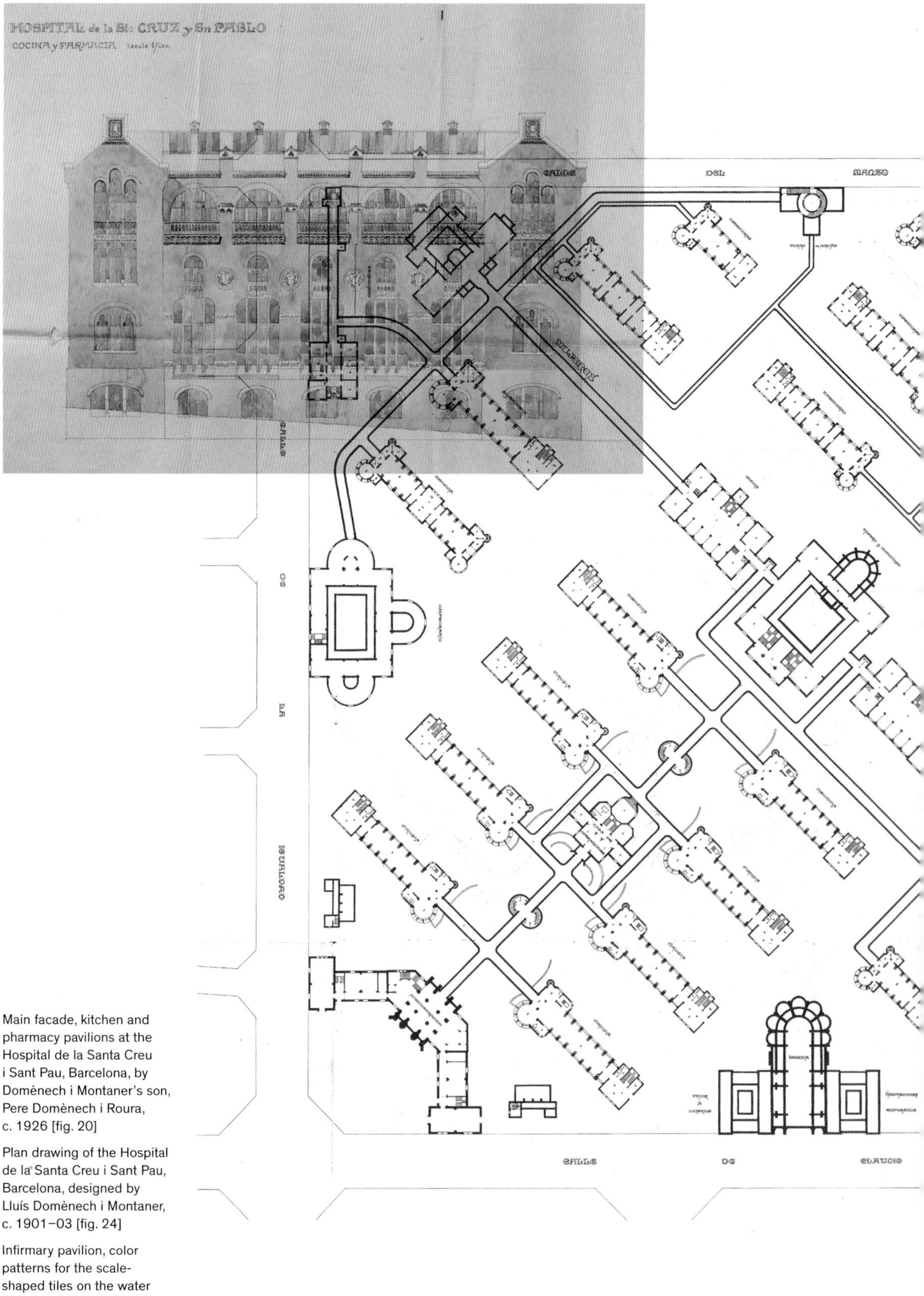

Main facade, kitchen and pharmacy pavilions at the Hospital de la Santa Creu i Sant Pau, Barcelona, by Domènech i Montaner's son, Pere Domènech i Roura, c. 1926 [fig. 20]

Plan drawing of the Hospital de la Santa Creu i Sant Pau, Barcelona, designed by Lluís Domènech i Montaner, c. 1901–03 [fig. 24]

Infirmary pavilion, color patterns for the scale-shaped tiles on the water tower, designed by Lluís Domènech i Montaner c. 1907 [fig. 21]

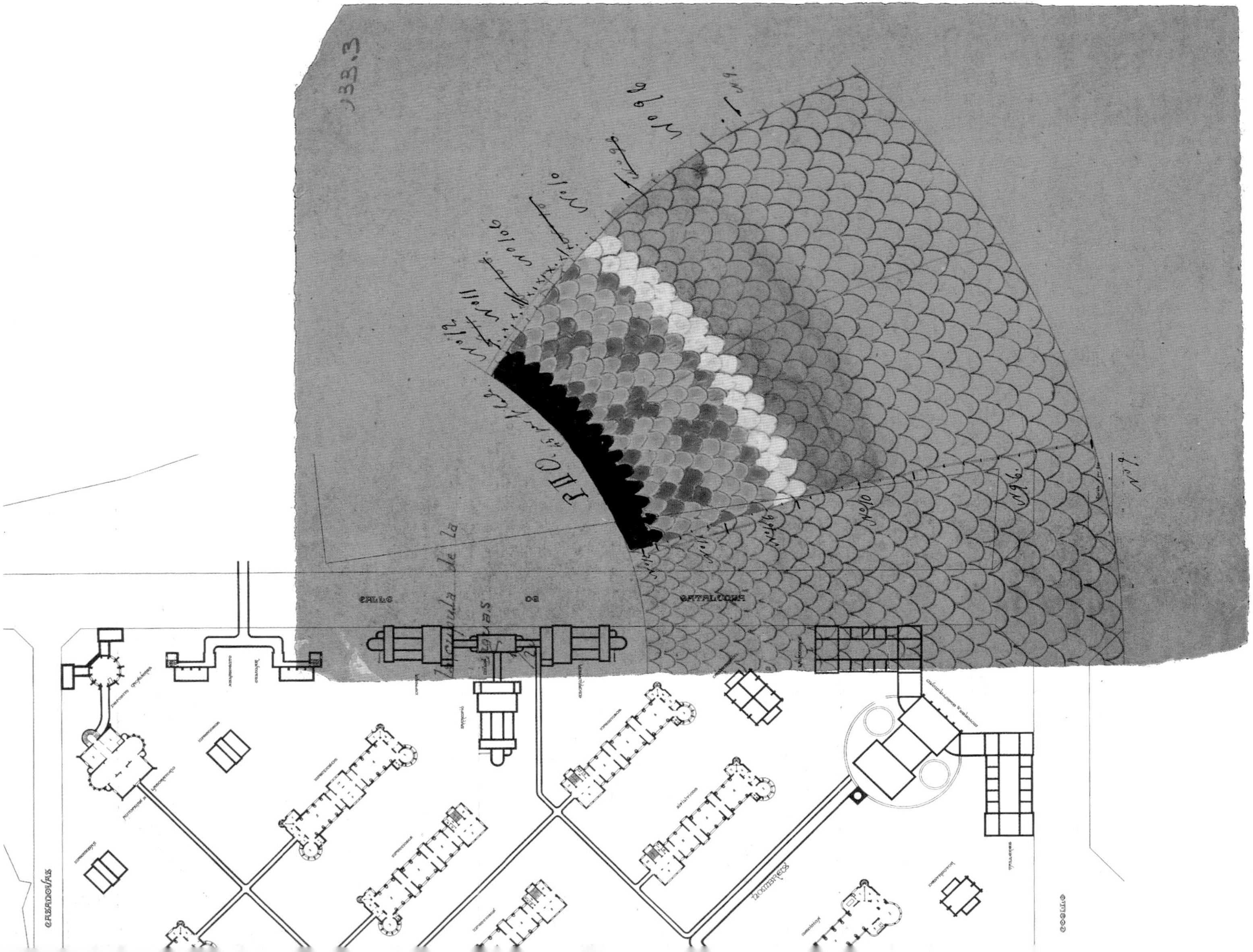
133.3
P II O.
Nº12
Nº11
Nº106
Nº10
Nº96
Nº9
CALLE
DE
CATALUÑA
CASANOVAS

Typical plan of a Nightingale ward (redrawn by MASS Design Group) [fig. 15]

Typical plan of a pavilion, Hospital de la Santa Creu i Sant Pau, Barcelona, designed by Lluís Domènech i Montaner, c. 1901–03 (Fundació Hospital de la Santa Creu i Sant Pau) [fig. 25]

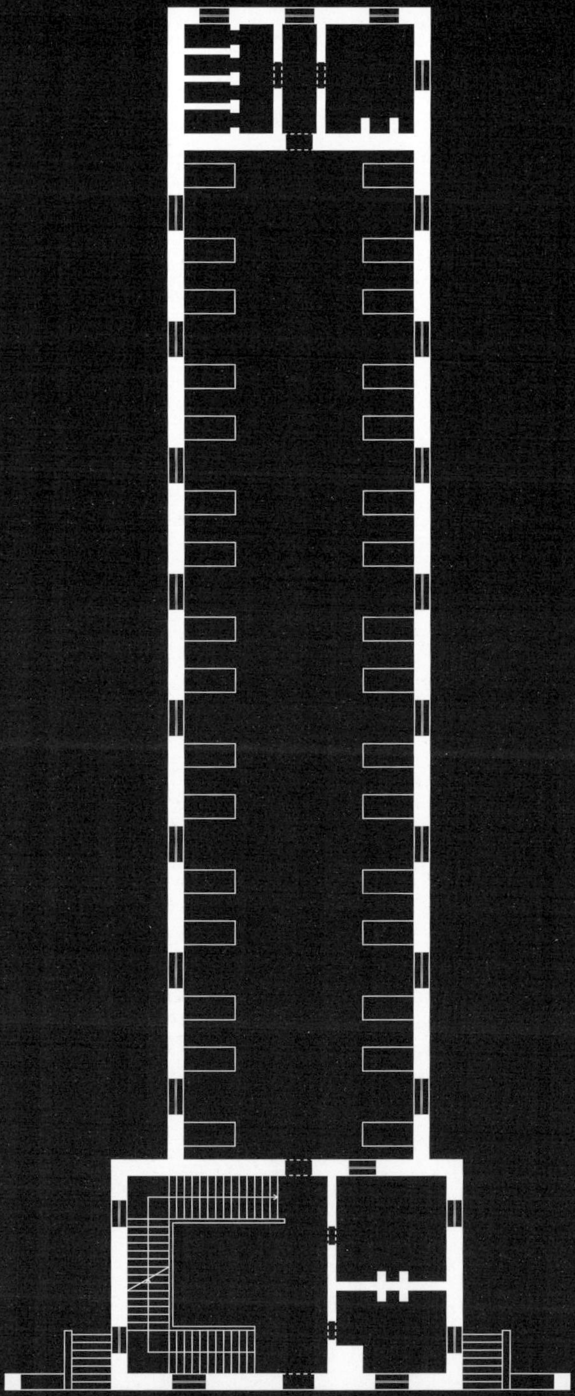

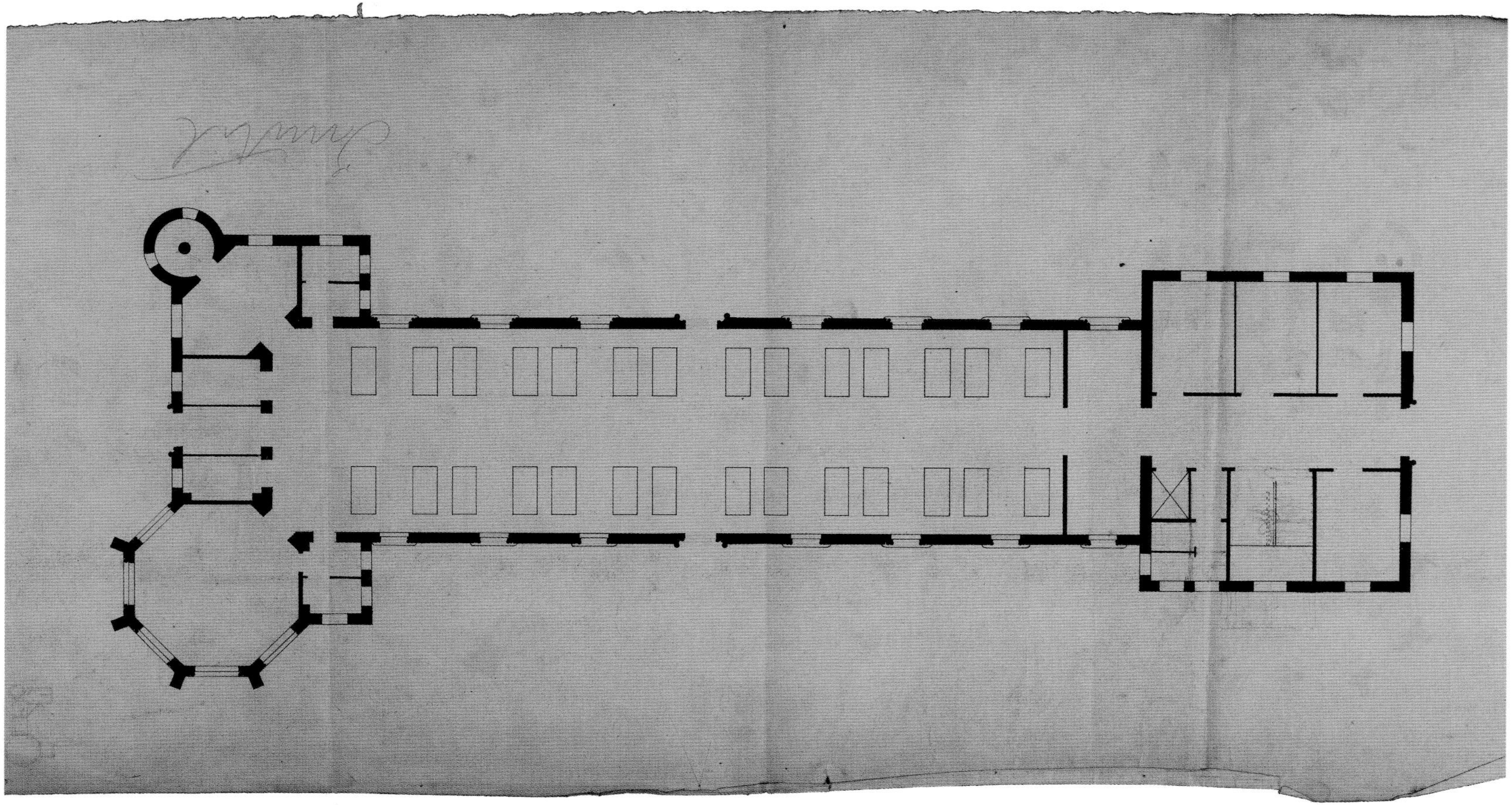

Chapter 3
Imperial Forms and the Medical Mission

Exporting the Pavilion

Florence Nightingale was a polymath: her writing, designs, teachings, and data visualizations all launched new disciplines (fig. 1), and nursing, medicine, statistics, and architecture all credit her as a foundational thinker. Nightingale's work had political implications too; as an advocate and lobbyist, she influenced British policy, fighting for a national health care system and health care investment throughout the British Commonwealth. But for all her contributions to medicine, she also propagated certain imperialist concepts that were subjugating, racist, and dismissive, including the notion of civilizing uplift and the perceived moral supremacy of British scientific knowledge.[1] The public hospital was a conduit and symbol of both political power and charitable responsibility, but it also embodied a moral defense of the colonial project. Hospital architecture, no matter its impact on public health, was a reflection of the British crown's conception of its responsibilities and its power over its subjects, at home and in its colonies.

The pavilion hospital was particularly exportable and replicable. It was standardized, simple, and self-contained, and its logic — if not always its specific forms — could be applied consistently across a vast range of climates and sites. As an element of British public health initiatives in the late 1800s, it was expressive of the state's responsibility to the public, but it also was used, especially in the colonies, to reinforce power structures favorable to the British. Defined through a language of scientific analysis, the pavilion hospital communicated privilege, racial difference, and cultural control, weaponizing apparently neutral concepts such as hygiene and sanitation in the service of dominance and segregation.

In the nineteenth and early twentieth centuries, corporate and state entities invested heavily in hospitals, as their profits were predicated on colonized labor, and health care kept the laborer fit to work.[2] A patient placed in a hospital ward also *becomes a ward* of the authorities — the doctor, the administrator, the colonizer — that oversee care, reinforcing social orders of subjugation and difference.[3] In this way, the hospital is both a humanitarian service (a provider of charity) and an enforcer of power (a system of control) — roles that are contradictory yet inherently intertwined.

New Somerset Hospital, Cape Town

In 1859, construction began on New Somerset Hospital in Cape Town, South Africa (fig. 2), designed by the British-born colonial engineer John Scott Tucker (1812–1882). When the hospital opened, in 1864, it recruited its staff from Nightingale's London School of Nursing and Midwifery, importing, along with its workers, the Victorian era's aesthetics, charitable ideals, and ethos of colonial domination.

At the time, eclectic period revivals were all the rage in architecture, with buildings designed in neo-Gothic, neo-Tudor, and neoclassical styles, among others. For New Somerset, Scott Tucker chose a medieval style, designing the hospital like a twelfth-century British castle, with keep, turrets, and towers. Now a provincial heritage site, it was an imperial fortress: a defensive structure designed to keep people out instead of welcoming them in (fig. 3). Visitors were greeted by an impressive entry parlor and a handcrafted wooden staircase (figs. 4, 5) below tiled archways intermixed with decorative crests. On the second floor were pavilion wards, on either side of a central corridor. They followed Nightingale's guidelines, featuring high ceilings, large windows, fireplaces, and a unique clerestory hopper window designed to pull air through the wards and out over the hallway roof (fig. 6). In addition, long, shaded wooden verandas lined the windowed exterior walls of the wards, creating outdoor spaces for patients (figs. 7, 8).

1

2

3

4

5

6

7

8
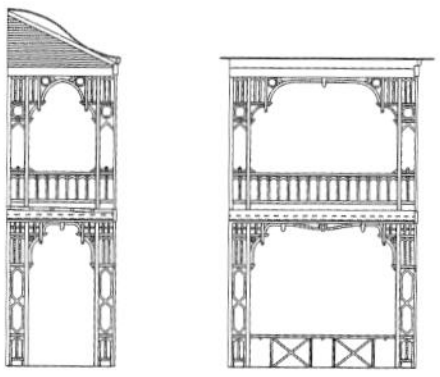

1 See, for example, Florence Nightingale, *Sanitary Statistics of Native Colonial Schools and Hospitals* (London, 1863).

2 "The United Fruit Company . . . seems to have spent the most money on protecting the health of its worker. By the late 1920s, the Company . . . had yearly net earnings of nearly £20 million. From these earnings, the Company spent £1 million per year for medical expenses, and £500,000 for sanitation and street-cleaning operations." John Farley, *Bilharzia: A History of Imperial Tropical Medicine* (London: Cambridge University Press, 1991), 117.

3 This process of subjugation, which Michel Foucault called "biopower," can be understood as a regulatory mechanism — and the hospital as a disciplinary apparatus — that links medical practice to broader agendas of disease control, patient supervision, public health, and population control. Biopower, according to Foucault, is "an explosion of numerous and diverse techniques for achieving the subjugations of bodies and the control of populations." Foucault, *The History of Sexuality*, vol. 1, *The Will to Knowledge* (London: Penguin, 1998), 140. The anthropologist Jean Comaroff elaborated, writing, "Notwithstanding its status as emerging science, medicine drew upon social images to mediate physical realities, giving colonial power relations an alibi in the ailing human body. And colonial regimes, in turn, drew upon medical icons and practices to impose their domination upon subjects and collectivities." Comaroff, "The Diseased Heart of Africa," in *Knowledge, Power, and Practice*, ed. Shirley Lindenbaum and Margaret Lock (Berkeley: University of California Press, 1993), 307.

The veranda is among the most identifiable tropes in early British colonial architecture, and it was (and is) a recognizable symbol of the colonial tropical lifestyle.[4] Functionally, it served a double role: it cooled the building by shielding the walls from the sun and also created an "outdoor comfort zone" that accommodated the preferences of the colonizers, providing shade, protection from rain, and management of mosquitoes **(figs. 9, 10)**. It was, like most colonial "climate control features" from the nineteenth century, adapted from local building practices;[5] in Cape Town, it mirrored the intricate structures on the exteriors of commercial buildings in the old city core as well as the verandas common on local homes. Mosquito-borne diseases such as malaria plagued European colonists in many regions of the world, leading to various types of spatial investment in addition to verandas. Strategies like draining areas of standing water led to the creation of "hygienic" zones that divided cities into native and colonial communities **(figs. 11–15)**. Colonial housing was constructed on higher ground than where the natives lived, and the resulting "malaria line" became a barrier for segregation.

New Somerset Hospital was imposing. It represented permanence. Wings named for Queen Victoria, Queen Alexandria, and King Edward **(fig. 16)** communicated the supposed largesse of the mother country **(fig. 17)**, and high-quality craftsmanship and materials and state-of-the-art technology indicated that the investment would not be a temporary one. This was an architecture of nation building **(figs. 18, 19)**. Locally, the hospital also reinforced colonial hierarchies: the Cape Colony, infamously segregated, built the hospital primarily to serve the British. Many colonies also built hospitals for indigenous communities (care was necessary to keep laborers healthy), but they often featured less ornamentation and appeared more temporary **(figs. 20–23)**. The articulation and detailing of these structures communicated the colonists' perceptions of power, hierarchy, and permanence — and of whom was worth designing for.

4 Jiat-Hwee Chang and Anthony King, "Towards a Genealogy of Tropical Architecture: Historical Fragments of Power-Knowledge, Built Environment and Climate in the British Colonial Territories," *Singapore Journal of Tropical Geography* 32, no. 3 (November 14, 2011): 283.

5 Chang and King, "Towards a Genealogy," 286.

9

10

11

12

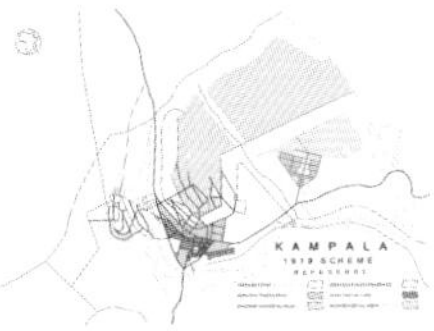

13

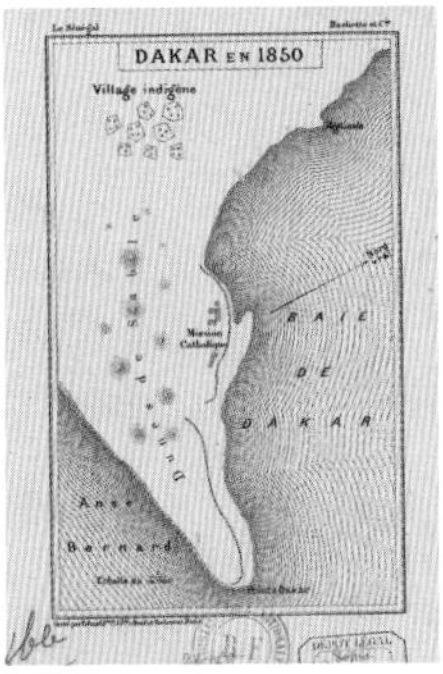

14

15

16

17

18

Through the next century and a half, as the British colonial regime and then the Afrikaner apartheid regime rose and fell, New Somerset remained. Today, the hospital continues to provide a location for health care and research **(fig. 24)**, suggesting that an architectural structure such as the pavilion hospital, designed to function in changing environmental conditions, may also acclimate to fluctuating political and social conditions, regardless (or in spite) of the intent of its patrons.

Renkioi and Deployability

The seeds of Nightingale's pavilion ward are located in a specific moment in time and place: a military hospital in the Turkish town of Renkioi during the Crimean War (see chapter 2). Another key concept in hospital design also emanated from Renkioi, and it also began with Brunel's field hospital. Erected rapidly, and serving over a thousand patients (with a capacity for three thousand), the field hospital was deconstructed after a year of use, in 1856, at the end of the war.[6] From this origin point came two divergent concepts in hospital infrastructure. The first is permanent, inflexible, locally made, handcrafted, and institutional — call it the Nightingale line. The other is temporary, flexible, prefabricated, deployable anywhere, and a prototype — call it the Brunel line **(figs. 25, 26)**.

While permanence played a key role in state-sponsored colonial architecture, impermanent and temporary structures were also essential to the imperial project, although they were often built by nongovernmental actors. Deep in the hinterland, Christian missionaries and corporations set up field outposts for labor, for missionary service, and for souls. Often made with low-cost materials, either locally harvested or easily portable into difficult terrain, Brunel's deployable huts were an economical solution for colonial medical infrastructure.

6 Pieces of the Renkioi hospital were auctioned off, and the buildings were donated to the Ottoman Empire. Some were re-erected within a year in Salonika to provide aid after an earthquake. C. G. Merridew, "I. K. Brunel's Crimean War Hospital," *Anaesthesia and Intensive Care* 42, history supplement (July 2014): 18.

19

20

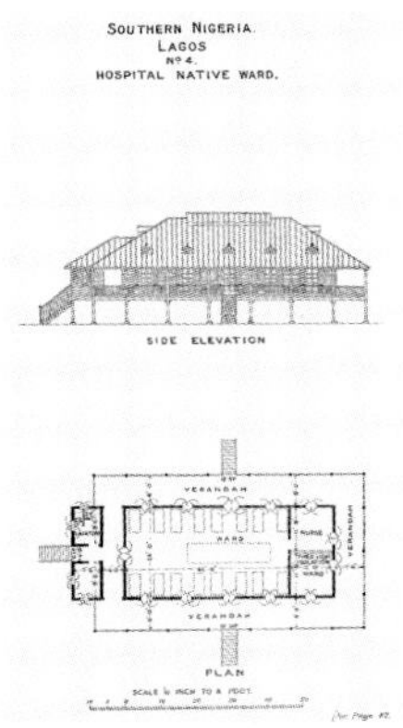

21

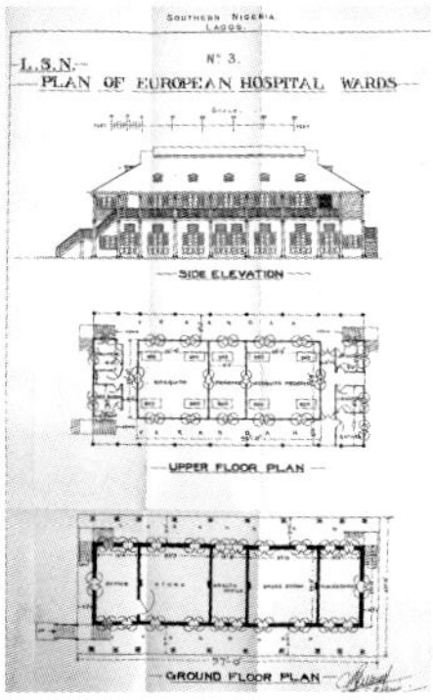

22

23

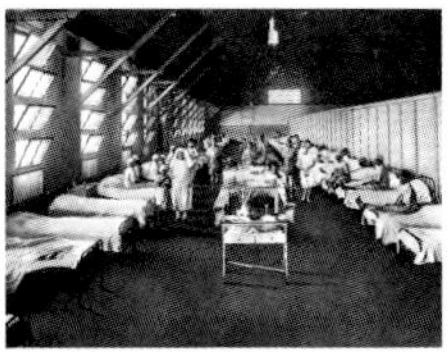

24

25

26

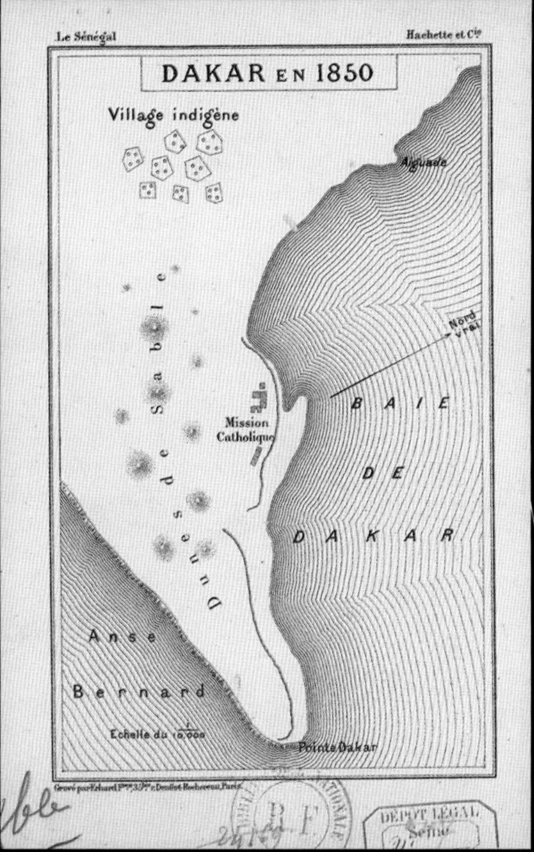
Le Sénégal
Hachette et Cie
DAKAR EN 1850
Village indigène
Aiguade
Nord vrai
Dunes de Sable
Mission Catholique
BAIE DE DAKAR
Anse Bernard
Echelle du 1/10.000
Pointe Dakar
Gravé par Erhard Fres, 35bis r. Denfert-Rochereau, Paris
DÉPOT LÉGAL
Seine

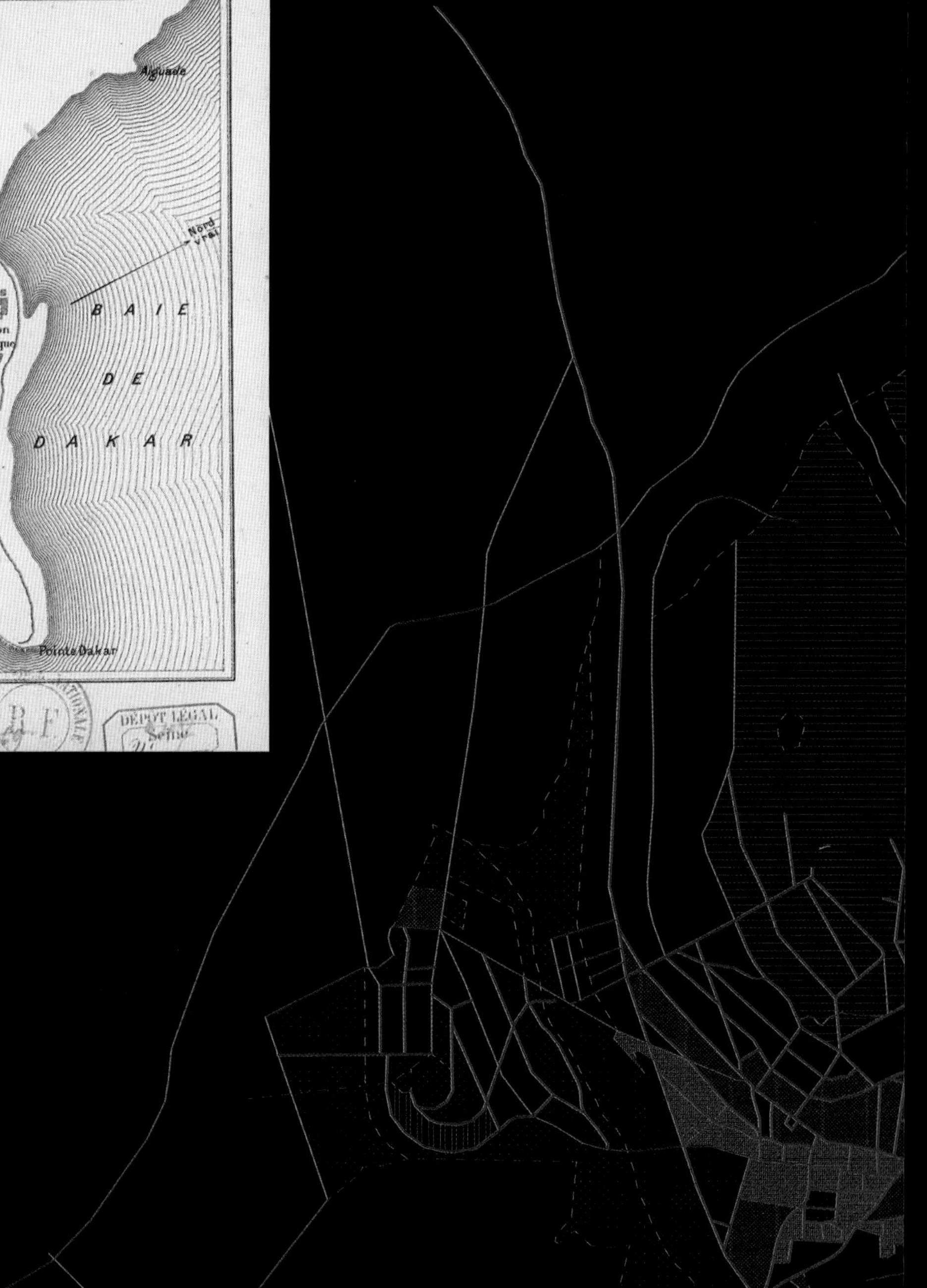

Plan of Dakar, Senegal, in 1850, showing the European Quarter and the Indigenous Quarter. Drawing by Jules Charles, 1889 [fig. 13]

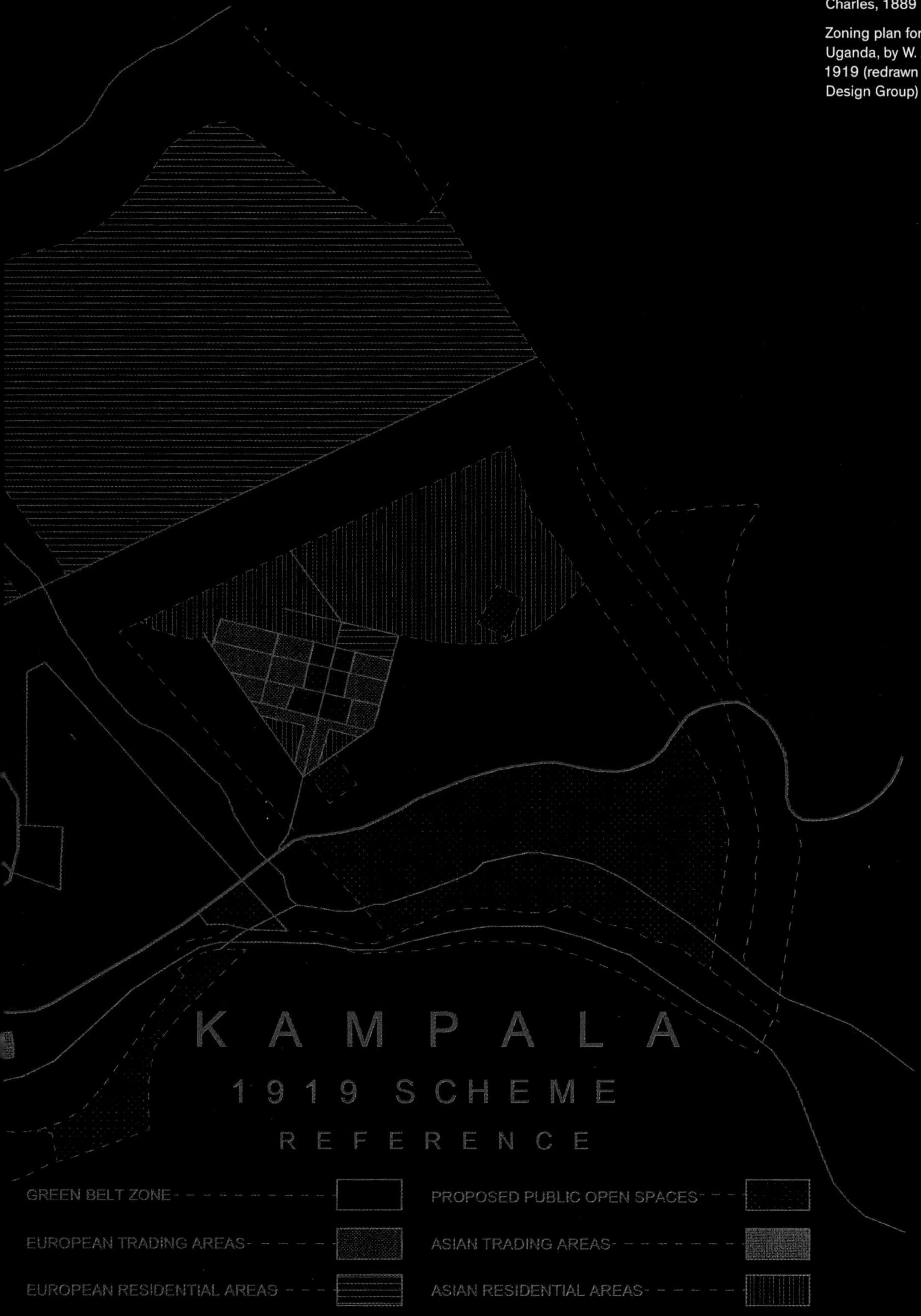

Zoning plan for Kampala, Uganda, by W. J. Simpson, 1919 (redrawn by MASS Design Group) [fig. 12]

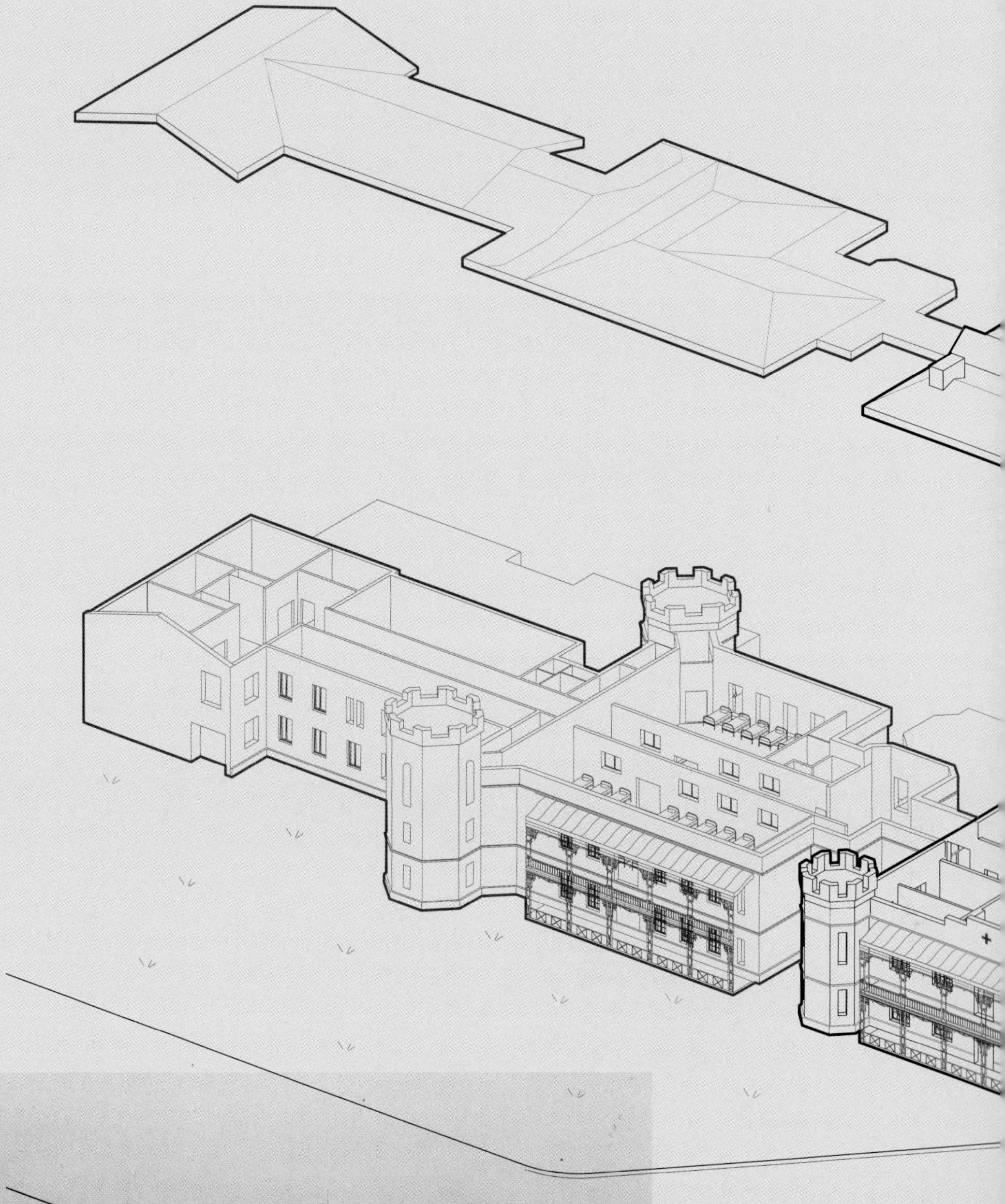

Axonometric drawing of New Somerset Hospital, Cape Town, showing the original building in black and later additions in red: the Queen Victoria Wing (left) and the King Edward and Queen Alexandria Ward (right) [fig. 16]

New Somerset Hospital, Cape Town, South Africa, 1899, designed by John Scott Tucker, 1864 [fig. 3]

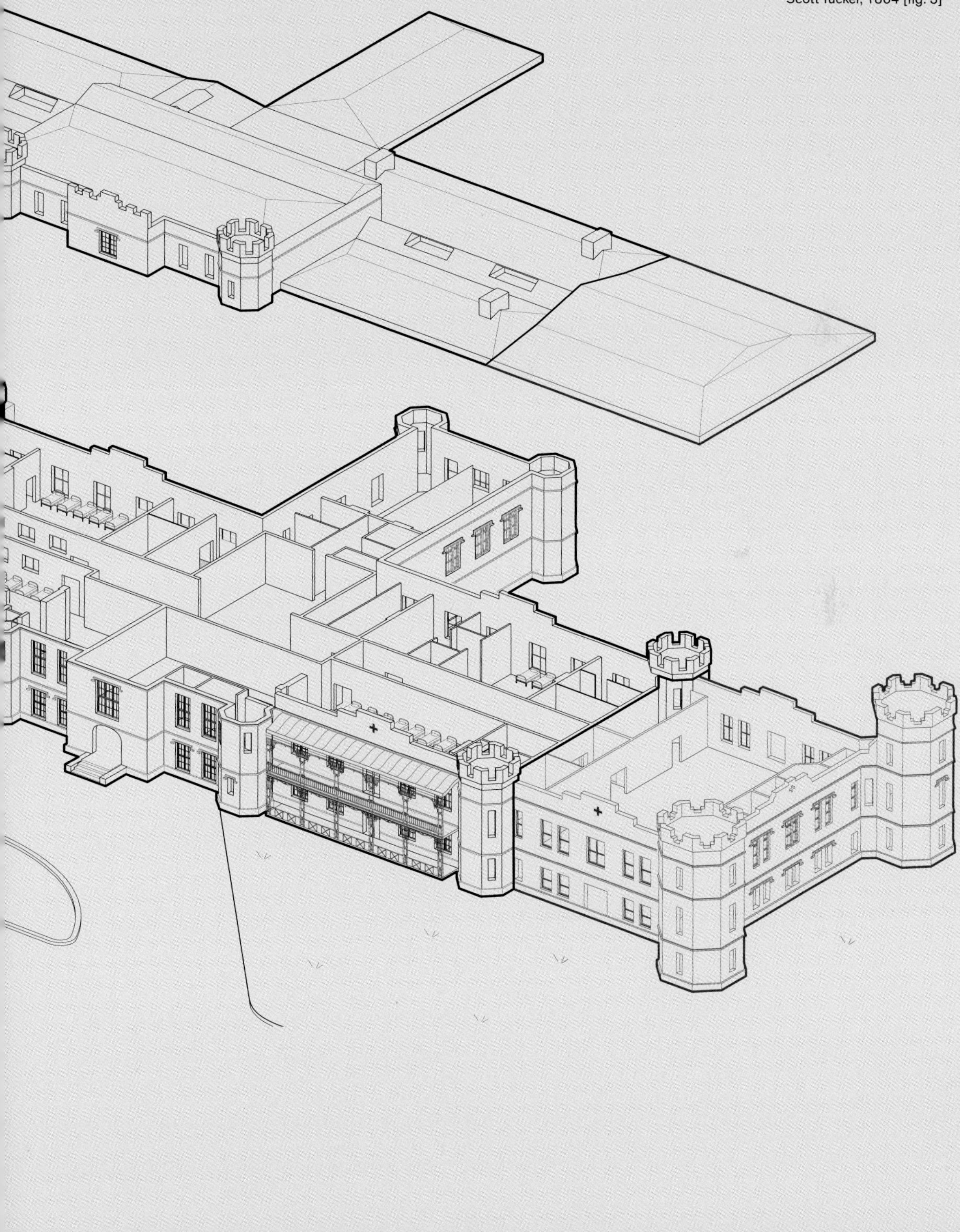

Plan and elevation drawings of the ward for indigenous patients at Lagos Hospital, Nigeria, 1901 [fig. 20]

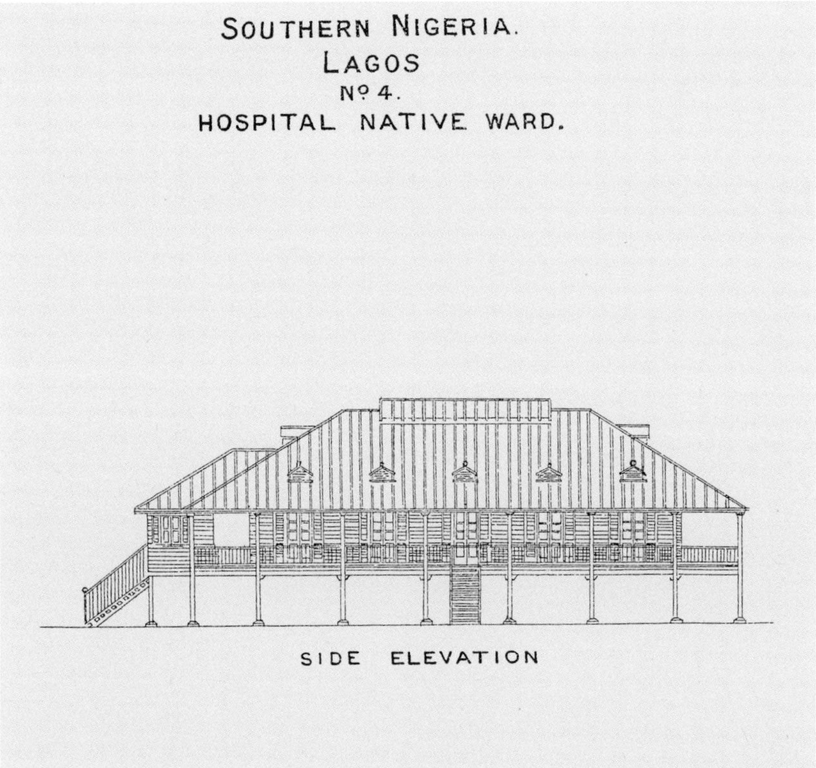

SOUTHERN NIGERIA.
LAGOS.

L.S.N.

No. 3.

PLAN OF EUROPEAN HOSPITAL WARDS

SCALE.

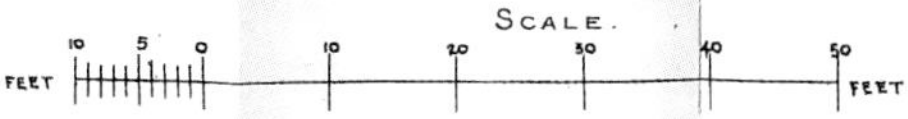

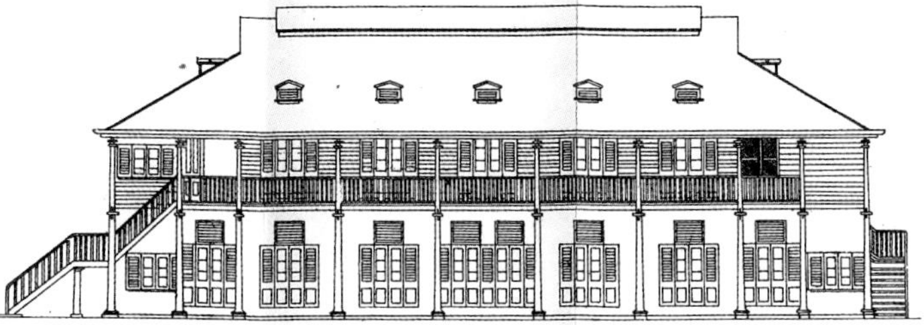

SIDE ELEVATION

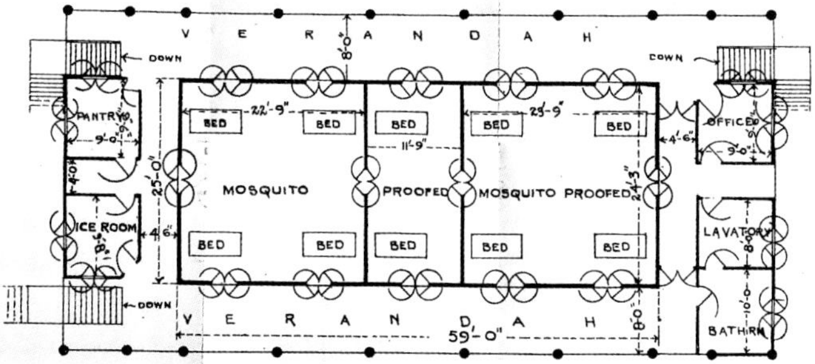

UPPER FLOOR PLAN

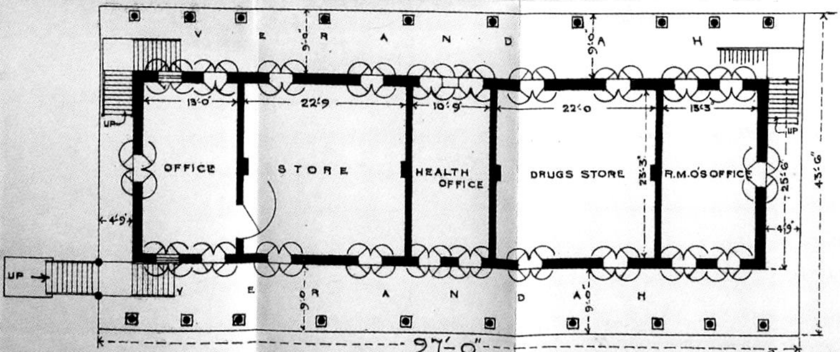

GROUND FLOOR PLAN

Humanitarianism and Paternalism in the Field Hospital

With the advance of scientific proof of the causes of disease, and as death became more preventable, access to health care science was understood within the imperial project to be a moral and humanitarian responsibility. Christian organizations funded medical outposts and encouraged European doctors to participate in a form of medical service tourism, seeking to provide European-style medicine where it was not otherwise available. Often built alongside company towns organized around extractive industries, these missionary settlements mixed charity with imperial and industrial goals, serving, through the medical clinic, the laborer and the sick and the poor. Lambaréné, in French Equatorial Africa (now Gabon), home to a field clinic founded by Dr. Albert Schweitzer, was one of the most influential of these outposts (figs. 27, 28).

27

28

29

30

31

32

33

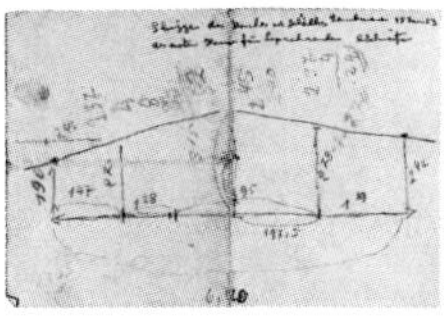

34

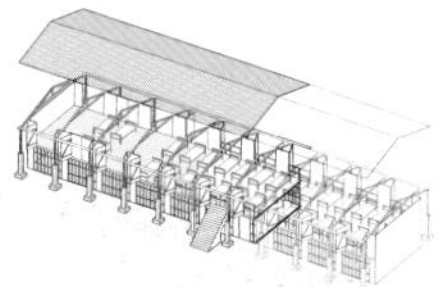

35

36

37

38

Hôpital Albert Schweitzer, Lambaréné

Lambaréné is sited at the confluence of two tributaries of the Ogooué River (fig. 29), which deposits its waters into the Atlantic Ocean two hundred miles (322 kilometers) downriver at Port Gentil. Albert Schweitzer (1875–1965), an Alsatian physician, musician, theologian, and philosopher, and his wife, the German nurse and social worker Helene Breeslau Schweitzer (1879–1957), moved to Lambaréné in 1913 with the goal of setting up a hospital for Africans at the outpost established there by the Paris Missionary Society (fig. 30). Initially, they provided medical services out of a chicken coop, before erecting a pavilion-style structure at the river's edge (fig. 31). The Hôpital Albert Schweitzer was modest and economical. In its construction and fabrication, it resembled other buildings of the region, made of locally available wood and bricks of river clay and capped with inexpensive tin roofing (figs. 32, 33).

In response to insect-driven disease and the presence of sleeping sickness and other supposed miasmic maladies, the hospital was placed above the ground on pilasters, and a cushion of air flowed not only through but underneath the buildings, insulating them from the "contaminated" ground. The facades of the buildings, lined with screens and jalousie blinds, opened almost completely to allow breezes off the water to pass through. The movement of air dissipated mosquitoes, and verandas, blinds, and the buildings' elevated position accommodated river flooding and allowed for modulations in response to diurnal fluctuations in heat and light (fig. 34). These effective methods of environmental cooling were borrowed from local settlement patterns and styles as well as colonial guidebooks.

Schweitzer's hospital required near-constant expansion and maintenance (fig. 35). He had a full-time carpenter on staff to fabricate structural changes and fix floorboards eaten by termites (fig. 36), and over time he added dormitories for a leper colony, staff housing, and administrative structures, followed by a surgical suite and a water-filtration system. Sanitation was unintegrated, and nurses were not stationed at checkpoints, as each ward stood on its own pilasters (fig. 37).

These were not great buildings. Simple, open to the air, and austere, they were improvisations, responding to needs on-site, and though they were not prefabricated they had much in common with Brunel's prototype, which he had described as "a sober exercise in common sense."[7] Unlike permanent structures of colonial occupation, they communicated the temporary and adaptable passions of a single individual. Despite their flimsiness and architectural irrelevance, they are still standing today and are under consideration to be named a UNESCO World Heritage Site because of Schweitzer's influence on global humanitarian service (fig. 38).

7 Isambard K. Brunel, letter to William Brunton (1856) on the disassembly of Renkioi, cited in David Toppin, "The British Hospital at Renkioi 1855," in *Arup Journal* 16, no. 2 (July 1981): 17.

Albert Schweitzer (right) and workers cut a log that has drifted from a lumber camp on the river to use at Hôpital Albert Schweitzer, Lambaréné, Gabon [fig. 28]

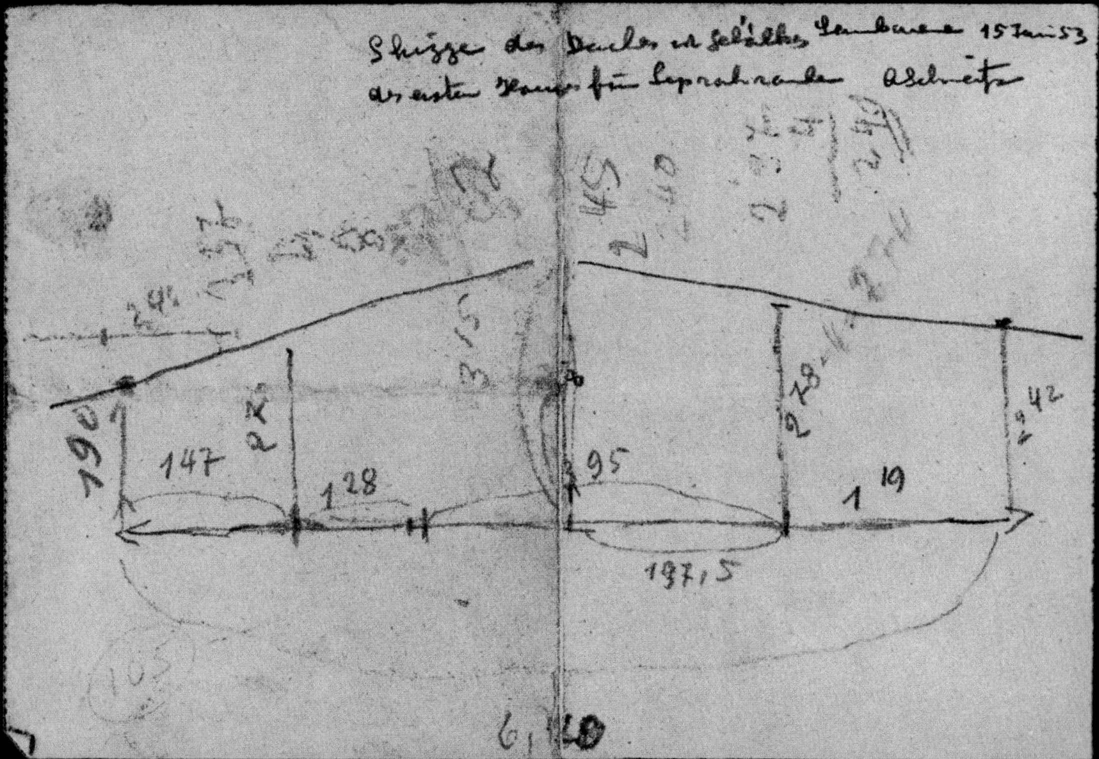

Sketch for the roof and construction of the first house for the leper village, by Albert Schweitzer, June 15, 1953 [fig. 33]

Concrete foundations being constructed for the leper village at the Hôpital Albert Schweitzer, Lambaréné, Gabon [fig. 37]

Albert Schweitzer in the workshop at the Hôpital Albert Schweitzer, Lambaréné, Gabon [fig. 27]

The leper village at the Hôpital Albert Schweitzer, Lambaréné, Gabon, c. 1960–65, designed by Albert Schweitzer, c. 1952–53 [fig. 32]

. . . Oh, this "noble" culture of ours! It speaks so piously of human dignity and human rights and then disregards this dignity and these rights of countless millions and treads them underfoot, only because they live overseas or because their skins are of different color or because they cannot help themselves. . . . Think of the atrocities that were perpetrated upon people made subservient to us, how systematically we have ruined them with our alcoholic "gifts," and everything else we have done. We decimate them, and then, by the stroke of a pen, we take their land so they have nothing left at all. — Albert Schweitzer, 1905

The Paradox of Humanitarianism

Schweitzer lived the rest of his life in Lambaréné, and he and Helene are both buried there. An ardent neocolonialist, he developed a pointed critique of colonial power and white supremacy. In 1905, he censured colonial occupiers for the racial hierarchies they created and for murderous crimes committed "under the pretext of justice," and denounced the hollow arguments of European powers who disregarded cultural value abroad in the name of civilization.[8] He also made a case for human rights and the protection of human dignity regardless of origin, nationality, or race.

However, despite being a harsh critic of colonialism, Schweitzer was also, as Chinua Achebe later argued, a representative of its racist and paternalistic attitudes.[9] He was blamed for his reliance on European medical staff and for not offering training programs for Gabonese professionals. In 1924, he famously said of the Gabonese, "I am your brother, it is true, but your elder brother," a statement that reveals the deep connections between humanitarianism and paternalism.

Schweitzer later acknowledged the racism inherent in his early statements and sought to move beyond it. His philosophy evolved into a belief system he called "reverence for life," according to which all life, from the plant to the animal to the human, wherever it is found, is owed respect, humility, and reverence. This theory of universal human rights grounded his anti-nuclearization activism, which in turn led to his Nobel Peace Prize in 1952. His writings influenced the modern environmental movement; Rachel Carson dedicated her foundational 1962 book *Silent Spring* to Schweitzer, quoting him in the dedication: "Man has lost the capacity to foresee and to forestall. He will end by destroying the earth."[10] His philosophy also presaged the arguments for indigenous autonomy, independence, and sovereignty that would inform postcolonial thought. In this way, the Hôpital Albert Schweitzer was a crucible in which the charitable strain in medical work was transformed — from an impulse predicated on a paternalistic Christian missionary philosophy to a more humanitarian point of view based on respect for life and opposed to hierarchies of difference.

Maternity patient being carried from the delivery room to the ward, Hôpital Albert Schweitzer, Lambaréné, Gabon, 1954 [fig. 38]

8 Albert Schweitzer, "The Call to Mission," a sermon preached on January 5, 1905, repr. in *Reverence for Life: Sermons 1900–1919* (New York: Irvington, 1993), 53.

9 Chinua Achebe, "An Image of Africa: Racism in Conrad's *Heart of Darkness*," *Massachusetts Review* 18, no. 4 (Winter 1977).

10 Rachel Carson, *Silent Spring* (New York: Houghton Mifflin, 1962), epigraph.

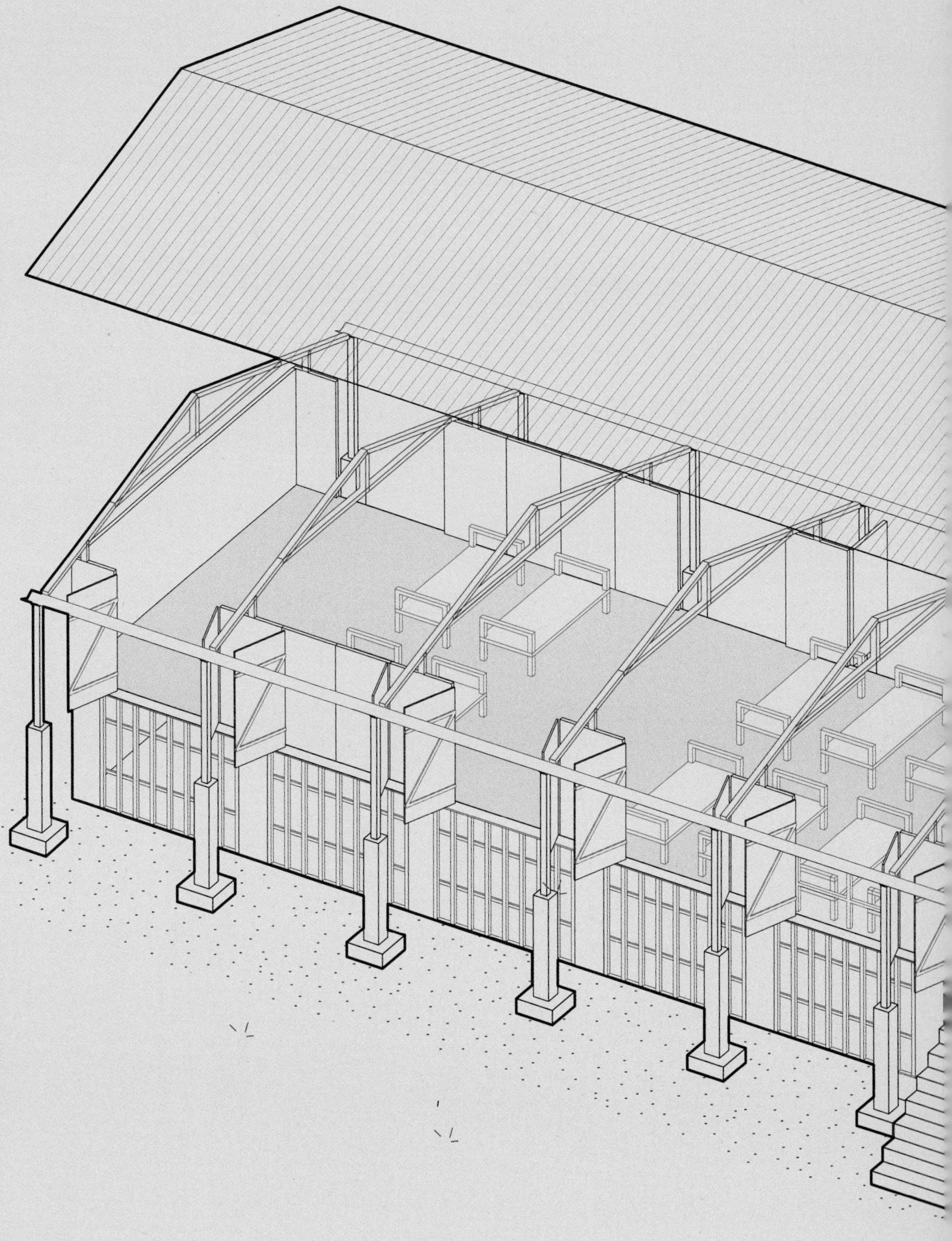

Axonometric drawing of ward building at the Hôpital Albert Schweitzer, Lambaréné, Gabon, designed by Albert Schweitzer, 1913 [fig. 34]

The Hôpital Albert Schweitzer, overlooking the Ogooué River, Lambaréné, Gabon, c. 1960–65 [fig. 31]

Chapter 4
Modernism and the Factory

The Hospital as Factory

The emerging modern project, privileged forms that could be distributed at scale, and modernism became indelibly intertwined with industrial fabrication and mass public services. Modern architects made the moral argument that by borrowing factory processes and spaces they could expand access to design and thus improve society. The factory, with its spatial optimization and efficient assembly lines, dictated the new modern aesthetic as functionalism. Industrial processes and the buildings that housed them were newly conceived as empowering, and the former aversion to the factory as alienating — by thinkers such as William Morris (see chapter 3) — fell away.

Functionalism, then, was about societal improvement, and it was expressed in architecture in two distinct strands. The first addressed issues of social health: universal, rationalist designs were proposed to solve broad social issues — such as disease, poverty, and poor housing and sanitation — at scale, and often at the expense of the individual. The second sought to create spaces that would improve the life and experiences of the individual through purposeful designs, regardless of scale or replicability.

The Frankfurt Kitchen and the Ford Assembly Line

Designed in 1926 by Austrian architect Margarete Schütte-Lihotzky (1897–2000), the Frankfurt Kitchen was a prefabricated room intended to be inserted into public housing projects **(fig. 1)**.[1] With dimensions optimized for efficient movement and reach, the insert shrank the kitchen to its essential components, thereby ostensibly reducing domestic labor **(fig. 2)**.[2] In this way, the Frankfurt Kitchen is the preeminent example of rationalist functionalism distributed at scale.

Although it was intended as a liberating force for women and was originally praised for unshackling homemakers from domestic labor, the Frankfurt Kitchen — designed for all, regardless of culture, class, or cuisine — came to represent the over-optimization of the individual. In fact, critics said, the so-called optimizations built into the kitchen increased the labor needed for cooking — one size did not fit all — and the application of the principles of factory efficiencies to individuals and families was experienced as dehumanizing and alienating. Distinctiveness, individual identity, and personal desire were secondary considerations when it came to design for the masses.

1

2
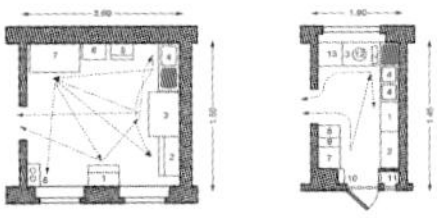
3

4

5

Nevertheless, some ten thousand of these kitchens were built in the late 1920s as part of the Neue Frankfurt housing program designed by the architect and city planner Ernst May (fig. 3). In 1930, the Soviet government requested the Frankfurt Kitchen for new town developments, and an international utopian project of "housing for the masses" emerged. At the same time, a hypercapitalist ethos of mass production entered the global lexicon with Henry Ford and his innovative Model T assembly line in Detroit.

Fordist concepts also infected hospital design. Products began to be optimized for the average user (the rationalized body), and architecture was increasingly considered a commodity to be plugged in, replicated, and distributed from a factory to the home — an assembly-line mode of thinking. The global problem of access to health care, it was theorized, could be solved by new efficiencies in design and manufacturing. Albert Kahn (1869–1942), the architect of Ford Motor Company's factory complexes — including those in Highland Park, Detroit (1910; fig. 4), and Charlotte, North Carolina (1924; fig. 5) — was also responsible for the University of Michigan's Old Main Hospital (1925), where he incorporated Fordist ideals of rationalist functionalism in a hospital-as-factory.[3]

University Hospital, Ann Arbor, Michigan

Kahn's task was significant. The population of Michigan was growing rapidly, and health care services were required for the burgeoning industry that would make Detroit a capital of US innovation. The giant University Hospital (later called Old Main) was a massive central-bar building, nine stories high. Each end of the bar split into a V, and the bar itself was intercepted in the middle by a T (figs. 6, 7). Medical operations took place on the first six floors; above them were the patient wards. Thin floorplates oriented to the south optimized patients' sun exposure for heliotherapy and facilitated cross-ventilation by ensuring that breezes passed through operable windows on either side. The hospital — designed to sleep more than a thousand patients — boasted two miles (more than three kilometers) of hallways, nearly three thousand windows, and 280,000 square feet (26,000 square meters) of floor space overall.[4] It was the twenty elevators, however, that decisively differentiated the new hospital from its pavilion ancestors: no longer laid out horizontally among gardens, the entire complex could be traversed vertically, floor by floor.

Patient rooms were also transformed in this configuration. With ventilation stacks moving air, large open wards were no longer preferable, and the rooms at Old Main (each holding fewer beds) were organized along hallways. The building's form changed too, shifting from the rectangle-shaped pavilion designed around the ward to the thin and elongated, Y- and T-shaped bar hospital, composed of a bed tower designed around the hallways. Nurses' stations were located at hallway intersections and sunrooms at the end of each floor. Elevators allowed for the vertical movement of both patients and waste materials, and pneumatic tubes and electric dumbwaiters in the walls transported samples and devices between surgical suites and labs. New technologies

1 Karen Melching, "Frankfurt Kitchen: Patina Follows Function," *Conservation*, no. 53 (Summer 2006), 18.

2 Schütte-Lihotzky wrote, "The problem of rationalizing the housewife's work is equally important to all classes of the society. Both the middle-class women, who often work without any help [i.e., without servants] in their homes, and also the women of the worker class, who often have to work in other jobs, are overworked to the point that their stress is bound to have serious consequences for public health at large." Margarete Schütte-Lihotzky, "Rationalisierung im Haushalt," *Das neue Frankfurt*, no. 5 (1926–27), 120–23.

3 Nitin K. Ahuja has thoroughly explored the emergence of Fordist ideals at Old Main. See "Fordism in the Hospital: Albert Kahn and the Design of Old Main, 1917–25," *Journal of the History of Medicine and Allied Sciences* 67, no. 3 (July 2012): 398–427.

4 James Tobin, "150 Years at the Hospital," University of Michigan Heritage Project, https://heritage.umich.edu/stories/150-years-at-the-hospital/.

6

7

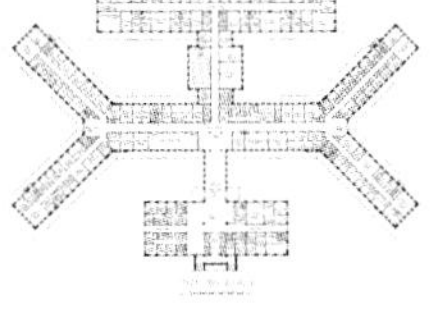

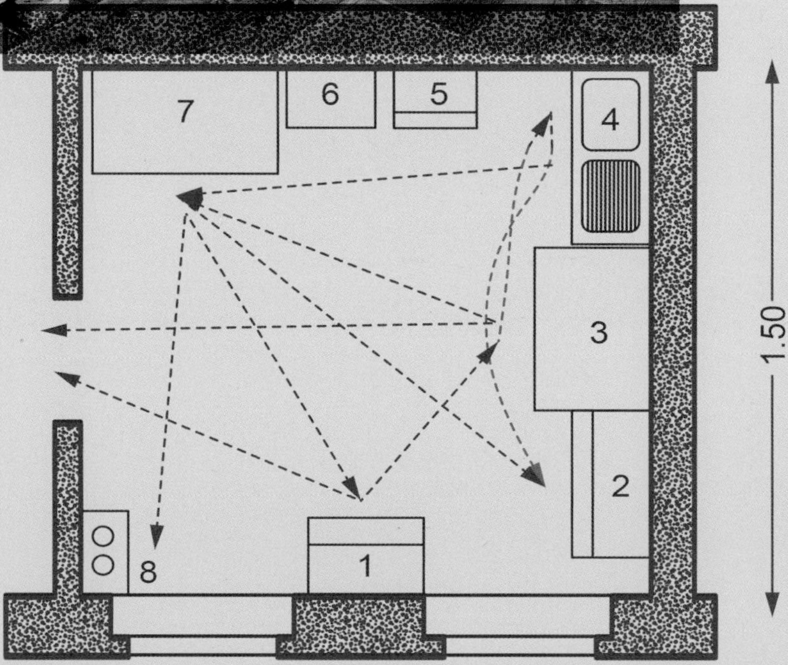

Aerial view of Estate Westhausen, one of several housing projects built in the late 1920s as part of Ernst May's Neue Frankfurt housing program [fig. 3]

Plan of the Frankfurt Kitchen by Margarete Schütte-Lihotzky (redrawn by MASS Design Group) [fig. 2]

The Frankfurt Kitchen, designed by Margarete Schütte-Lihotzky, 1926 [fig. 1]

In 1930, the Soviet government requested the Frankfurt Kitchen for new town developments, and an international utopian project of "housing for the masses" emerged. At the same time, a hypercapitalist ethos of mass production entered the global lexicon with Henry Ford and his innovative Model T assembly line in Detroit.

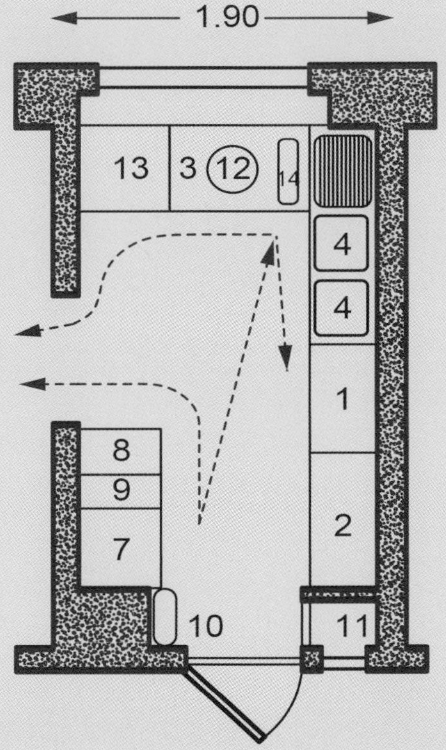

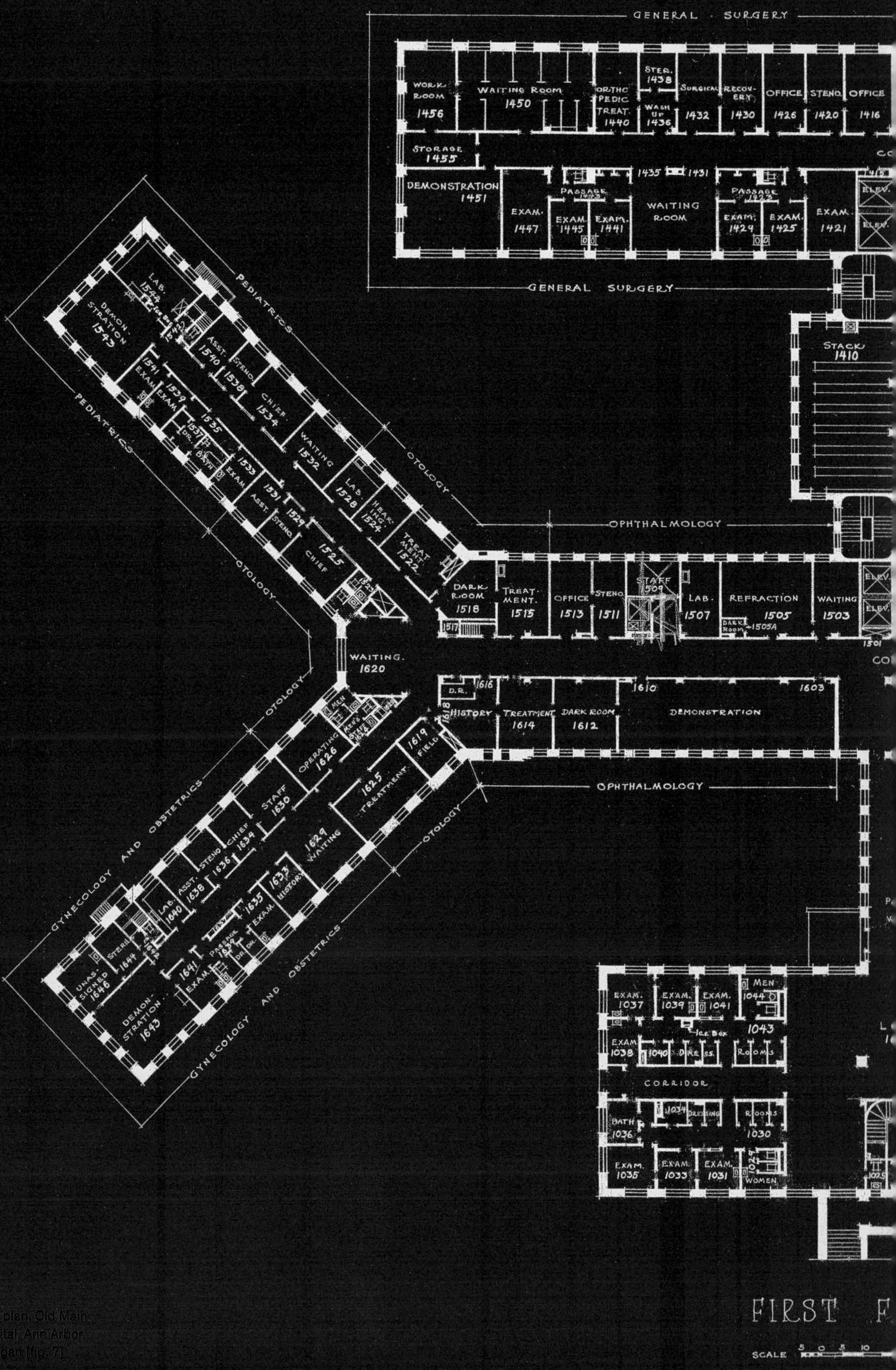

Floor plan, Old Main Hospital, Ann Arbor, Michigan [fig. 7]

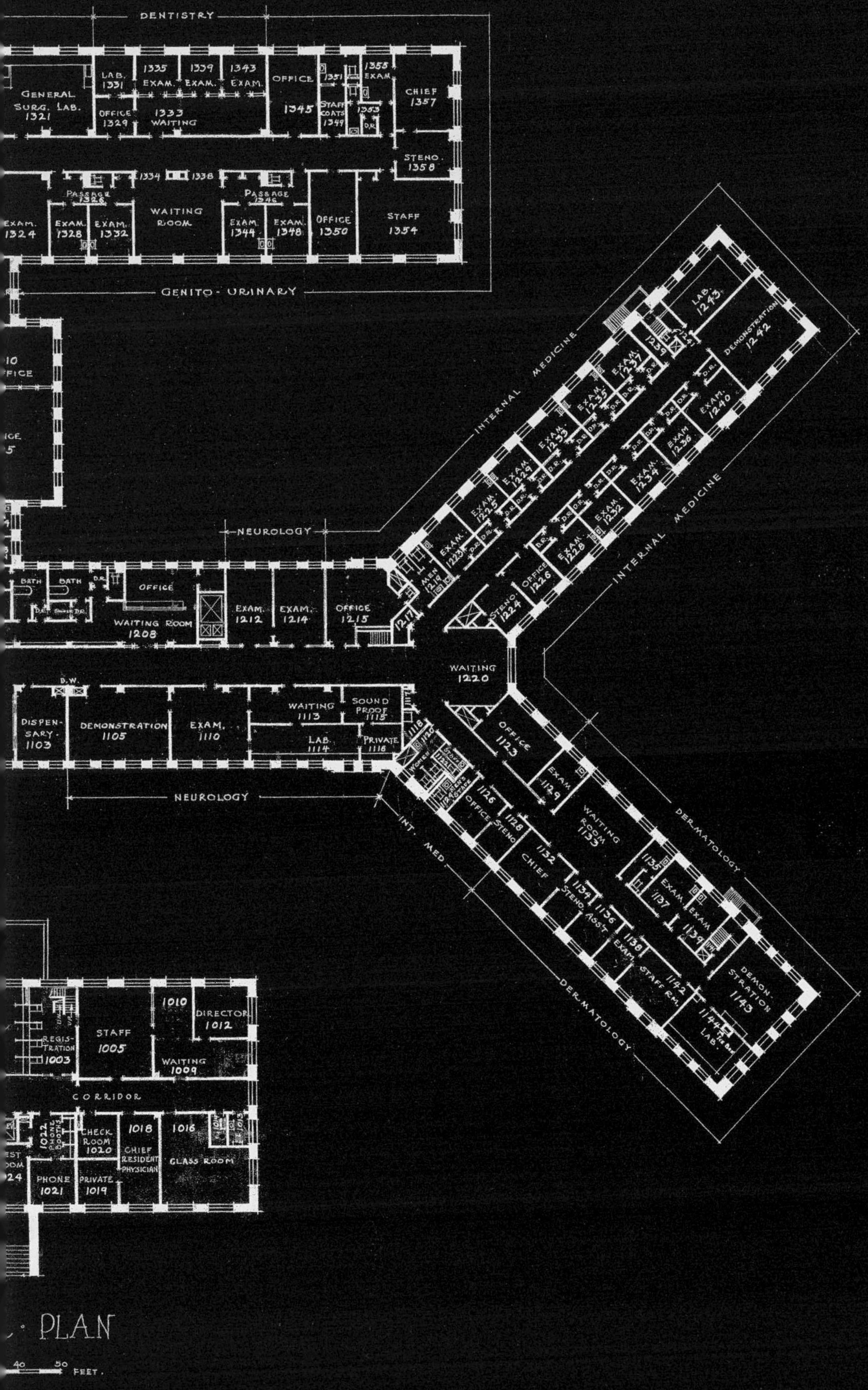
DENTISTRY
GENERAL SURG. LAB. 1321
LAB. 1331
1335 EXAM.
1339 EXAM.
1343 EXAM.
OFFICE 1329
1333 WAITING
OFFICE 1345
1351
STAFF COATS 1349
1355 EXAM.
1353
D.R.
CHIEF 1357
STENO. 1358
1334
1338
PASSAGE 1326
PASSAGE 1346
EXAM. 1324
EXAM. 1328
EXAM. 1332
WAITING ROOM
EXAM. 1344
EXAM. 1348
OFFICE 1350
STAFF 1354
GENITO-URINARY
INTERNAL MEDICINE
LAB. 1243
DEMONSTRATION 1242
1239
EXAM. 1237
EXAM. 1235
EXAM. 1233
EXAM. 1229
EXAM. 1225
EXAM. 1223
EXAM. 1240
EXAM. 1236
EXAM. 1234
EXAM. 1232
EXAM. 1228
OFFICE 1226
STENO. 1224
D.R.
MEN 1219
1217
NEUROLOGY
BATH
BATH
D.R.
OFFICE
WAITING ROOM 1208
EXAM. 1212
EXAM. 1214
OFFICE 1215
WAITING 1220
D.W.
DISPENSARY 1103
DEMONSTRATION 1105
EXAM. 1110
WAITING 1113
SOUND PROOF 1115
LAB. 1114
PRIVATE 1116
1118
1120
WOMEN
OFFICE 1123
EXAM. 1129
WAITING ROOM 1133
1126 OFFICE
1128 STENO.
1132 CHIEF
1134 STENO.
1136 ASST.
1138 EXAM.
1142 STAFF RM.
1135
EXAM. 1137
EXAM. 1139
DEMONSTRATION 1143
1144 LAB.
INT. MED.
DERMATOLOGY
DERMATOLOGY
REGISTRATION 1003
STAFF 1005
1010
DIRECTOR 1012
WAITING 1009
CORRIDOR
1022 PHONE BOOTHS
CHECK ROOM 1020
1018 CHIEF RESIDENT PHYSICIAN
1016
GLASS ROOM
PHONE 1021
PRIVATE 1019
40 50 FEET.

· PLAN

FIR

like the X-ray and advanced laboratories completed the hospital: it was a closed system in which patients moved along an assembly line from one service to another — a factory for healing.[5] Five years after it was completed, three more floors were added to Old Main, expanding the factory and its output.

Rational, logical, serviceable, and huge, the early modern hospital functioned as a deterrent for disease and mortality. These buildings, with their flexibility and adaptability, were precursors to the glass-and-steel boxes of midcentury's more corporate modernism. As in Schütte-Lihotzky's design, the individual was converted into a statistical body to be quantified and measured, an efficiency that for modernists equaled progress. Under the rubric of rationalism, universalizing principles were brought to bear, esteeming sameness rather than uniqueness.

Kahn was aware of the risk of dehumanization. To counter a feeling of institutionalization or alienation, he suggested small flourishes such as painting the walls green instead of white, but in massive projects such as Old Main, these attempts at softening the individual experience were insufficient. The institution was a representative of the state, to which individuals must surrender for the sake of their health, and this reality was inescapably linked to its design.

Like Lluís Domènech i Montaner in his Hospital de la Santa Creu i Sant Pau in Barcelona (see chapter 2), practitioners of the second strand of functionalism considered the individual's experience. The designers of smaller, more intimate spaces — such as the Paimio Sanitorium — focused on individual well-being, and their projects in some cases took on a dual role as both hospital and center for recuperation. As Beatriz Colomina has detailed, their ideas of beauty, cleanliness, hygiene, and healthy living would influence the modern style, spreading worldwide in the first half of the twentieth century.[6]

Paimio Sanitorium, Finland

In his design for the Paimio Sanitorium, constructed in Paimio, Finland, in 1932, Alvar Aalto (1898–1976) focused on one climate, one region (southwestern Finland), and one specific population: those suffering from the tuberculosis pandemic (fig. 8). The sanitorium's form was based on the best science available at the time, which called for heliotherapy and natural cross-ventilation to both mitigate the spread of the respiratory disease and provide a cure (fig. 9). Aalto's project was a total work of art: he reconsidered everything from chairs and sinks to closets and beds (figs. 10, 11). In Paimio, Aalto demonstrated that fabrication of customized and personalized solutions could solve universal problems.

The sanitorium's inflexibility was its least-acknowledged innovation yet its most enduring legacy. The tall, thin structure, with curved floorplates and a spidery, site-driven plan, resisted addition, extension, or replication (fig. 12). The natural functionality of this thin bar — the optimization of sunlight through its south-facing orientation and the movement of fresh air through the volume — was primary, and the design elements at Paimio, including large, open-air verandas designed for outside convalescence in the cold Finnish winters, presupposed that even the climate may be harnessed for health.

5 Nitin Ahuja observed the parallels between the Ford assembly line and Old Main: "This description [of the hospital] dovetails neatly with the image of the assembly line facilitated by Kahn's designs for Ford. It closely matches the architect's description of factories designed for rational flow: [as Kahn noted,] 'raw material enters at one point, finds its proper place without unnecessary rehandling, passes in orderly manner through the manufacturing process, [and] arrives at the finished stock room ready to crate and ship.' Likewise, at Old Main, patients were to arrive at a common physical location, be rigorously evaluated by a sequence of clinicians, and deposited into a bed as required." Ahuja, "Fordism in the Hospital," 417. See also Albert Kahn, "How Building Design Affects Production Efficiency," November 15, 1939, Box 1, Albert Kahn Papers, Bentley Historical Library, University of Michigan.

6 Beatriz Colomina, *X-Ray Architecture* (Zurich: Lars Müller, 2020), 61.

The sanitorium's furnishings and finishes were unique, with many features specifically designed for those suffering from tuberculosis. The Paimio Chair, for example, was intended to straighten the patient's back to improve breathing **(fig. 13)**. It has since become a modern classic, used in all sorts of domestic, commercial, and health care settings; in solving for one condition, Aalto created a universally appealing design. The Paimio Sanitorium was functional, yet it was not rationalized on a grid or organized via a consistent logic. The design and its fabrication reaffirmed the presence of individuals; their needs were considered. It was not so much a critique of functionalism as a critique of rationalism at scale.

Such a critique could be summarized as "designed for all, but for no one person in particular." Initially launched, via the Frankfurt Kitchen, with a liberatory intention, rationalized modernism would come to represent alienation, institutionalization, and domination for those who grew up within it. Architects of the modern era began to bifurcate their work, alternating between the sculptural specificity of designs like the Paimio Sanitorium and the machine aesthetic demanded by large institutions such as Old Main. Modernist ideals fed both strands, leading to dramatically different buildings and, eventually, to the rejection of modernism as a philosophy.

10

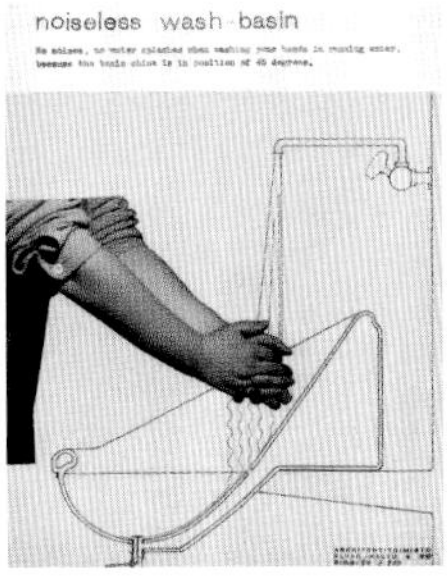

12

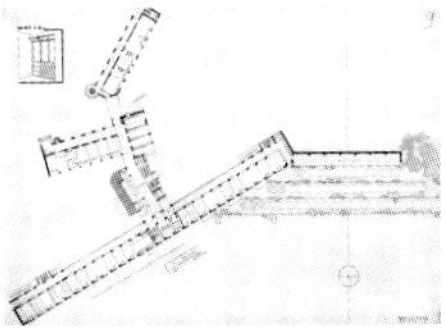

8

13

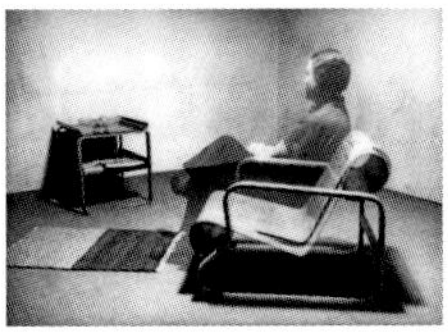

9

11

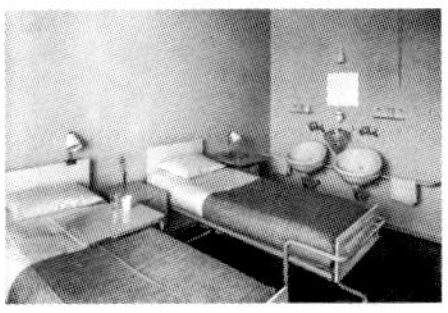

Paimio Sanatorium, Paimio, Finland, designed by Alvar Aalto, 1932 [fig. 8]

Site plan, Paimio Sanatorium [fig. 12]

Typical patient room at the Paimio Sanatorium [fig. 11]

Paimio Chair at the Paimio Sanatorium [fig. 13]

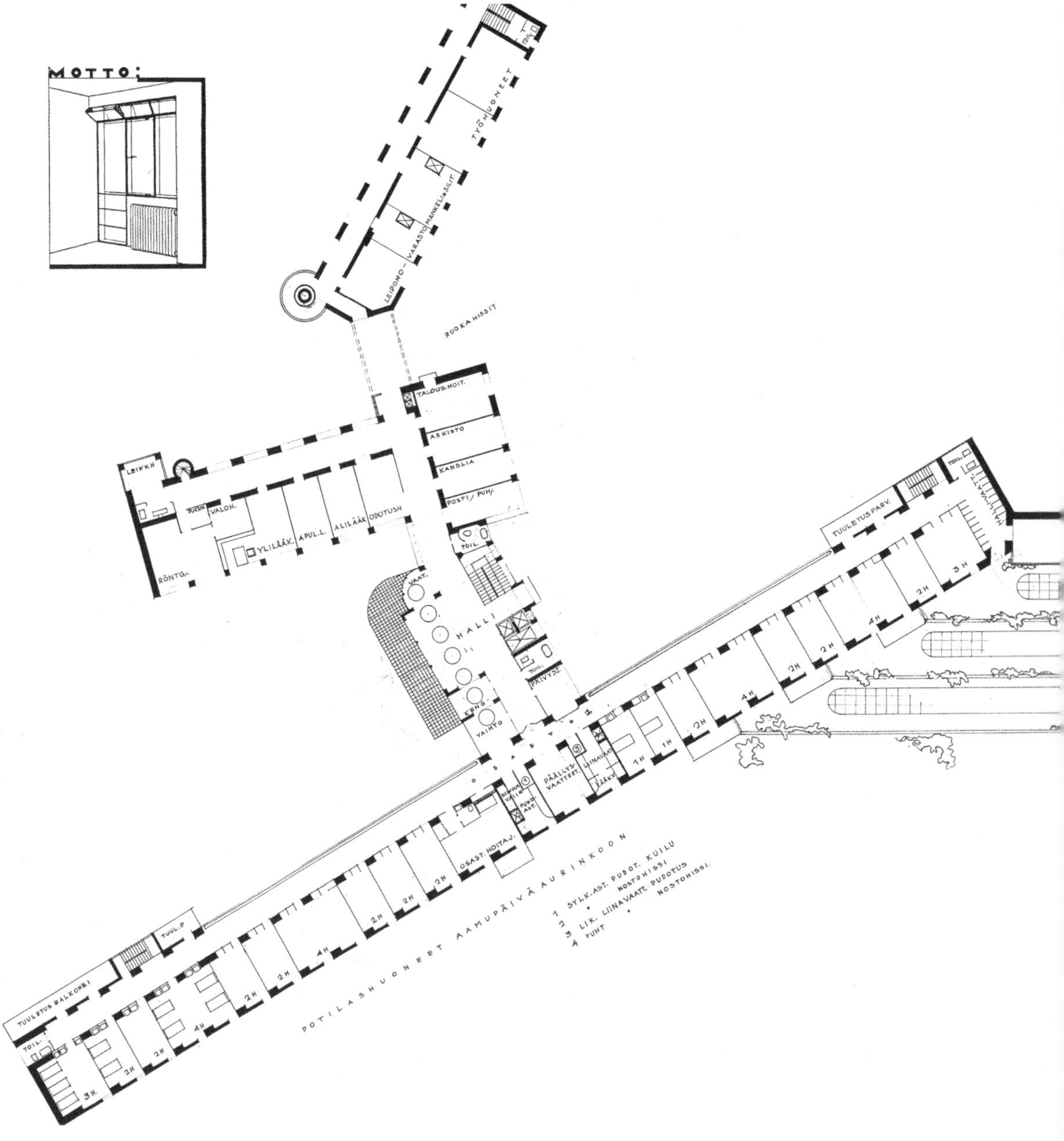

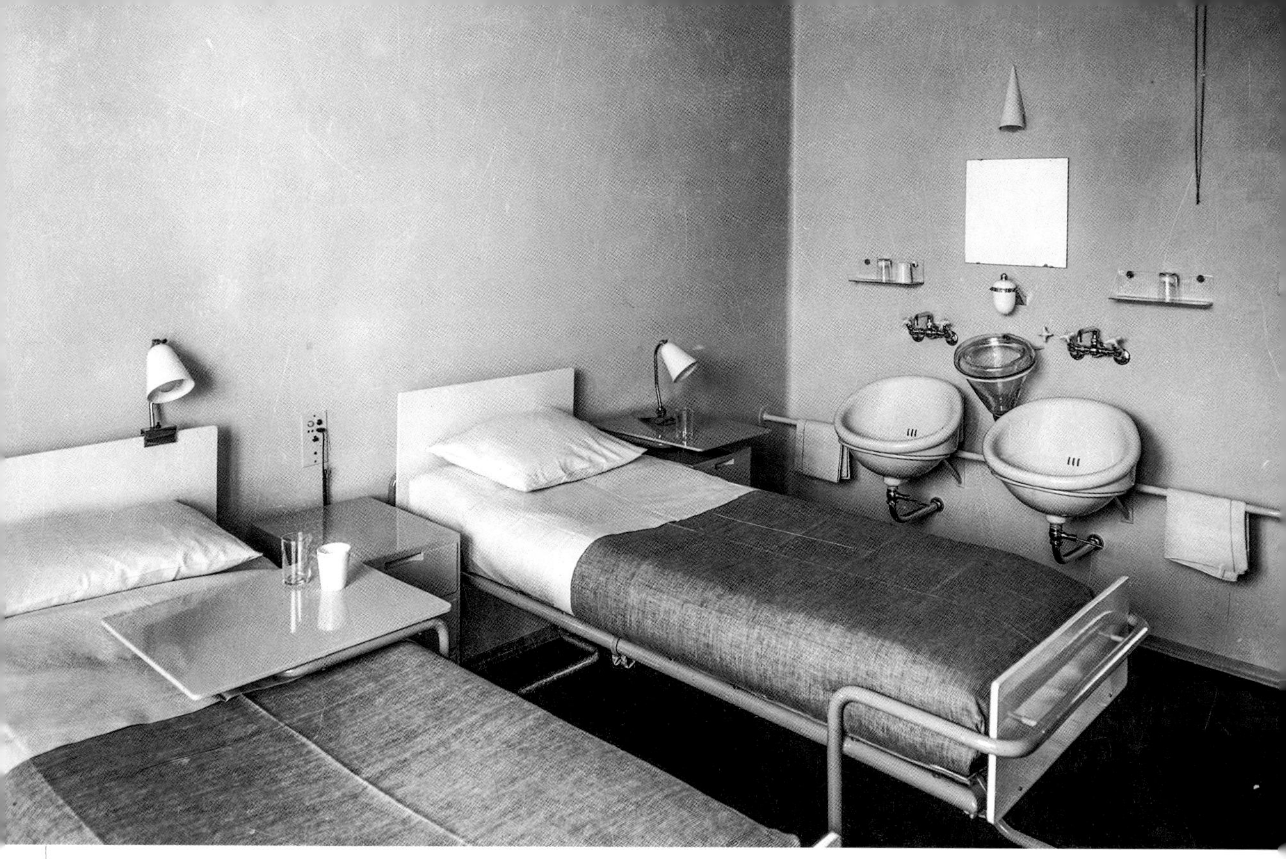

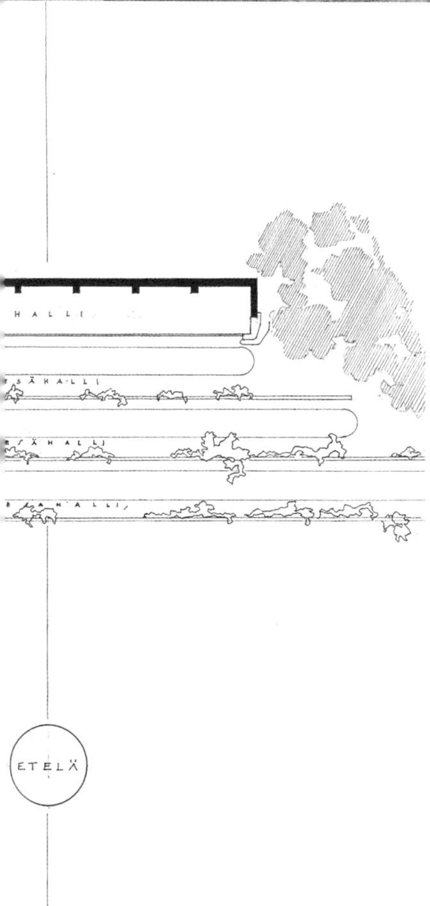
HALLI
SÄHALLI
SÄHALLI
ETELÄ
ARKKITEHTITOIMISTO
ALVAR AALTO & CO
SIGN 50 /26

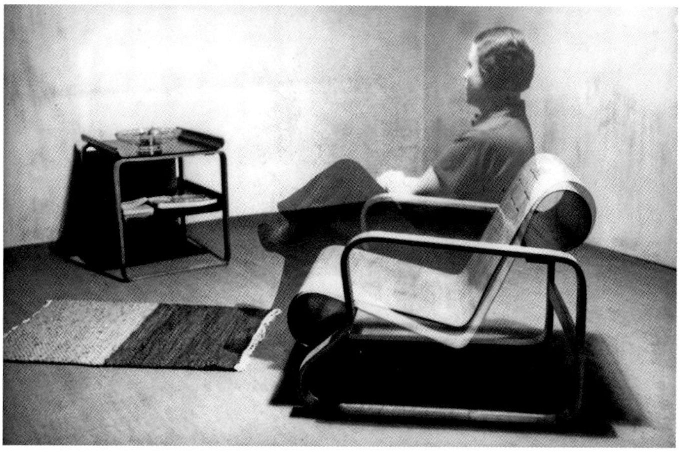

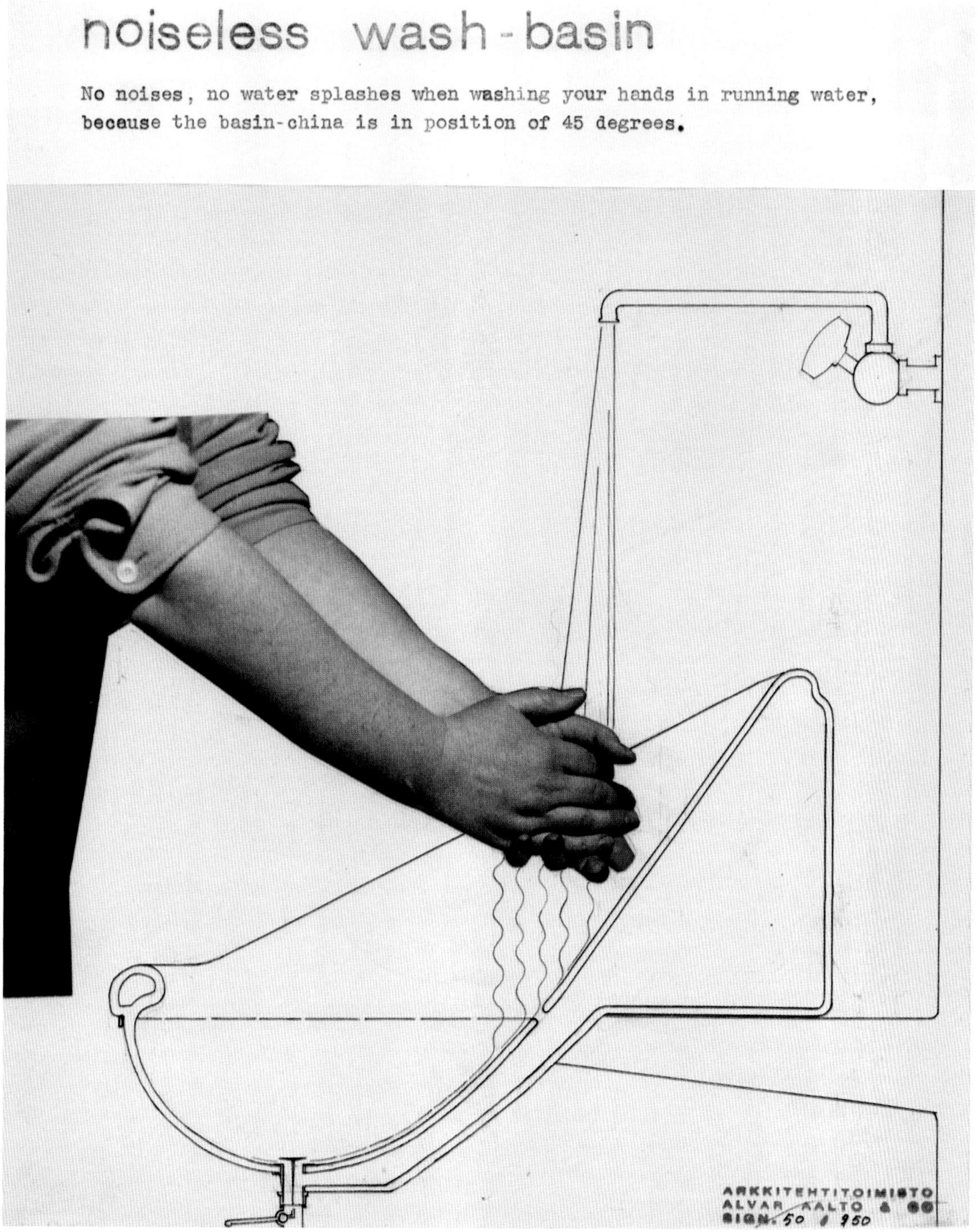

Design for "noiseless" sinks
at the Paimio Sanatorium
[fig. 10]

Chapter 5
The Medical Machine

After the Pavilion
The Royal Vic and the Foundations of Modernism

"You will not find the Royal Victoria Hospital mentioned in any of the standard histories of modern architecture."[1] So wrote Reyner Banham (1922–1988), theorist, advocate, author, and pointed critic of the contradictions of the modern movement.[2] Belfast's Royal Victoria Hospital (fig. 1), designed by Thomas Cooper (born 1847) and William Henman (1846–1917) and completed in 1903, predated by a few years the early modern buildings designed by Peter Behrens in Berlin. Walter Gropius, a protégé of Behrens, proclaimed that the core theoretical tenet of modernist architecture was "the synthesis of art and technology";[3] Banham argued that this ideal was already present in Ireland before the inception of the modern movement. In his 1967 essay "The Architecture Below," he panned the architectural historians who ignored the Royal Vic (as the hospital became known), criticizing them for reflecting on the "stylistic concerns" of modernism instead of digging beneath the topsoil into the bowels of the technological "architecture below." Hidden away amid the industrial smog of pre-secessionist Belfast, he wrote, was an overlooked and underappreciated germ of the modern movement.[4]

Which is not to say that the Royal Vic was a masterpiece. Banham referred to the building as "a stinker" and to its Queen Anne style as debased and mongrelized. But in its conceptualization, it did something that no building had done before. Harnessing ingenious machine innovation and environmental modeling, it was the first to implement forced-air ventilation as a means of controlling the indoor air environment and regulating its heat and humidity (fig. 2).

The technique of chemically cooling air had been invented just a year earlier in Buffalo, New York, as a climate-control solution for the printing industry (fig. 3).[5] That a hospital would adopt the technology so swiftly suggests the scale of the need for innovation in public health. The implementation of the new system required the reconfiguration of the entire hospital: from staffing, services, patient experiences, and user behavior to the space itself. It was now necessary, for example, to have a team of facilities engineers constantly at the ready to feed the boilers and tweak the air handlers. Nurses no longer assisted patients by opening windows and pulling curtains aside. The treatment of air and the treatment of patients became synonymous, and the hospital was transformed into an *instrument* that could be tuned for social progress.

Form followed suit, and radically. With all air movement to the wards controlled by massive air ducts and mechanical fan rooms, the long, high-ceilinged pavilion ward was made obsolete. Wards were ganged in a row, ceilings were lowered so air flowed more rapidly, and the party wall replaced the window wall, eliminating direct natural light and a view of the outdoors **(figs. 4–6)**. Clerestory punctures were a source of indirect light and views, but only for patients lying supine and staring up toward the ceiling. The individual, rendered anonymous, was lost among the environmental controls, completely dependent on the proper functioning of the technology.

The Royal Vic was a hermetically sealed box, an architectural innovation that embodied, Banham wrote, "the exact point and crisis of the transition from the ancient to the modern."[6] It would be another sixty years before controlled air handling was adopted in medical spaces worldwide. But in this forgotten "stinker" of a hospital — the first to integrate mechanical technology into its structure and its very soul — a seed of the modern movement sprouted.

1

2

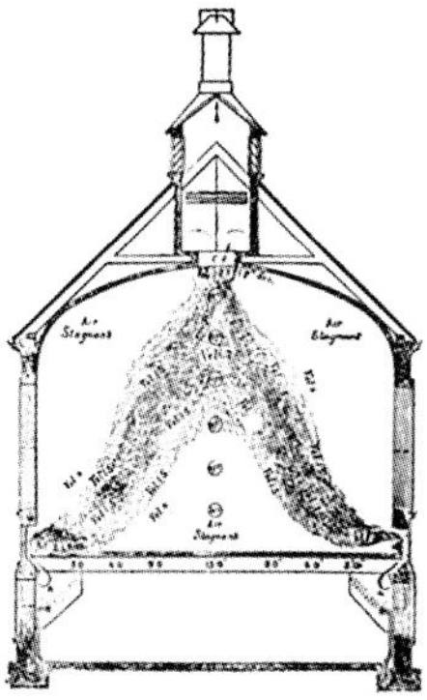

3

4

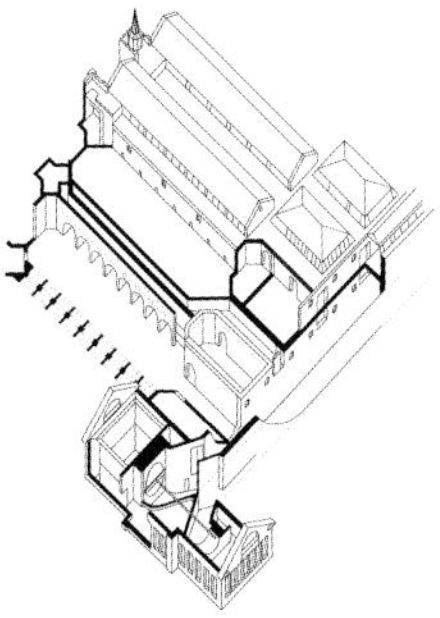

5

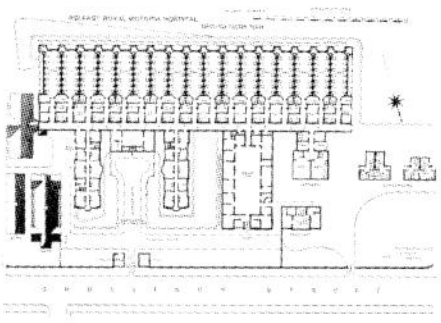

6

1 Reyner Banham, "The Architecture Below," *Listener* 77, no. 9 (February 1967), 196–97.

2 Banham reinterpreted key structures to reveal a through line in the modern movement and illuminate its ideals and contradictions. In his introduction to a reissue of Banham's 1976 book *Megastructure*, Todd Gannon wrote, "Banham established himself as a vociferous critic of modern orthodoxy with his celebrated revisionist history 'Theory and Design in the First Machine Age (1960),' and a formidable body of critical journalism that stretched back to the 1950s. In these writings, Banham often included dire prognostications about modern architecture's future, as in the famous conclusion to 'Theory and Design,' in which he warned that an architect unwilling to keep up with technology risked being left behind by technological culture." See introduction, in Reyner Banham, *Megastructure: Urban Futures of the Recent Past* (1976; repr., New York: Monacelli, 2020), 6.

3 Banham, quoting Gropius, "The Architecture Below," 196.

4 Banham, "The Architecture Below," 196.

5 In 1902, a printing company tasked Willis Carrier with developing a way to prevent paper from warping in the summer heat and humidity. Carrier's solution, which reversed coil-heating principles for cooling, led to the invention of the modern air conditioner. Banham, "The Architecture Below," 197.

6 The quote continues, "...from an architecture in which the building of massive structures was virtually the only way of modifying the human climate, to an architecture in which climate could be manufactured to taste, and the structure served merely to stop it blowing away." Banham, "The Architecture Below," 197.

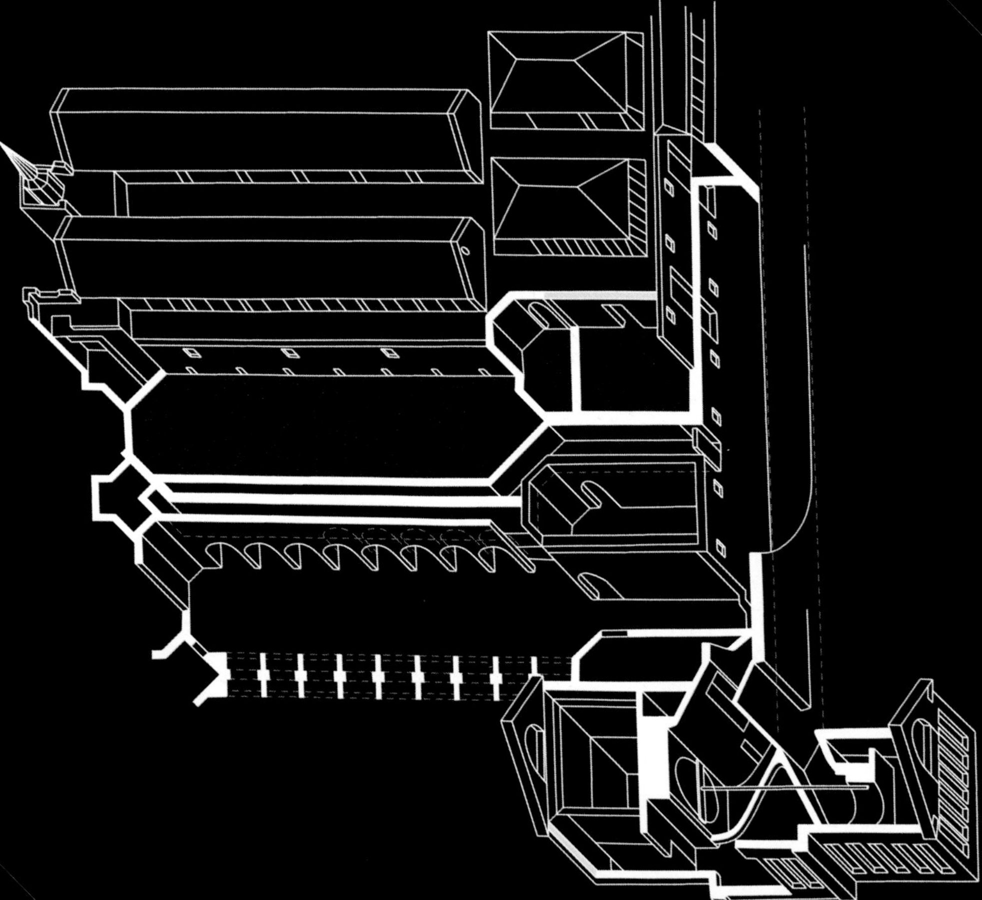

You will not find the Royal Victoria Hospital mentioned in any of the standard histories of modern architecture. — Reyner Banham

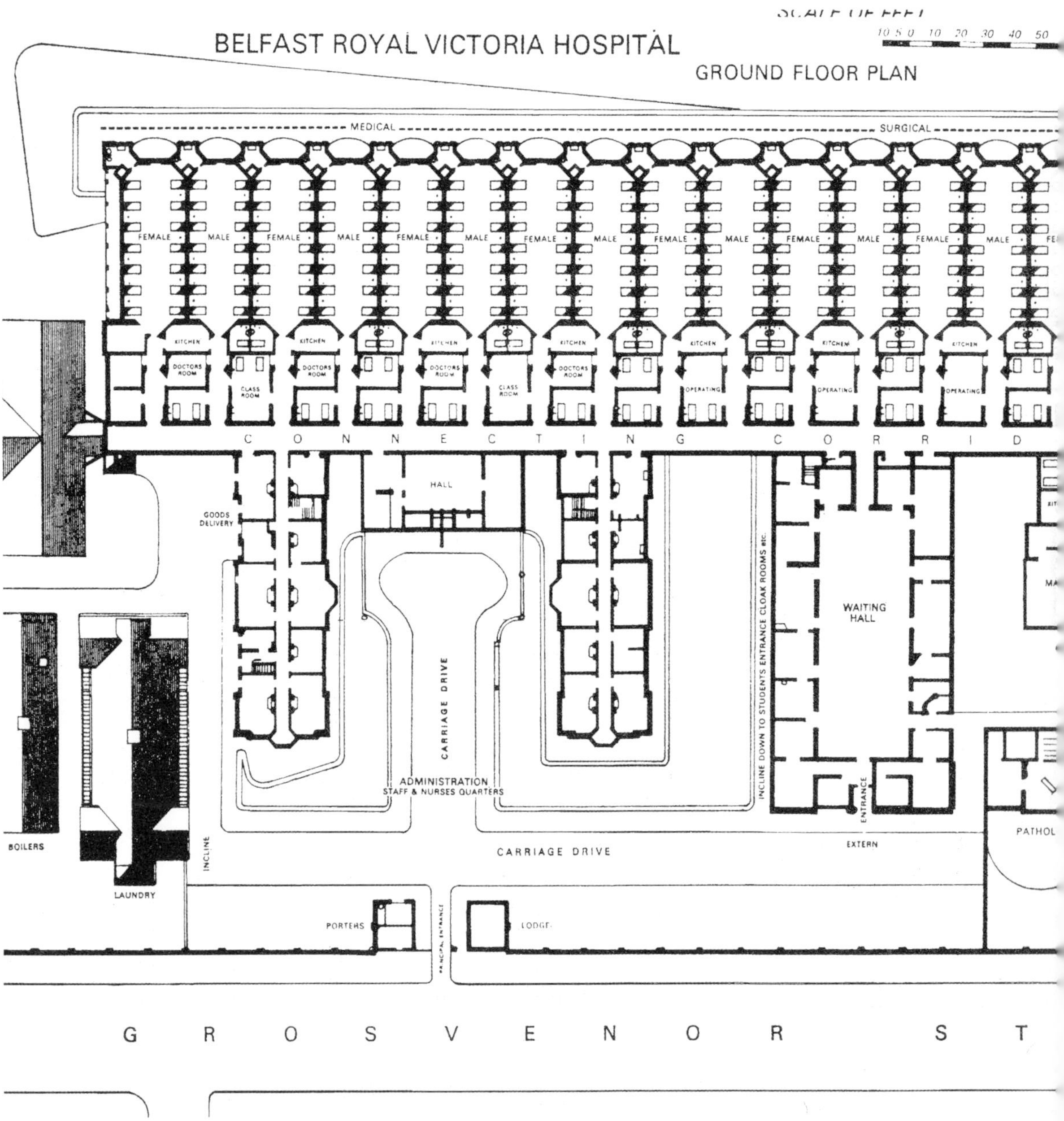

Plan, Royal Victoria Hospital, Belfast, designed by Henman and Cooper, 1899–1903 [fig. 5]

Larkin Office Building, Buffalo, New York, designed by Frank Lloyd Wright, 1906 [fig. 3]

Corridor, Royal Victoria Hospital, Belfast [fig. 6]

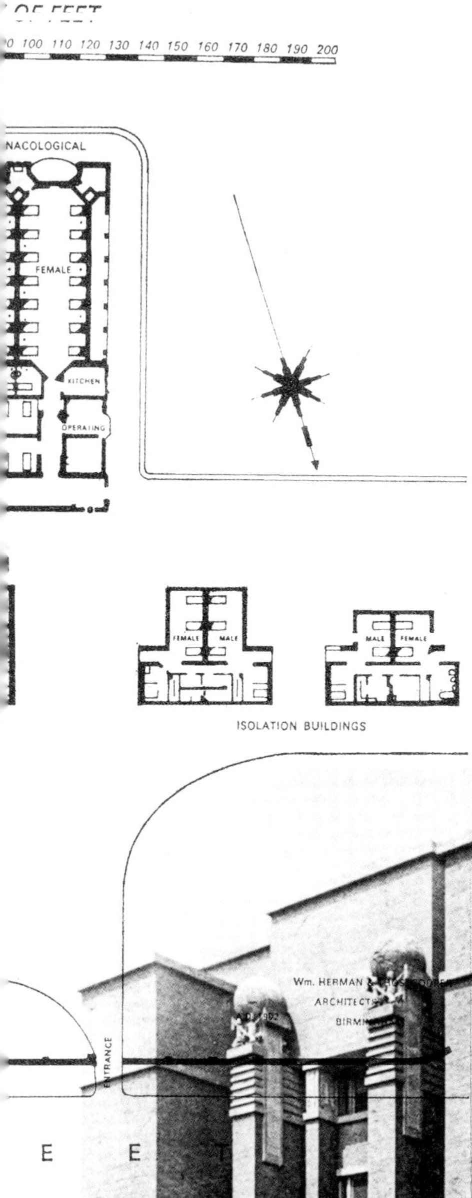
0 100 110 120 130 140 150 160 170 180 190 200
NACOLOGICAL
FEMALE
KITCHEN
OPERATING
FEMALE MALE
MALE FEMALE
ISOLATION BUILDINGS
ENTRANCE
E E

Wm. HERMAN &

The Block Hospital

On Medical Innovation

Innovation often grows exponentially, beginning slowly and cresting into a wave. Early modern medicine made way for germ theory (1870), the X-ray (1897), controlled environments (1903), and penicillin (1928), and by midcentury the rate of technological and medical invention outpaced design.[7] With these advances, newly erected hospitals faced obsolescence even before they opened. They attempted to keep up, however, struggling resolutely to accommodate novel machines, performance expectations, and medical specializations.

The same strategies necessitated by forced-air ventilation and moisture control in the Royal Vic — larger floorplates, fewer operable windows — were useful in accommodating advances in medical equipment later in the century. The machines and devices that now made medicine possible, plus the equipment and computational requirements of air handling, exhaust, and storage, took over the facility from within. Accordingly, the hospital's core began to swell — from the panoptic nurses' station to the war-room control tower, it soon managed millions of inputs, outputs, and throughputs **(fig. 7)**. Hallways followed suit, wrapping the core in hard circulatory tissue, while pressure was released vertically through elevator cores and waste-control stints. The use of artificial ventilation systems and the concurrent emergence of steel framing allowed hospital designers to abandon the bar form, which was replaced by expanded floorplates stacked vertically. At the same time, specialized care and the growing middle class drove demand for smaller private rooms.[8] A new taxonomy emerged of single-patient rooms and semiprivate wards accommodating two to eight patients, accessible via labyrinthine interior hallways. These rooms pressed outward, lining the buildings' exteriors but sealed behind inoperable curtain-wall fenestrations. The skin of the building became a liability. Window handles — a mundane detail — were removed, and the public interface was hermetically sealed. This was the block hospital.

Gordon Friesen

Gordon Friesen (1909–1996) was one of the mid-twentieth century's most ardent evangelists of technology, championing it as a form of humanism for its liberating and democratizing potential. Friesen had an enormous influence on hospitals from the 1960s on, but instead of taking a role as an architect, a trade whose practitioners he dismissed as distracted by form, he created a new discipline: systems engineering — an elevation of technology over art **(fig. 8)**. Friesen theorized that efficiency would be of ultimate service to the patient and proselytized for technical modeling as the future of medical spaces.

Friesen's systems interventions were intended to create a new model for what he termed "patient-centered" care by freeing nurses from busywork to focus on the patient. The result, however, as David Theodore has observed, was a hospital that looked and performed (even more) like a factory, with new machines and systems;[9] Friesen's Automated Cart Transport system, for example, was designed to deliver

7 The postwar years saw the polio vaccine (1952), the heart-lung machine (1953), the first kidney transplant (1954), cardiopulmonary resuscitation (1960), the wide dissemination of oral contraception (1960), the artificial heart (1963), commercial fetal ultrasound (1965), magnetic resonance imaging (1970), and positron emission tomography (1975), among a dizzying array of medical advancements.

8 Annmarie Adams, *Medicine by Design: The Architect and the Modern Hospital, 1893–1943* (Minneapolis: University of Minnesota Press, 2008).

9 David Theodore, "Towards a New Hospital: Architecture, Medicine, and Computation, 1960–75" (PhD diss., Harvard University, 2014). "The new hospital [Friesen] championed is not actually centered on the patient, but rather on the machines, objects, furniture, technologies, and building components that freed up the nurse. In short, patient-centered care was Friesen's counterintuitive proposal that achieving better care would come through making the hospital more like a factory" (54).

7

8

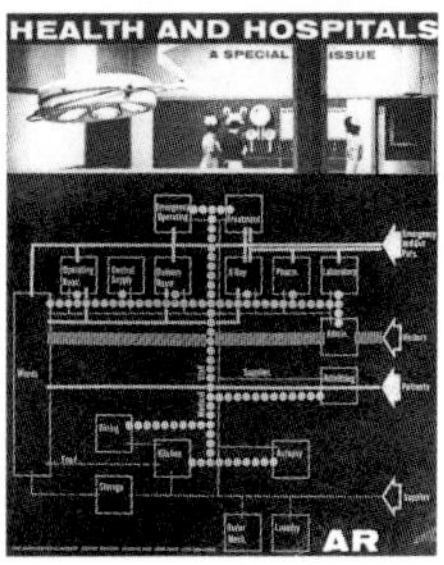

supplies to patients and nurses on an in-house track (fig. 9). However, for certain treatments, he argued, it was the patients who should be moved, transported along an assembly line of medical procedures. Using the Prototype Patient Capsule by William E. Berger (1969; fig. 10), a nurse, with the push of a button, could send a patient — recumbent in a space-age pod — along a track to specialists throughout the hospital. This design captures the techno-utopian, space-age spirit of the era; it also expresses a key dilemma in hospital architecture: the more technology is introduced into the hospital, the more inflexible the building is in accommodating future innovations. Though Berger's capsule system was decidedly future-oriented, it was not future-proofed. Essentially inadaptable, it would inevitably tether the building to a single transport system, hindering evolution in care programs, patient experience, and even maintenance and repair.

Around this time, the computer entered the hospital as a solution for health metrics and management. A far cry from the family practitioner who knows your health history and family dynamics, the faceless new hospital-machine could not remember the past — until the advent of medical-records technology, the next great advancement in the medical-industrial complex. In 1961, the Hospital Computer project at Massachusetts General Hospital in Boston introduced medical records into the vocabulary of care (fig. 11). This early experiment was fraught with difficulties. The learning curve was steep, the limited availability of computers and system downtime complicated access to medical records, and the large size and unwieldiness of early computers made them difficult to integrate into care spaces. Nurses' and other medical professionals' attention was inevitably drawn away from the patient and toward the workstation.[10] In addition, the project failed to fully take into account the human factor. Entering data into terminals doubled nurses' workloads (along with the training required to use the machines), and they rejected the premise that computers could achieve better results than their own expertise.

In the age of machine medicine, hospital designers wrestled with incorporating computers and other new technologies into their buildings and operations while also managing an ever-increasing workforce of care providers. The dichotomy between human and machine became ever more acute, and anxiety inside the hospital (for both patients and staff) grew increasingly delirious. In the new Bellevue Hospital in New York, this tension was inescapable.

Bellevue Hospital, New York

The block hospital is a facility whose interior environment is entirely controllable and sterile. By midcentury, as demand outpaced capacity, many existing institutions had added block structures to their sprawling expanded campuses. Historic medical entities like Philadelphia's Pennsylvania Hospital (1751; see chapter 1) and Massachusetts General Hospital in Boston (1811) built new facilities to accommodate changes in policies, services, capacities, and treatments after World War II. The US Congress passed the Hospital Survey and Construction Act (commonly known as the Hill-Burton Act) in 1946, opening up federal

10 Theodore, "Towards a New Hospital," 103–13.

9

10

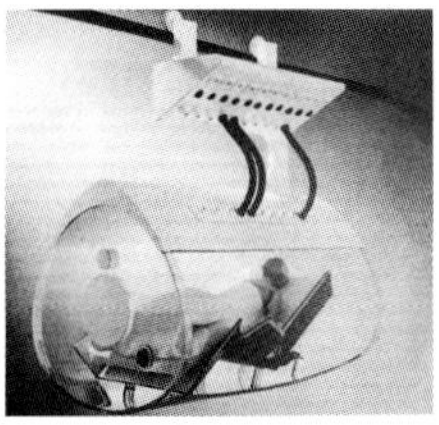

11

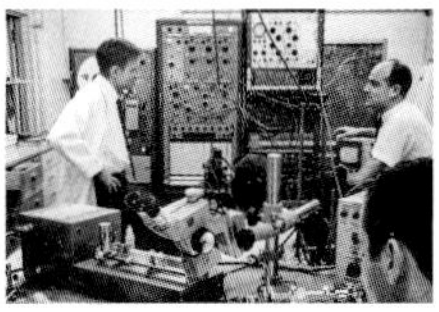

Stony Brook University Medical Center, Stony Brook, New York, designed by Bertrand Goldberg, 1980 [fig. 7]

Automated Cart Transport system, designed by Gordon Friesen, 1970 [fig. 9]

Prototype Patient Capsule, designed by William E. Berger, 1969 [fig. 10]

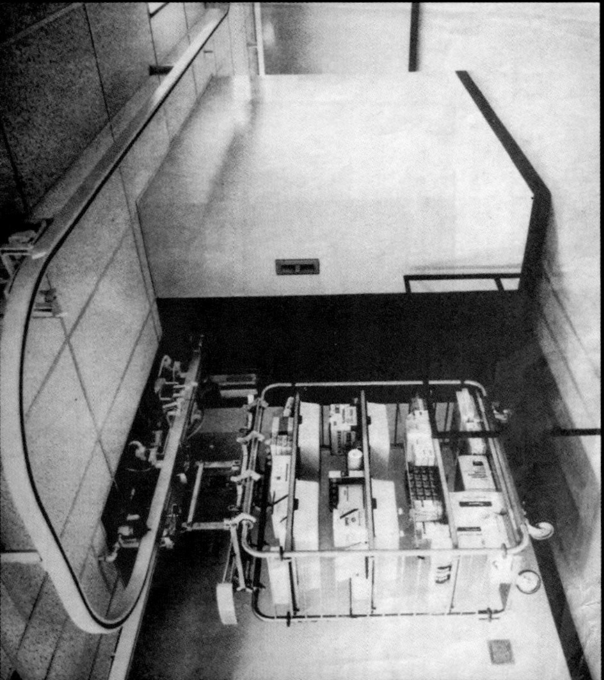

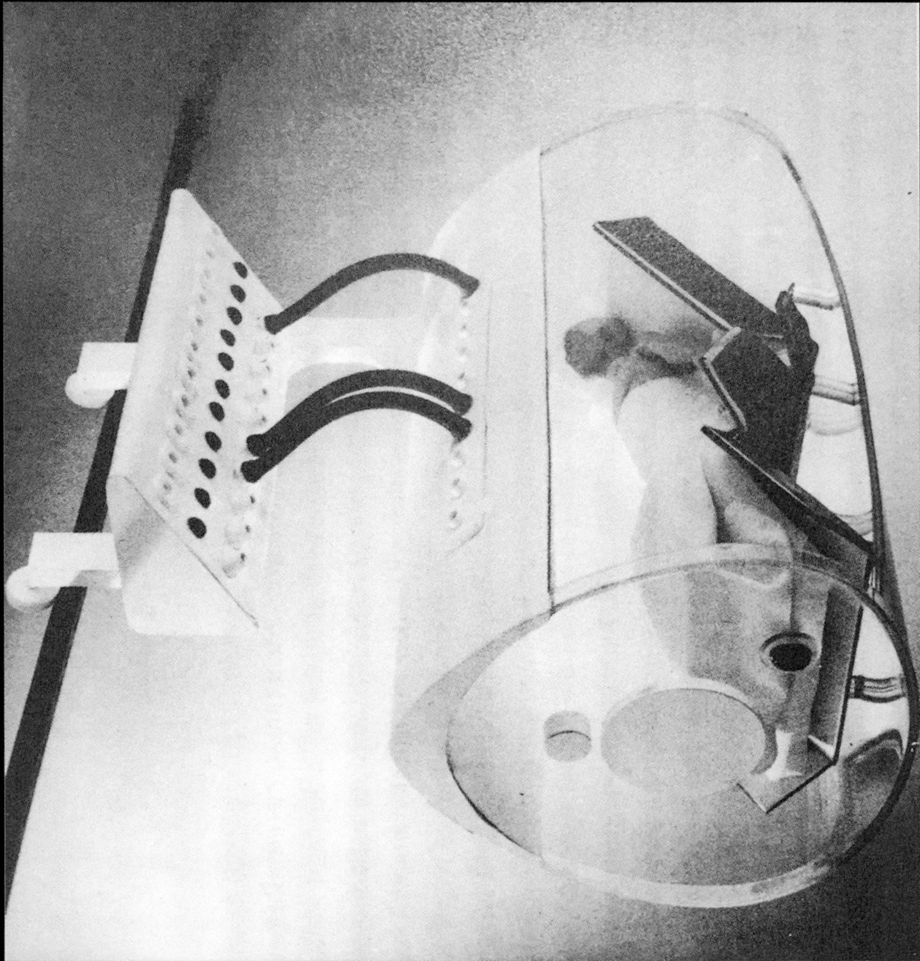

11 Bernard M. Weinstein, quoted in Deirdre Carmody, "Ancient Bellevue Is About to Open New Building," *New York Times*, October 3, 1973.

12 "Bellevue 'New Building,'" NYC Urbanism, https://www.nycurbanism.com/brutalnyc/bellevue-new-building.

13 Stephen Verderber and David J. Fine, *Healthcare Architecture in an Era of Radical Transformation* (New Haven, CT: Yale University Press, 2000), 63–129.

funding for many new hospital projects (fig. 12). Among these was the new home of the United States' oldest hospital, Bellevue.

Bellevue Hospital was established in New York City in 1736 where City Hall stands today. In 1811, it moved to Manhattan's East Side, where a distributed campus was established on a former farm (Belle Vue) near the East River. By the 1950s, the hospital, which served psychiatric patients and the poorest city residents, was in need of an upgrade. Its executive director, Bernard M. Weinstein, claimed, "If the devil himself had been commissioned to build a hospital facility, this is how he would have designed it."[11] Planning began in 1957, and after many changes in medical regulations and treatments, redesigns, and amendments, Bellevue "New Building" — also known as "the Cube" — opened its doors in 1973 (fig. 13).

Bellevue New Building was the largest hospital of its type in the United States, and it confirmed the complete victory of the block over the pavilion. Designed by the firm Pomerance and Breines in association with Katz, Waisman, Weber, Strauss, and Blumenkranz, the hospital was a monster, rising twenty-five stories. The services provided by fourteen previous buildings were consolidated into one tower, each floorplate of which covered over an acre of land, and the entire hospital could accommodate more than two thousand patients and fifteen hundred staff members. Its windowless core was transversed by heating and cooling ducts, sanitary chases, breakout rooms, nurses' stations, and bays upon bays of elevators (figs. 14, 15). In the pavilion hospital, outdoor spaces between ward buildings created courtyards and allowed natural light to penetrate into the interior. In contrast, Bellevue New Building's massive floorplate sprawled over and enclosed an entire Manhattan city block.

Functionalism and the Machine

The block hospital is a closed system. It requires a defined nurse capacity, an air-handling budget, a mechanical-systems team, fossil fuel, and its own energy-production capabilities. Where the pavilion — an open system — was reliant on the movement of natural air, the block is dependent on its suppression. Its skin is a liability. It looks inward. The architect is left to dream of a system so well automated that care is managed less by the judgment of an attendant than by the performance of the equipment. With self-monitoring gadgetry, observation and measurement are transformed into surveillance, while the block as a technological concept supersedes the architecture, erasing uniqueness, character, and humanity. The block hospital is defined not only by the bed, the privy, the window, and the altar, but also by the *machinery* of health care — a new strand in the DNA of the medical space.

Bellevue New Building was the perverse outcome of the techno-utopian promise foisted on hospitals at midcentury. With enough standardized "stuff, systems, and staff" (to quote Dr. Paul Farmer; see chapter 1), we were assured, the environment of our most difficult public building could be hardwired, rewired, and controlled. But workers at Bellevue almost immediately questioned the building's scale and lack of light and bemoaned the isolation engendered by its design.[12]

Even architects critiqued this branch of architecture for its rigidity, its reliance on technology, and its soullessness — the indignity engendered by its design. Modern "stinkers" such as Bellevue demonstrate the limits of this type of design futurism: notably, its complete indifference to human experience, its inflexibility of form, and its reliance on machines running without interruption. Historians Stephen Verderber and David Fine have claimed that tethering the hospital to technology was a Faustian bargain that will plague medical architecture for generations to come.[13] Mies's "less is more" became more and more and *more*. The failure of the block hospital spelled the end of the modernist box.

When Louis Sullivan theorized that "form ever follows function," he was constructing an argument for his own block structure, the skyscraper, whose height, made possible by elevators, had previously been unattainable (see introduction). But mechanical functionality, privileged above all else, created a leviathan, a *formless* architecture beholden to the machines that supported its existence. The block hospital is a sterile instrument, an institution stripped of its humanness. As a machine tuned and engineered for a single, overarching purpose (to fight death), the block abandoned the other mission of medicine: to give life. And to give life, the hospital must be designed for humanity.

In the hospital, function cannot be abandoned, but neither can it be privileged above all else. It must instead be considered parametrically, incorporated into the structure with more or less flexibility or rigidity, depending on the goals of the design. Pure functionality abandons form, and with it the possibility of beauty, authorship, identity, and, ultimately, human dignity. The block hospital engendered a sense of institutionalization and dehumanization, that particular loss of individual identity that functionalist modernism unleashed across built forms. The public demanded an alternative, and architects responded with systems designed to nurture self-determination, adaptation, and individualization.

12

13

14

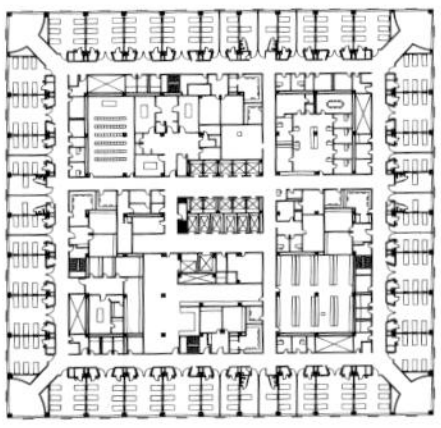

15

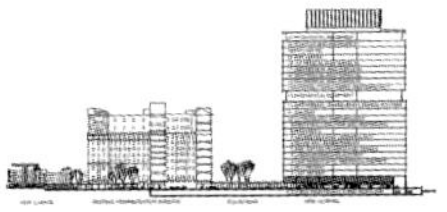

Mechanical functionality, privileged above all else, created a leviathan, a *formless* architecture beholden to the machines that supported its existence. The block hospital is a sterile instrument, an institution stripped of its humanness.

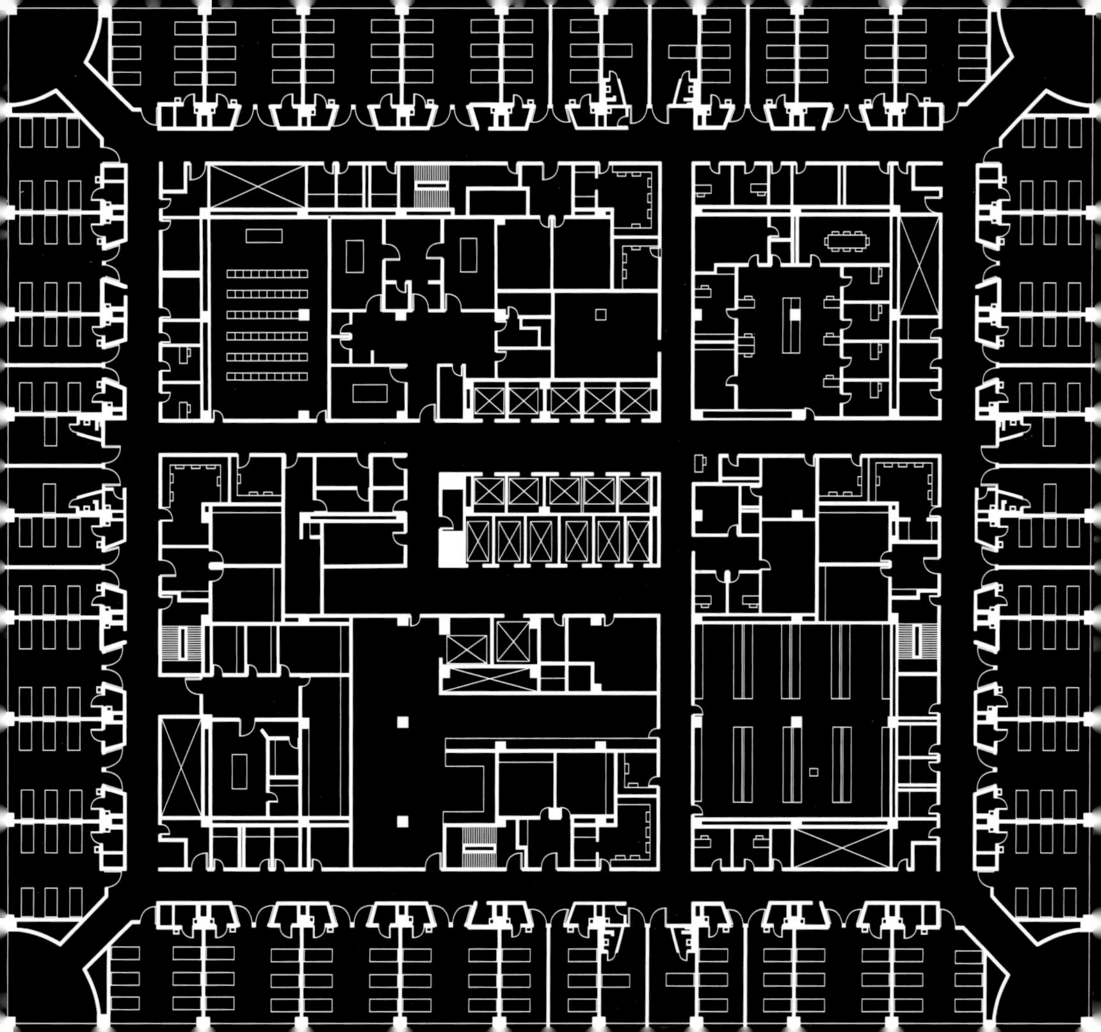

Section diagram of Bellevue Hospital, designed by Pomerance and Breines in association with Katz Waisman, Weber, Strauss, and Blumenkranz (redrawn by MASS Design Group) [fig. 15]

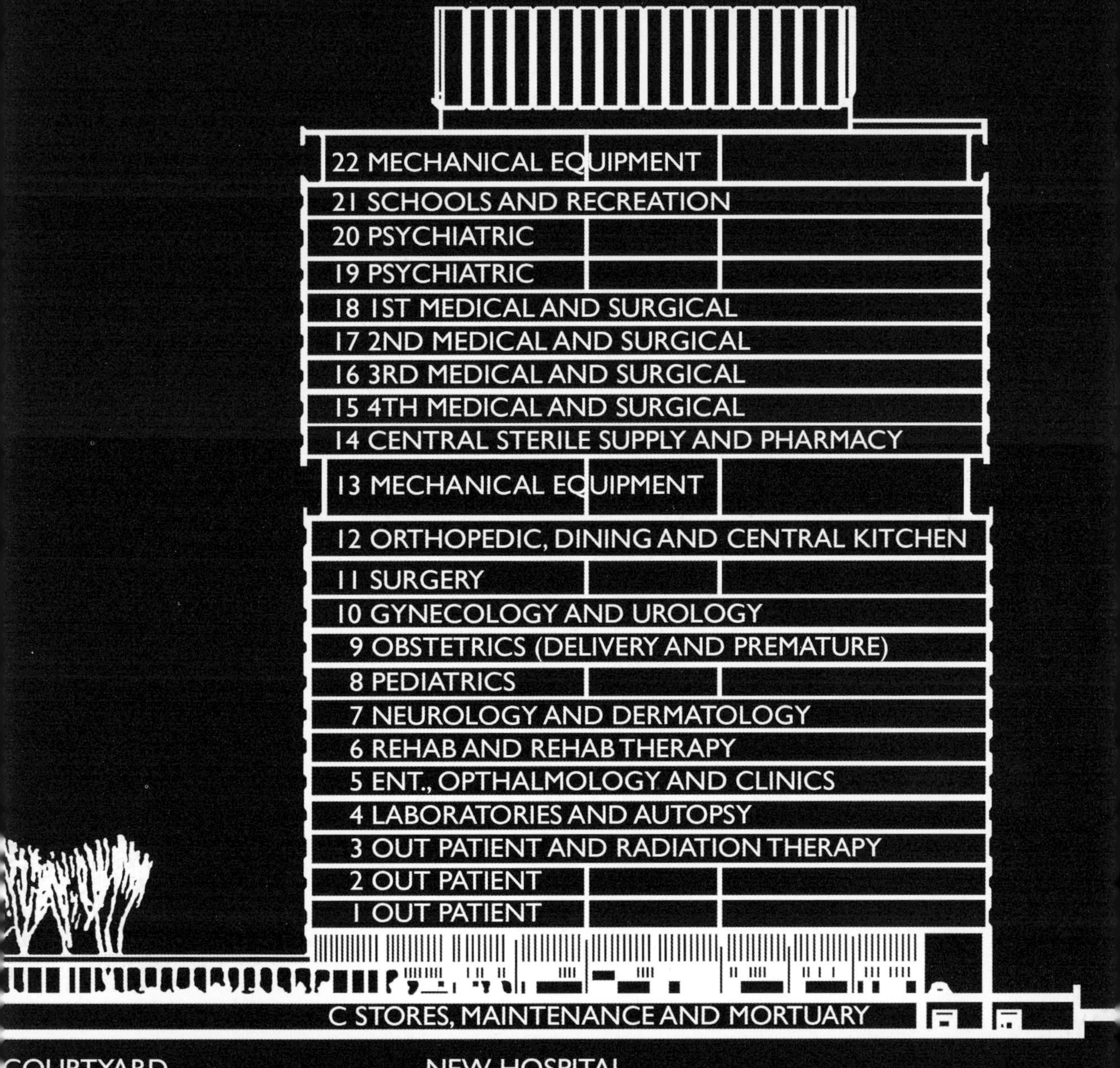
22 MECHANICAL EQUIPMENT
21 SCHOOLS AND RECREATION
20 PSYCHIATRIC
19 PSYCHIATRIC
18 1ST MEDICAL AND SURGICAL
17 2ND MEDICAL AND SURGICAL
16 3RD MEDICAL AND SURGICAL
15 4TH MEDICAL AND SURGICAL
14 CENTRAL STERILE SUPPLY AND PHARMACY
13 MECHANICAL EQUIPMENT
12 ORTHOPEDIC, DINING AND CENTRAL KITCHEN
11 SURGERY
10 GYNECOLOGY AND UROLOGY
9 OBSTETRICS (DELIVERY AND PREMATURE)
8 PEDIATRICS
7 NEUROLOGY AND DERMATOLOGY
6 REHAB AND REHAB THERAPY
5 ENT., OPTHALMOLOGY AND CLINICS
4 LABORATORIES AND AUTOPSY
3 OUT PATIENT AND RADIATION THERAPY
2 OUT PATIENT
1 OUT PATIENT
C STORES, MAINTENANCE AND MORTUARY
COURTYARD
NEW HOSPITAL

Chapter 6
The Mega-Hospital

As the machines inside the hospital demanded more and more space and the box hospital swelled to consume entire city blocks, the limitations and contradictions of its universalizing form became apparent, and architects began to search for an alternative. But instead of looking to hyperlocal, personal solutions like Alvar Aalto's Paimio Sanitorium (see chapter 4), they went in a new direction, opting to explicitly acknowledge the mechanical, social, and political forces shaping their designs.

Some architects began complicating the box, combining block-consuming rectilinear podium buildings with expressive bed towers and annex structures with different forms and functions. More radical designers abandoned the box altogether and began to experiment with forms that allowed for infinite expansion, an approach that constituted a shift from *architecture as building* to *architecture as a system*. This concept energized an emerging generation of designers, whose works Reyner Banham and the architect Fumihiko Maki characterized as *megastructures*.[1] The megastructure, Banham theorized, was a sort of "superbuilding" whose component pieces plugged into a framework or an armature that supported changeable elements — such as housing units or hospital wards — that could be replaced over time. Banham noted that megastructures were difficult to define and even more difficult to build: "Megastructures in their time were all large buildings — but not all large buildings of the time were megastructures."[2]

Hundreds of such modular and adaptable buildings were proposed, and radical young architectural collectives such as the London-based Archigram and the Italian Superstudio designed enormous — even nation-sized — structures **(fig. 1)**. Most of these were speculative, however, and only a dozen or so megastructures were actually built.[3] Across the Atlantic, E. Todd Wheeler, a partner at the firm Perkins and Will, was also experimenting with novel mega-forms, putting them to work in medical facilities and health systems.

1

2

3

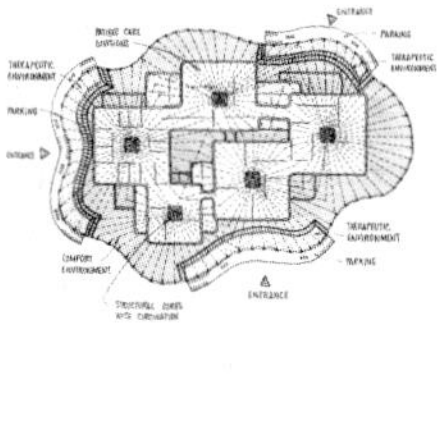

E. Todd Wheeler
Unbuildable Provocations

Wheeler (1907–1987), like Gordon Friesen (see chapter 5), was a systems thinker. In wrestling with the design of the medical facility, he began to sketch vast, siteless structures that could evolve over time. In one speculative hospital drawing, the Tent Hospital or Tropicarium (1971), Wheeler envisioned a massive canopy structure that stretched over a series of vertical masts housing elevator and equipment cores **(figs. 2, 3)**. Reconfigurable floorplates supported patient and procedure rooms that were in turn plugged into the masts and that could be exchanged and amended over time. Another megastructure from the same year, the Tree Hospital, similarly supported reconfiguration, featuring a grid-like cubic armature that a hospital's departmental volumes could plug into and out of, with core services provided in the negative space between the "branches" **(fig. 4)**. In a third project from 1971, Wheeler imagined an underwater hospital filling an Atlantis-like bubble, surrounded by unclaimed territory into which it could expand as needed **(fig. 5)**.

In these speculative, unbuildable projects, Wheeler was investigating methods of designing and controlling the indeterminate systems of the hospital. His sketches acknowledge the then-emergent truth that hospitals will inevitably experience constant change and will demand ever-larger spaces over time. They are also dystopian provocations; his underwater sites and canopies in the air acknowledge a shift in architects' understanding of the immensity of the environmental and social challenges they were facing. When applied to an actual commission, Wheeler's ideas were tempered by the constraints of budget, location, and scale **(fig. 6)**. His St. Mary of Nazareth Hospital in Chicago is bipolar, a transitional building that is neither strictly a block nor a fully realized megastructure.

St. Mary of Nazareth Hospital, Chicago

Like New Somerset Hospital (see chapter 3), St. Mary of Nazareth is a fortress and a beachhead of "progress" and modernity — in this case, in Chicago's lower-income West Side. When Wheeler, with Sheldon Schlegman and Perkins and Will, designed St. Mary of Nazareth, its Gotham City–style aesthetic was futuristic; today it evokes a utopia of futures past. The concrete tower and podium, completed in 1975, take up an entire city block on Division Street. Like Prentice Women's Hospital, which opened across town the same year (see introduction), St. Mary of Nazareth is a podium building with a bed tower sprouting from its core. Unlike Prentice, however, it merged its two divergent functional components into a singular composition: a hulking, brutalist superbuilding.

The bed tower at St. Mary of Nazareth is less experimental than Prentice's cloverleaf plan. Wheeler and Schlegman designed a pinwheel-shaped plan with vertical stems defining single patient rooms. These rooms are all in earshot of nurses' stations, although (in contrast to Prentice's geocentric solution) the distances from bed to station vary. In general, St. Mary of Nazareth is a more flexible design in terms of plan configurations, room sizes, and patient loads. Later additions — made to accommodate the growing hospital — are sited across the street and are connected to the original structure by a bridge. Unlike Prentice, St. Mary of Nazareth is still in operation today.

While Prentice's form resembled a concrete flower sprouting delicately from a single stem, St. Mary of Nazareth's formal language is much heavier. The hybrid form evokes a grotesque concrete monster whose belching and breathing is managed through the multistory air-handling vents sandwiched between the podium and the bed tower **(fig. 7)**. Where Prentice's form was based on the double patient room,

1 Reyner Banham, *Megastructure: Urban Futures of the Recent Past* (1976; repr., New York: Monacelli, 2020), 13.

2 Banham, *Megastructure*, 13.

3 Fumihiko Maki, *Investigations in Collective Form* (St. Louis, MO: School of Architecture, Washington University, 1964), 8–13. Cited in Banham, *Megastructure*, 223.

4

5
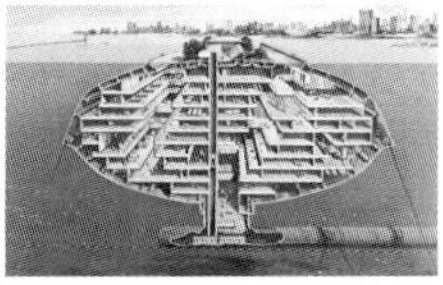

6

7

Concept rendering of Tent Hospital by E. Todd Wheeler, 1971 [fig. 2]

Concept plan of Tent Hospital by E. Todd Wheeler, 1971 [fig. 3]

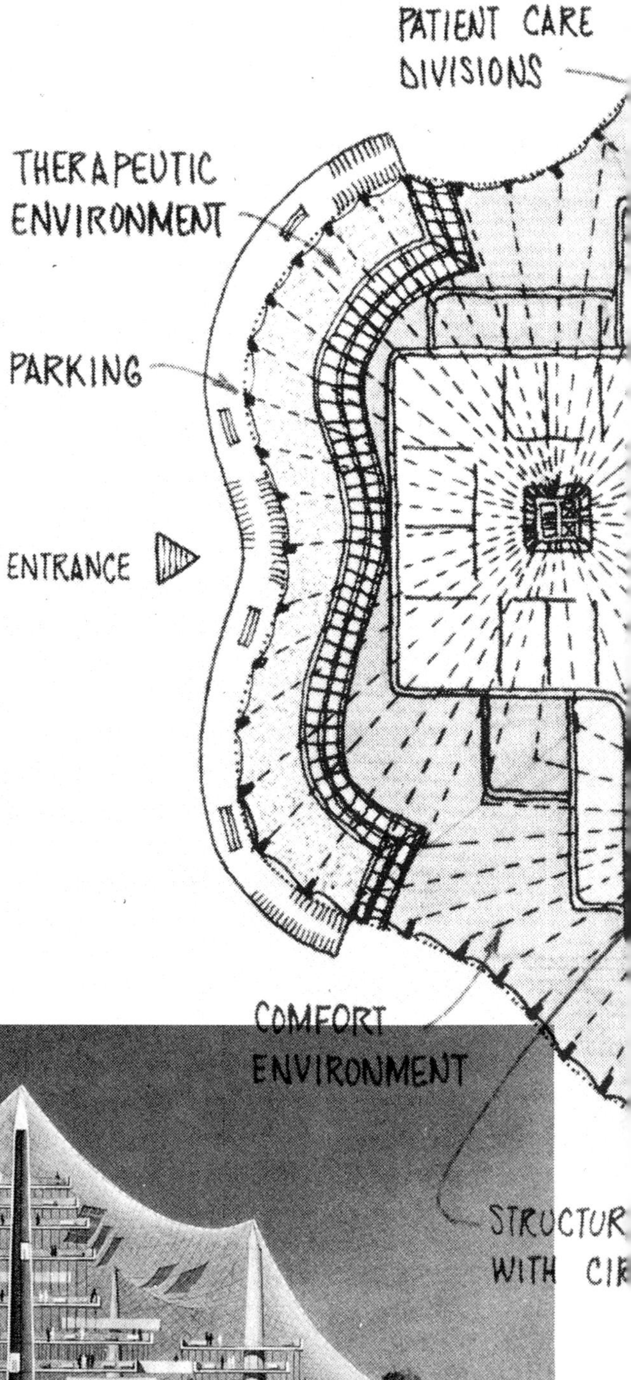

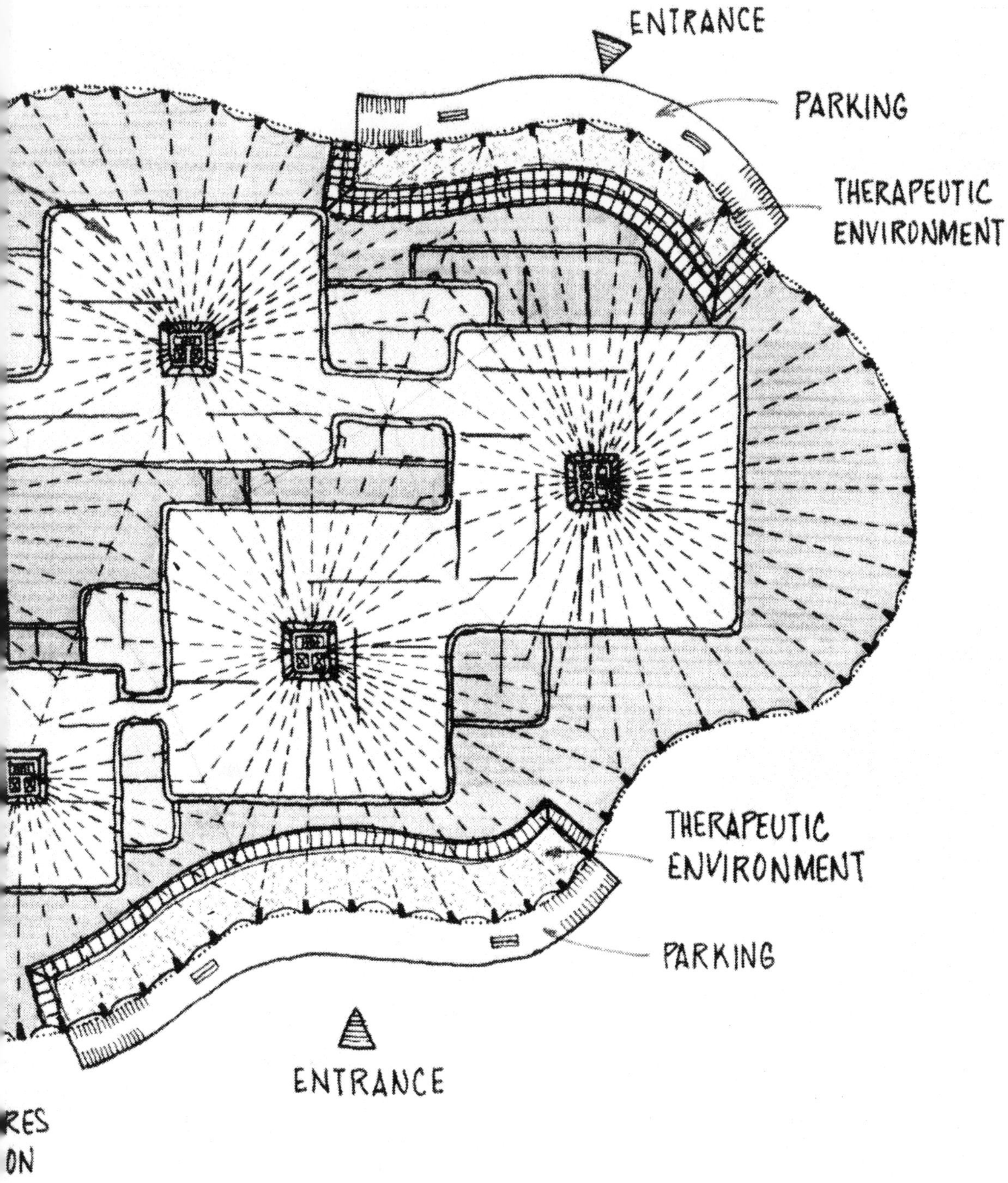
ENTRANCE
PARKING
THERAPEUTIC ENVIRONMENT
THERAPEUTIC ENVIRONMENT
PARKING
ENTRANCE

Concept rendering of the Tree Hospital by E. Todd Wheeler, 1971 [fig. 4]

Concept rendering of Inverted Pyramid Hospital by E. Todd Wheeler, 1971 [fig. 6]

In these speculative, unbuildable projects, Wheeler was investigating methods of designing and controlling the indeterminate systems of the hospital. His sketches acknowledge the then-emergent truth that hospitals will inevitably experience constant change and will demand ever-larger spaces over time.

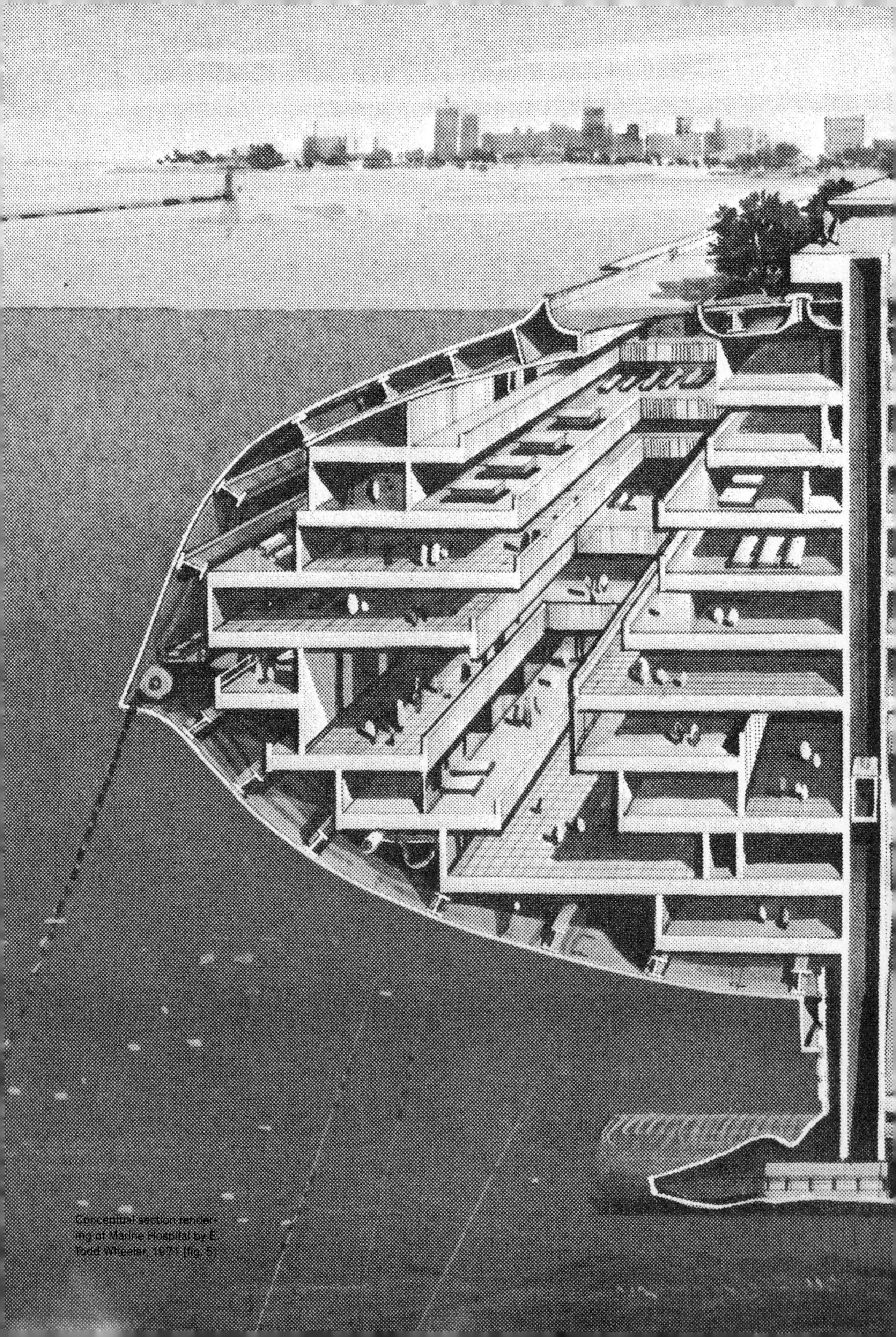

Conceptual section rendering of Marine Hospital by E Todd Wheeler, 1971 [fig. 5]

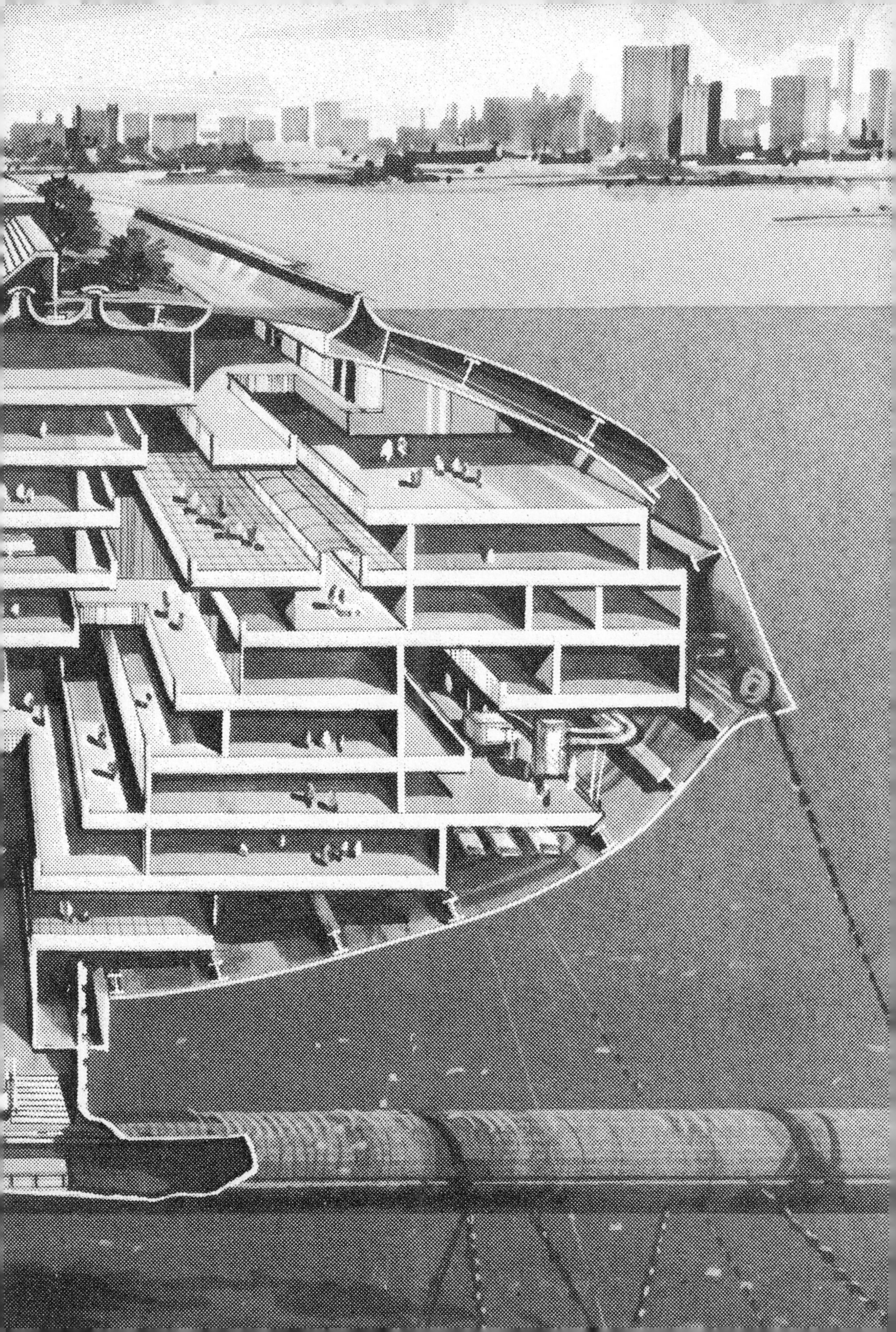

Il monumento continuo (The Continuous Monument), by Superstudio, 1979 [fig. 1]

4 Banham, *Megastructure*, 220.

Wheeler was inspired by the movement of air. In an acknowledgment of the dominance of the hermetically sealed hospital, he elevated the mechanical exhaust vent to a driver of form. The massive, multistory air vents loom over the hospital's podium base, emitting God knows what into the surrounding community. In the process, they articulate an immutable rule: regardless of what happens outside, the space in here breathes.

Other buildings of this period also harnessed functional components as expressive architectural elements, notably the Centre Pompidou in Paris, completed in 1977 and designed by Richard Rogers (born 1933), Renzo Piano (born 1937), Su Rogers (born 1939), and Gianfranco Franchini (born 1938). The Centre Pompidou is a scaffolded mass whose air ducts, escalators, and "systems wall" wrap around the exterior of its boxy form (fig. 8). Although the building was not necessarily big enough to be a megastructure, Banham proclaimed, it passed the "acid test of looking like one."[4]

St. Mary of Nazareth, the building as air duct, also passes the test. Wheeler staked an architectural claim against the invisible forces (airflow guidelines, mechanical specialists, technological expectations) that were taking over the hospital, explicitly acknowledging and aesthetically exploiting a mechanical system — airflow — that was usually hidden behind walls or beneath floorboards. Airflow — or the window strand of the hospital's DNA — is the dominant function and aesthetic language of the hospital. Wheeler did not shy away from the dystopian implications of his moment, but in elevating the exhaust system and harnessing it aesthetically — creating a behemoth air duct on West Division — he communicated that the machine can be controlled.

St. Mary of Nazareth has one final key component. To service the vents, Wheeler created a discrete space between the podium and the tower that is devoted entirely to air handling. This move presaged a key element of the megastructure: the creation of controlled spaces allocated specifically to equipment, as distinct from undefined areas designed to be open and adaptable.

Louis I. Kahn: Servant and Served Spaces and the Interstitial Floor

8

9

In hospitals and medical-research spaces around midcentury, technological progress meant *stuff*, and lots of it. Hallways were half-filled with roaming carts, and rooms teemed with obsolete or highly specialized machines. In the most well-funded institutions, new devices emerged annually. The invisible ailments of the body required ever-evolving devices of discovery.

Alfred Newton Richards Medical Research Laboratory, Philadelphia

Louis I. Kahn (1901–1974), the architect who best exemplifies midcentury heroic architecture, wrestled with the growing spatial requirements of modern scientific research and the inflexibility of the international modernist style. His 1965 Alfred Newton Richards Medical Research Laboratory at the University of Pennsylvania, in Philadelphia, is considered by many to be an inflection point in the shift from the Miesian International Style glass box of the postwar years to the new monumentality and material authenticity of the concrete modernism that followed (fig. 9).[5] In the Richards building, Kahn made his spatial solution to the problem of medical detritus a key visible element, designing air ducts, chimneys, and even staircases that stand proud of the floorplates between them. Resembling a fortress or a walled city, the building references the medieval Tuscan town of San Gimignano, which Kahn had admired and sketched on his grand tour of Europe.

Moving the chimneys and other elements of the service core to the exterior was a conceptual adjustment, one that reengaged the surface of the structure as part of the program of the building (fig. 10). Kahn's famous "servant" and "served" spatial concept was first expressed in the Richards building: the *servant* spaces — those chimneys, ducts, stairs, and shafts — constitute an articulated system that surrounds the *served* spaces of the laboratories. Again, a paradigmatic shift in architecture emerged from the spatial needs of medicine — in this case, from the exhaust of medical research and experimentation. Kahn's next iteration of the concept — his laboratory complex for the virologist and medical researcher Jonas Salk — was a masterpiece of architecture that directly influenced hospital design for the next two decades.

Salk Institute for Biological Studies, La Jolla, California

In his design for the Salk Institute for Biological Studies, completed in La Jolla, California, in 1965 (fig. 11), Kahn rotated the chimney horizontally and spread it out to cover the entire floorplate. This created a servant space that was essentially half a building story, sandwiched between each laboratory floor. While the move was somewhat excessive in relation to needs at the time, the allocation of entire floors of the building for medical equipment, air handling, cleaning, and coordinating acknowledged the growth of the medical machine and the spaces required to house it. The mechanical floors, around six feet (two meters) high, can't be comfortably occupied for long periods, but they are serviceable for ongoing maintenance and provide the structural foundations for flexible, column-free research spaces above and below. They also allow complex plumbing, venting, and wiring schemes to remain out of view, even while undergoing adjustments as the institute's needs change (fig. 12). This setup was a form of future-proofing, ensuring that Kahn's building would be adaptable to changes that might otherwise render it obsolete. Technology now made up at least half of the building.

The interstitial hospital, as it came to be known, caught on as a design strategy in the 1980s. It was iterated in projects around the world, such as the Tufts Medical Center in Boston in 1982 (fig. 13), and the 1984 Groote Schuur Hospital addition in Cape Town (fig. 14). In the interstitial hospital, flexible and rigid spaces alternate: one floor for the undefined and evolving, and the next for the controlled and precise. This allows the hospital to cope with the building's swelling core but also with the ever-accumulating *stuff* of medicine.

In the Salk Institute, Kahn inserted a stent into the clogged arteries of the block hospital by casting form and function in supporting roles.

5 Vincent Scully was effusive in his praise of the Richards building, calling it one of the greatest of modern times. See *Louis I. Kahn* (New York: George Braziller, 1962), 27. See also Emily Copperman, "National Historic Landmark Nomination: Richards and Goddard Buildings" (Philadelphia: National Park Service, May 2008). The Richards building is also featured in William H. Jordy, *American Buildings and Their Architects*, vol. 5, *The Impact of European Modernism in the Mid-Twentieth Century* (London: Oxford University Press, 1986), 361–73, 393–407.

10

11

12

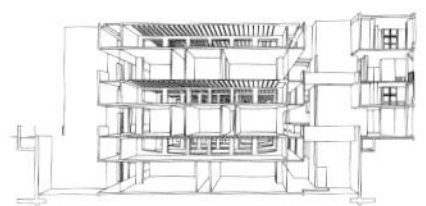

13

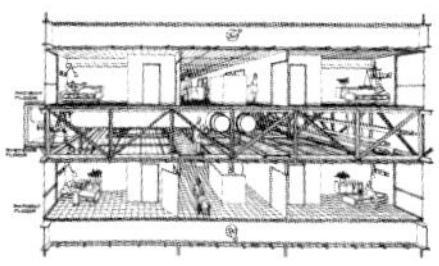

14

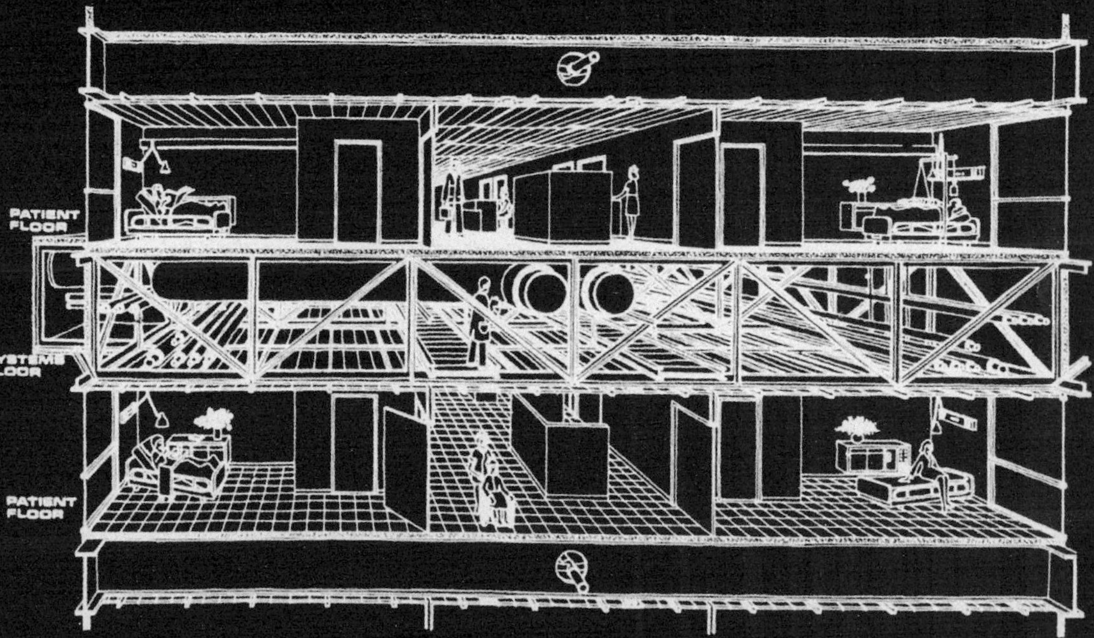
PATIENT FLOOR
SYSTEMS FLOOR
PATIENT FLOOR

Tufts Medical Center, Boston, 1982 [fig. 13]

The Centre Pompidou, Paris, designed by Richard Rogers, Renzo Piano, Su Rogers, and Gianfranco Franchini, 1977 [fig. 8]

Groote Schuur Hospital, Cape Town, South Africa [fig. 14]

Personnel

St. Mary of Nazareth Hospital, Chicago, designed by E. Todd Wheeler, 1975 [fig. 7]

Alfred Newton Richards Medical Research Laboratory at the University of Pennsylvania, Philadelphia, designed by Louis I. Kahn, 1965 [fig. 10]

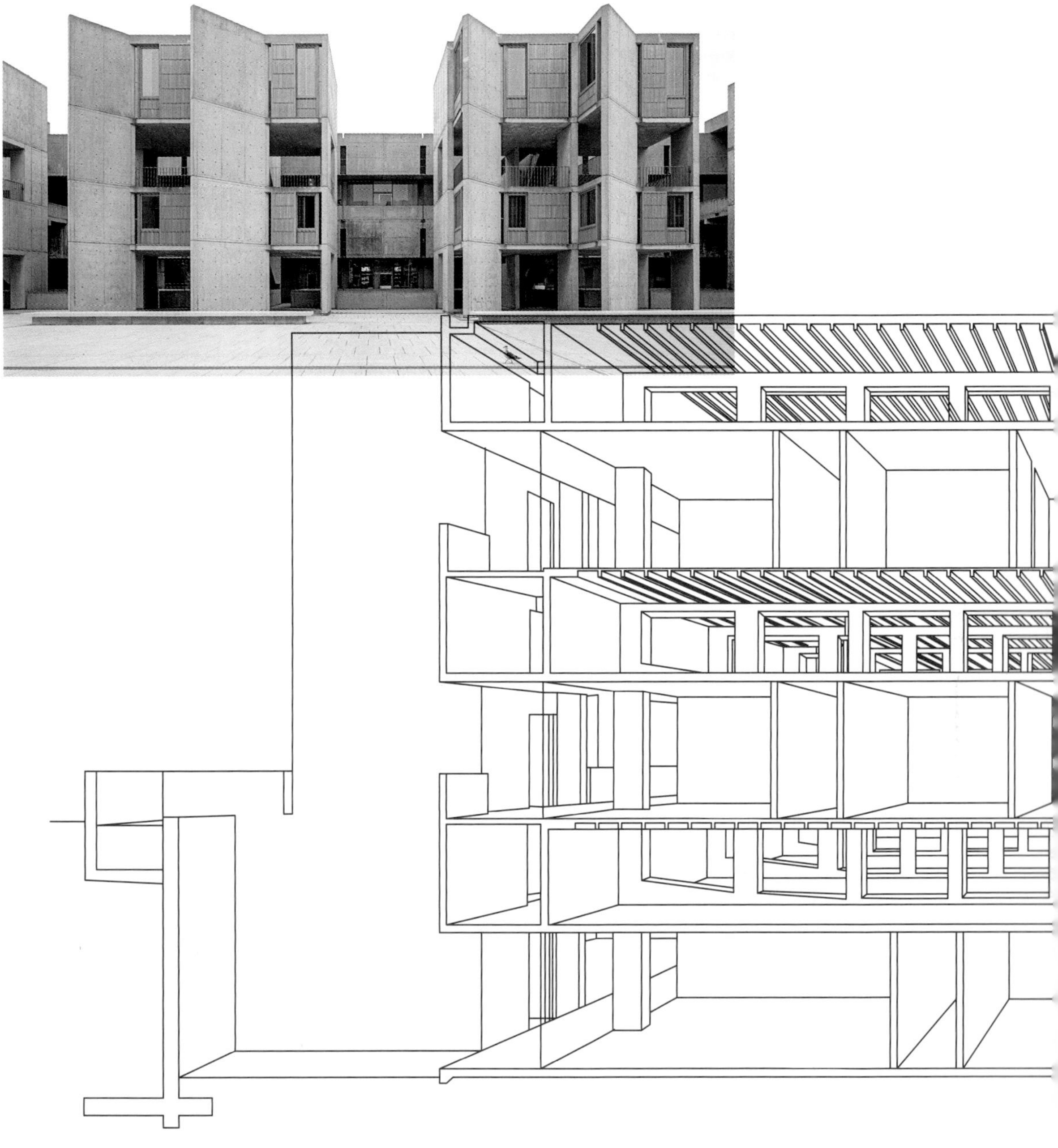

Salk Institute for Biological Studies, La Jolla, California, designed by Louis I. Kahn, 1965 [fig. 11]

Section drawing, Salk Institute for Biological Studies, La Jolla, California [fig. 12]

Alfred Newton Richards Medical Research Laboratory at the University of Pennsylvania, Philadelphia [fig. 9]

6 Banham, *Megastructure*, 185.

The artistry of the architecture takes center stage, exerting control over the demands of technology. Technology plays an integral and structural role in the design, but it does not dominate the beauty and humanity of the architecture. In his foray into medical research, Kahn gave medical spaces and the medical machine a long-overdue injection of dignity. In addition, his reconfiguration of the building as a mix of two integrated types (rather than two divergent types) created a pathway to the larger megastructure hospital, as exemplified by McMaster Health Sciences Center in Hamilton, Ontario, Canada, one of the few megastructures ever built.

The Mega-Hospital

McMaster Health Sciences Center, Hamilton, Ontario

It is difficult to describe the scale and complexity of the McMaster University Health Sciences Center except to say that it is massive — and even that might be an understatement (fig. 15). Designed by systems engineer Eberhard Zeidler (1940–2016) and completed by his firm Craig, Zeidler and Strong in 1972, McMaster resembles the open and extendable utopian ecosystems that Wheeler theorized but never built. It has the circuitry and connectedness of the block hospital but uses the skip-stop spatial framework of Kahn's interstitial plan to compose a health care city whose floors could be extended vertically and horizontally. Banham accurately described it as a maze of "indeterminate extensibility and variability,"[6] and yet it achieved a level of uniqueness in its interior — created by double-height spaces, skylights, interspersed outdoor patios, and health-specialty neighborhoods — that rendered it accommodating and warm at times, despite its dizzying complexity.

Zeidler designed McMaster as a series of repeatable modules layered between interstitial floors and supported by four vertical cores that extend past the building's roof (fig. 16). This forms a megamodule, which, when repeated dozens of times, creates health districts and service zones throughout the layout that allow for distinctness and memorable moments of pause (figs. 17, 18). This modular theory of construction was influenced by the Japanese Metabolists, specifically Arata Isozaki's Joint Core System project of 1960 (fig. 19). The interstitial floors contain venting, wiring, and lighting and have ceilings that are high enough to allow maintenance workers and contractors to walk upright.

With its modular construction, McMaster was designed so that in the future, if desired, it could be extended to more than double its current width and height (fig. 20). This gives the building a sense of unfinishedness and an aesthetic reminiscent of a space station occupied before completion (fig. 21). The vertical extension of the cores beyond the building floor also gives McMaster, which is almost *anti*-formal, its most visible aesthetic driver of form, an acknowledgment of its indeterminate and adaptable future.

Like Friesen and Wheeler, Zeidler was concerned with the effective distribution of stuff, systems, and staff throughout the hospital. At McMaster, he mapped relational flow patterns for patients and workers and for goods, laundry, and waste. This has resulted in highly rationalized movement within the building: maintenance staff move in certain places at certain times, as do nurses and patients. These flow patterns are supported by an innovative goods-distribution system that Zeidler named the Bulkveyor **(fig. 22)**. Essentially an electronic tug cart custom designed for McMaster, the Bulkveyor transports modular units — containing food, lab samples, and surgical supplies — to designated points, where they are collected by staff. Zeidler went so far as to design modular laboratory equipment that is transported on the Bulkveyor and that is proportionally and dimensionally optimized for the building.[7]

7 Eberhard Zeidler, *Healing the Hospital: McMaster Health Science Centre: Its Conception and Evolution* (Toronto: Zeidler Partnership, 1974).

17

20

15

18

21

16

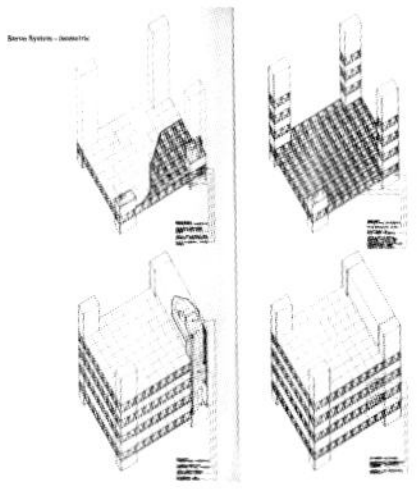

22

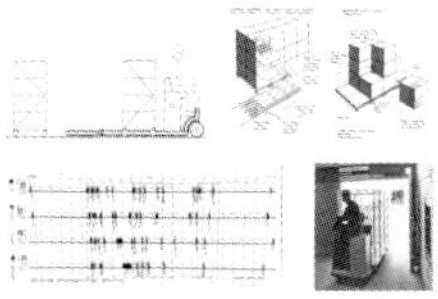

19

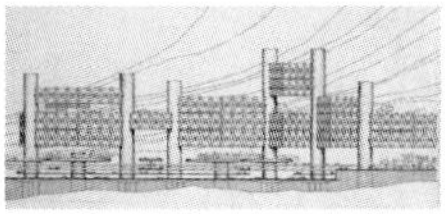

The vertical extension of the cores beyond the building floor also gives McMaster, which is almost *anti*-formal, its most visible aesthetic driver of form, an acknowledgment of its indeterminate and adaptable future.

Children's play area, McMaster University Health Sciences Center, Hamilton, Ontario [fig. 18]

McMaster University Health Sciences Center under construction [fig. 21]

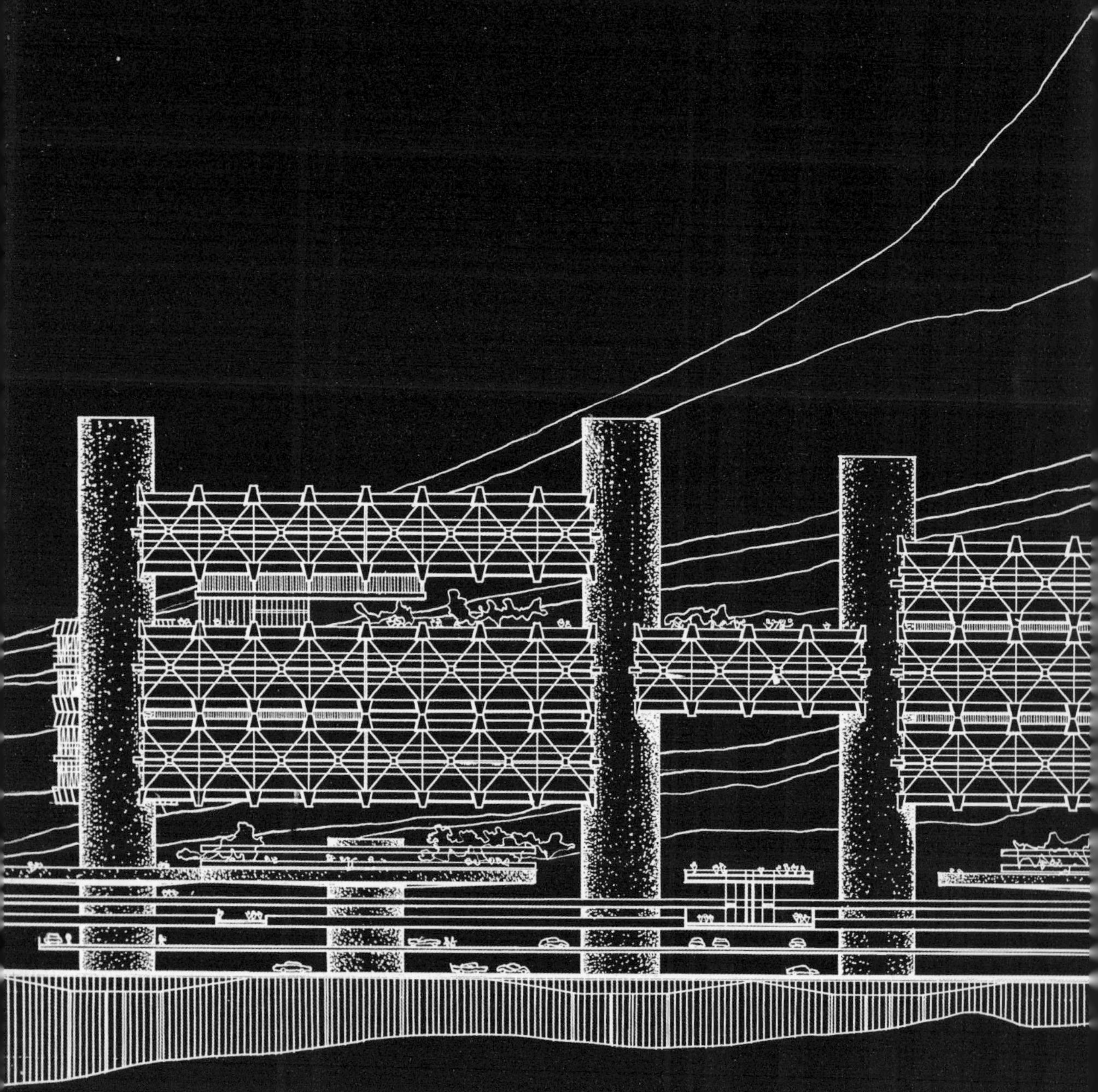

Section drawing of Joint Core System, by Arata Isozaki, 1960 [fig. 19]

Second-floor plan of
McMaster University Health
Sciences Center, Hamilton,
Ontario, by Craig, Zeidler
and Strong, 1972 [fig. 17]

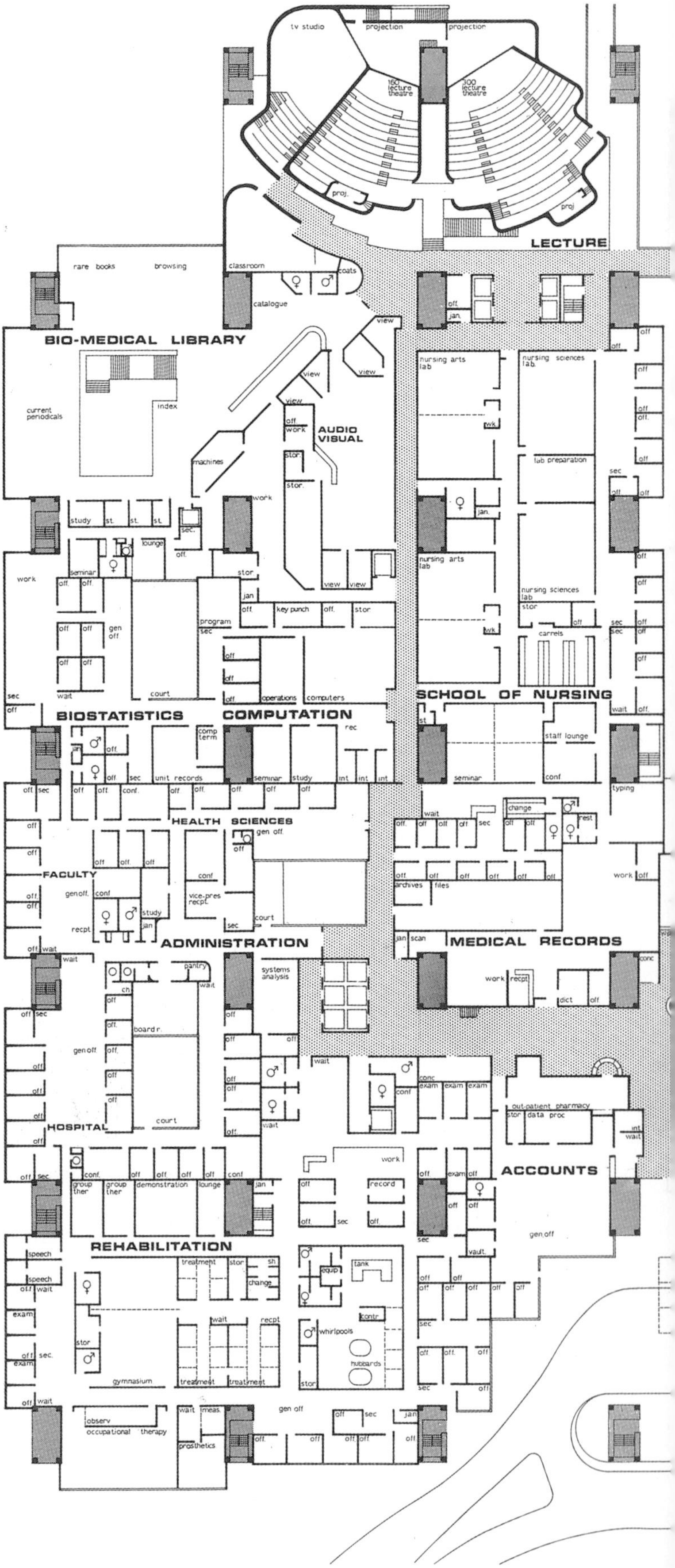

PATHOLOGY / POST MORTEM
OPERATING SUITE
RADIOLOGY
ROUTINE LABS.
INTENSIVE CARE
ADMITTING
FAMILY PRACTICE
EMERGENCY
2
0 5 15 35 75 140
ONE HALF MINUTE WALK

8 Todd Gannon, introduction to Banham, *Megastructure*, 5.

9 Maki, *Investigations in Collective Form*. Banham wrote, "No megastructure consciously designed as such was ever built without some architectural monomaniac scheming and pushing, wheeling and dealing to make it come about" (*Megastructure*, 217).

10 Banham, *Megastructure*, 222.

The hospital is divided into service and specialty districts, each characterized by a dramatic color scheme and supergraphics that transform dull corners into energizing and vibrant meeting areas. A play area features a custom-built topography of soft geometric spaces through which children can climb. Hallways are often single loaded (doorways along one side only) with skylights lining the ceiling above, while interior balconies overlook larger gathering spaces below. All these spaces are padded with a carpet in horizontal bands of primary colors, heightening what could be a mundane experience into one of delight, surprise, signal overload, and hopefully joy **(figs. 23, 24)**.

Everything about the hospital was deliberate and planned, but its success was not predetermined. On the exterior, its scale and complexity render it almost formless, mall-like **(fig. 25)**. Inside, a visitor risks getting lost in the labyrinth. Zeidler's attempts at creating moments of discovery and surprise were efforts to break up the banality latent within a system so overdetermined **(fig. 26)**. But its saving grace is neither the carpet nor the graphics but rather its inherent acknowledgment that hospitals will change over time. The module Zeidler and his team designed is adaptable enough to retain its uniqueness within a system of repeatable and expandable units **(figs. 27, 28)**. In this environment, function can be controlled and designed for without sacrificing the delight and dignity of the patients, the hospital staff, and the public. The interests of the public and the individual are placed in balance; the hospital is a labyrinth of discovery within a machine of precise functionality.

Utopia and Dystopia

In the 1970s, the very real functional dilemmas of the hospital — the demand for constant adaptability, changeability, and innovation within a controlled internal environment — overlapped with sociological criticism of the architectural planning of the era. Hierarchical top-down planning systems, critics said, were paralyzing, oppressive, destructive, and limiting to individual liberty. The megastructure movement grew out of the attempts of architects to "have it both ways," Todd Gannon has written, and "design their way out of an impasse to which half a century of contradictory impulses had led them."[8]

These architects found form in a higher level of functional design, in a structure so large that it was more a system of building-size modules than a building itself. In this way, the megastructure movement was more theory than practice; it was characterized by a speculative engagement with the indeterminate needs of systems rather than the ability to build them. It also signaled an end point in the search for beauty in craftsmanship and the demise of the total-design architect who would attend to details such as door handles and sinks. Instead, the beauty of these designs was found in well-resolved ecosystems, and the architect was more a world builder than a woodworker — what Maki called a "master-form" author.[9]

Because it was too flexible and because it rendered the building authorless and resistant to craft, Banham concluded, the megastructure as a theory of architecture was "self-cancelling" and "auto-destructive."[10]

The megastructure acknowledges that to be an architect is to be complicit in a system one can't fully control. However, the frameworks that define the megastructure can also be read as a way to shed the responsibility of authorship entirely. While this largely theoretical project led to few built structures, megastructure theories survive today in hospitals. The tensions inherent in the megastructure — between control and liberation, individual experience and functionalism, functionalism and constant adaptability — all persist in the medical institution, but the public requires a functioning health system, not a health building, and is willing, it seems, to accept a slightly alienating form if they can locate themselves in it from time to time.

Architects of the mega-hospital, such as Wheeler, Friesen, Zeidler, and even Kahn, challenged environmental and social forces by making space for them, elevating them, aestheticizing them, and composing them instead of allowing them to completely take over. In the fight against alienation, the megastructure is both utopian and dystopian, both labyrinth and machine. The hospital can protect against death and give life, but doing so requires a balance of flexibility and rigidity. It requires a design for adaptability. The designer must anticipate the indeterminate nature of all dynamic systems, none of which are more important than health care.

23

24

25

26

27

28

Eb Zeidler (right) with Dean of Medicine and Vice President of the Health Sciences Division, Dr. John Evans (left), and a model of McMaster University Health Sciences Center, Hamilton, Ontario, by Craig, Zeidler and Strong, 1972 [fig. 27]

Model, McMaster University Health Sciences Center, Hamilton, Ontario, by Craig, Zeidler and Strong, 1972 [fig. 25]

1970s photograph of McMaster University Health Sciences Center, Hamilton, Ontario [fig. 28]

Information desk, McMaster University Health Sciences Center, Hamilton, Ontario [fig. 23]

Interior lounge, McMaster University Health Sciences Center, Hamilton, Ontario [fig. 24]

NFO
ORMATION·INFORM

Chapter 7
The Mat and the Labyrinth

The Anxiety of Authorship

The rationalist, functionalist forms of the modern project had reached their peak in avant-garde circles and in public acceptance by the late 1960s, and in cities across the globe, grids and boxes were deployed in massive residential superblocks consisting of identical cubicles and promoting "universal clean living." Designed for all but for no one in particular, modernist architecture dominated and alienated those who lived among it. Michel Colle, writing in the journal of the artist group CoBrA (fig. 1), summarized the experience:

> We have been given the machine for living in, where very often nothing is sacrificed to the only truly human parts of life, to poetry and to dream. There is worse: for our intransigent rationalists, a residential building can be nothing other than the superimposition of four, ten, any number of linked machines for living in. . . . The ambiance is overwhelming: at the end of his day, man quits his factory for working in for his factory for eating and sleeping in.[1]

1

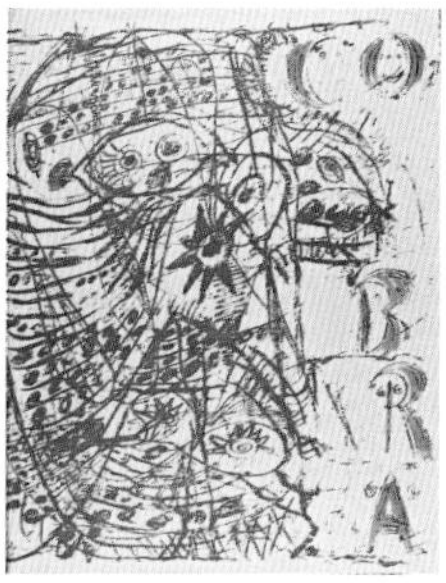

2

3

4

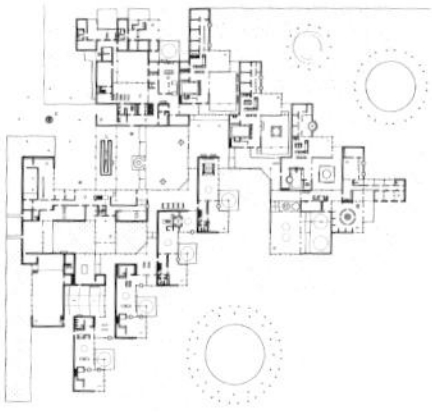

5

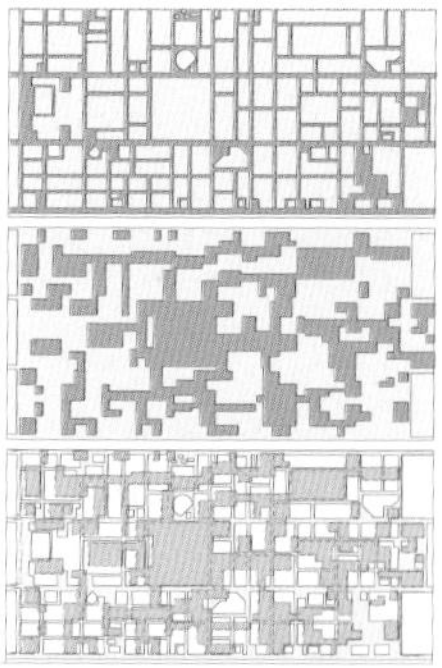

6

To reclaim a sense of identity, architects, activists, artists, and collectives of creators sought to challenge the totalizing effects of rationalist doctrine. Focusing on the user's journey through space, one new strand of architecture sought to embrace the unknown and celebrate the unintentional chaos, playfulness, interruption, chance, and learned agency of everyday life — what Henri Lefebvre called "moments out" and Constant Nieuwenhuys (fig. 2) described as an "architecture of situations."[2] The goal was not to design a new utopian world but rather to catalyze the positive transformation of society through the production of spaces for unique events authored in collaboration with the participants.

The megastructure, a response to the same conditions, was an acknowledgment of the dominance of rationalism, functionalism, and the machine in architecture (see chapter 6). Practitioners of this other strand sought instead to counter those principles, turning to an emphasis on form and individual authorship and aesthetics. Though their works were similar to some megastructures in appearance, they conveyed their authorship through empathetic designs that were intended to free the user from domination by offering a self-directed experience.

The Mat and the Labyrinth

In 1974, the British architect Alison Smithson (1928–1993) identified the "mat" building, an emergent form of architecture so called because it lies horizontally along the ground.[3] With its nonhierarchical interior spaces, the mat building was designed to reproduce the experience of, and restore a sense of dignity to the user. Call it the war against the hallway. The mat building — sometimes megastructural in scale and organization, but rarely modular — was made possible by the mechanical conditioning of interior air. Aldo van Eyck's Amsterdam Orphanage (1960; figs. 3, 4) and Shadrach Woods's 1962 proposal for the Free University of Berlin (figs. 5, 6) are vast, undifferentiated spaces, interrupted only by breaks in the roof plane that let in light or introduce courtyards. These designers, as Günther Feuerstein has written, resisted the image-making of the great classical institutions, whose creators had sought to communicate a nation's intellectual strength through their buildings.[4]

In the mat, form didn't follow function; form, rather, was meant to cultivate function by way of experience. These buildings didn't eschew craft or highly designed or "authored" spaces, but they sought to free users from the domination of the author by disorienting them, theoretically liberating them from the constraints of the building from *within* the building. Mat buildings asked new questions of architecture. Could moments of discovery create delight? Could a building recode the hierarchies of order that dominated the structures of cities and, indirectly, our minds?

When translated into structures, however, the mat often left these idealistic questions unresolved. The mat hospital, in particular — as exemplified by Le Corbusier's 1960s Venice Hospital design — was severely flawed. Notably, the attempt to cede control of the experience

1 Michel Colle, "Vers une architecture symbolique," *CoBrA* 1, no. 1 (Brussels, 1948): 21–23.

2 Henri Lefebvre, in "Lefebvre on the Situationists: An Interview," by Kristin Ross, *October* 79, no. 102 (Winter 1997): 70, cited in *Guy Debord and the Situationist International*, ed. Tom McDonough (Cambridge: MIT Press, 2002), 267–69. Also see Constant Nieuwenhuys, "For an Architecture of Situation" (1953) and "New Babylon," *Architectural Design* 34, no. 6 (June 1964): 304–5.

3 Alison Smithson, "How to Recognise and Read Mat-Building: Mainstream Architecture as It Has Developed towards the Mat-Building," in *Case: Le Corbusier's Venice Hospital and the Mat Building Revival*, ed. Hashim Sarkis (Munich: Prestel, 2001), 90–103.

4 Günther Feuerstein, *New Directions in German Architecture* (New York: George Braziller, 1968), 50. Feuerstein wrote of these designs, "All this might . . . be interpreted as a complete denial of the great educational institutions' traditional claims that their image expresses the source of the nation's intellectual strength." See Reyner Banham, *Megastructure: Urban Futures of the Recent Past* (1976; repr., New York: Monacelli, 2020), 148.

Constant Nieuwenhuys. *New Babylon*. 1961. Lithograph. [fig. 2]

Plan diagrams showing the orthogonal grid of inner corridors and courtyards at the Free University of Berlin, 1962 (redrawn from Shadrach Woods, Alexis Josic, Georgis Candilis, and Manfred Schiedhelm) [fig. 5]

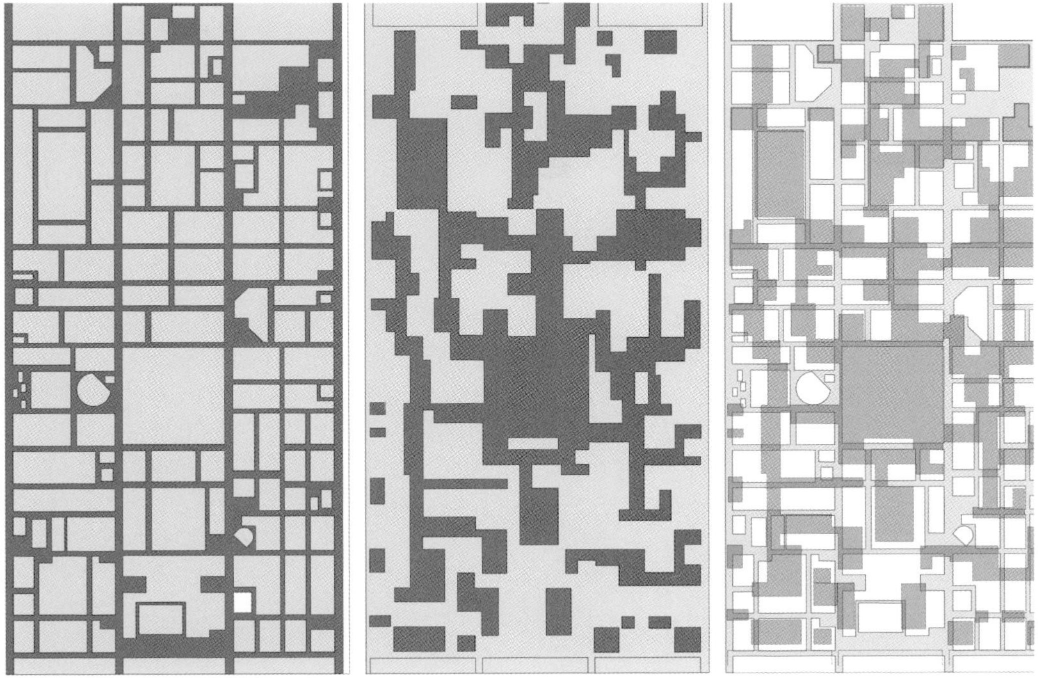

1974, designed by Shadrach Woods, Alexis Josic, Georgis Candilis, and Manfred Schiedhelm, 1962 [fig. 6]

Plan, Amsterdam Orphanage, designed by Aldo van Eyck, 1960 (redrawn by MASS Design Group) [fig. 4]

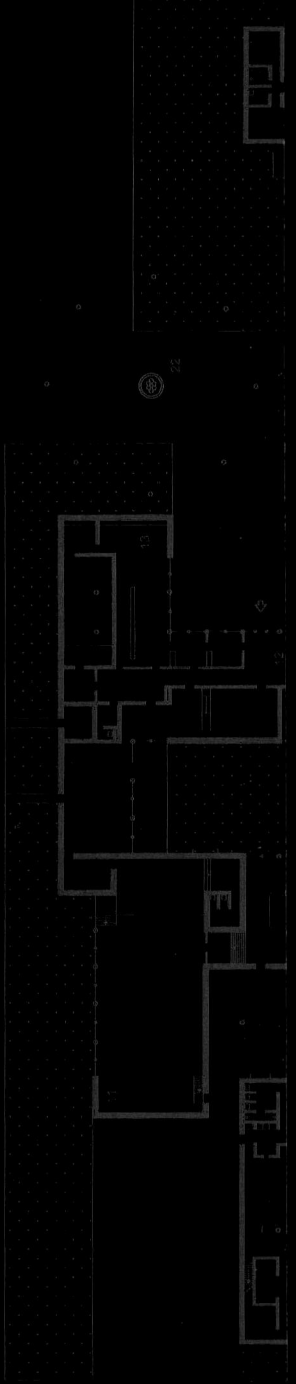

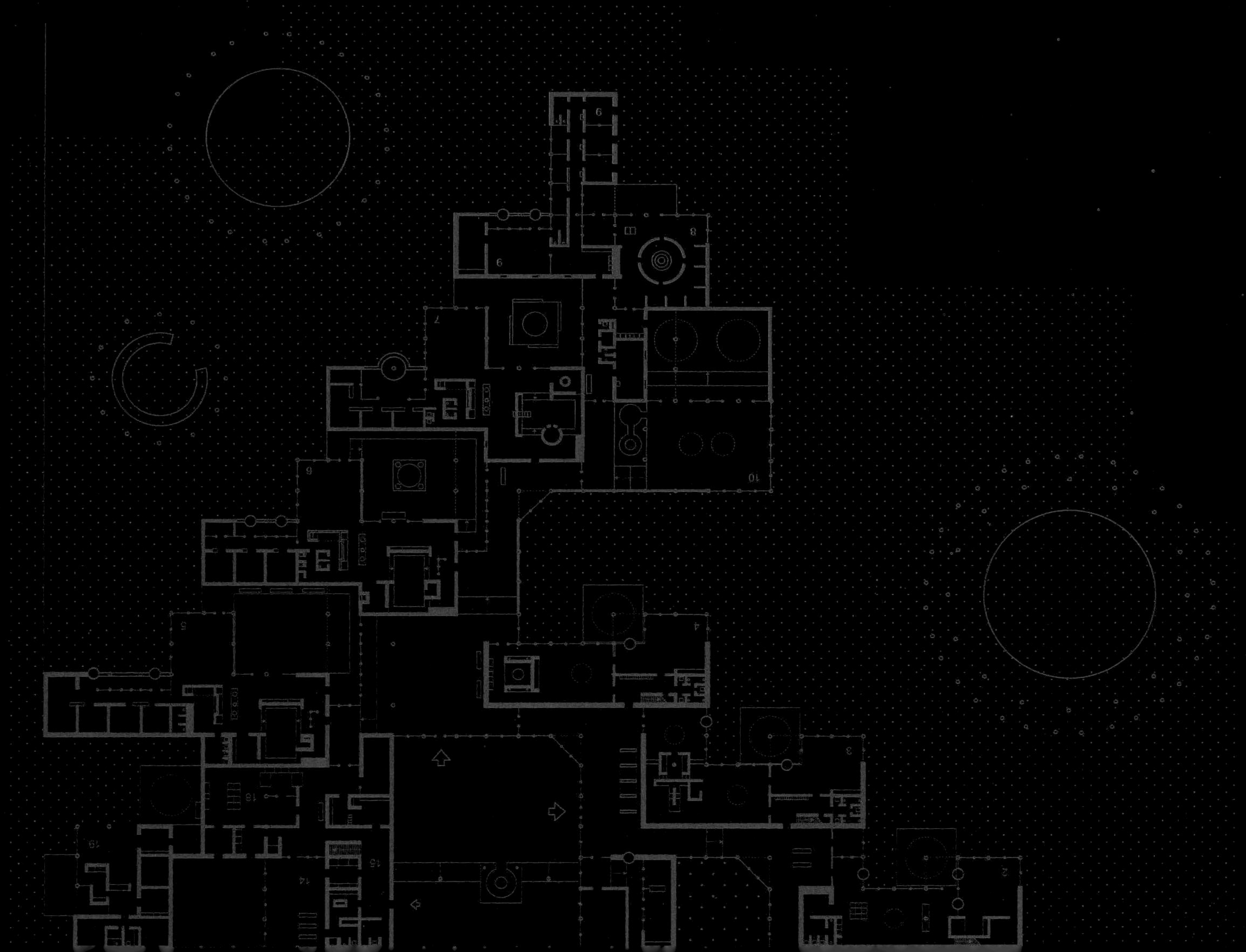

to the user disrupted the crucial balance of the systems of machines and expertise that were necessary for the hospital to function.

Venice Hospital

Charles-Édouard Jeanneret, known as Le Corbusier (1887–1965), the divining rod of twentieth-century architecture, died while designing his hospital for the city of Venice. Though unbuilt, the design was completed by Guillermo Jullian de la Fuente (1931–2008). As laid out on paper, the Venice Hospital is a sprawling horizontal maze, configured to spur discovery and encourage situational occurrences and chance encounters.[5] It exemplifies the mat building.

Venice, with its meandering streets, is itself a labyrinth of discovery and chance. Le Corbusier's hospital, like Todd Wheeler's speculative projects (see chapter 6), does not disrupt the existing city fabric but is, rather, supported on *piloti* over the Venetian Lagoon (figs. 7, 8). The hospital is a city unto itself, made of grids of buildings interspersed with courtyards (fig. 9). It is sectioned into two main levels, although it rises to five stories at various points. The hospital's lower floors are designed for surgery, medical procedures, circulation, and mechanical systems, while the upper floors contain bedrooms and garden courtyards. Simple in section (fig. 10), in plan the design is a nonhierarchical, orthogonal field, laid out in ordered contrast to the byzantine veins of Venice's canals and pathways. The design is hamstrung by the limitations of the horizontal form: despite Venice's strong sea breezes, the patient rooms do not feature fresh-air cross-ventilation. Le Corbusier, like Thomas Cooper and William Henman (see chapter 5), abandoned windows altogether. Instead, he proposed skylights for natural light and relied on later engineers to create a mechanically controlled climate. The drawing documents state that "the regulation of airflows and temperatures will be provided by a mechanical system especially *designed by engineers* to respond to the particular needs of a contemporary hospital's services."[6]

The phrase "especially designed by engineers" epitomizes late modernists' abandonment of core architectural responsibilities to the medical machine. Le Corbusier had been a leading proponent of facade systems that regulated sun and air to promote health and hygiene. In his unbuilt Barcelona Lotissements of 1931 (fig. 11), Daniel A. Barber has written, he considered the facade as a mediating device between the environmental conditions of airflow and the cultural symbolism of architectural language.[7] In 1965, however, with the interior conditioning of air now a requirement, Le Corbusier outsourced climate control to unknown future engineers whose work was not integrated into the design. A piece of the hospital's DNA — the window (or airflow) — was not fully resolved, and so the design could not address the full complexity of the medical facility or meet the needs of its users. In the mat hospital, idealism confronted reality, putting medical functionality in peril.

Nonetheless, Venice Hospital's speculative horizontality, nonhierarchical order, and aspirational user experiences were intoxicating to a rising class of postwar urbanists, who saw in it a solution to the ills of the alienating postwar city (fig. 12). For Alison Smithson and her partner Peter Smithson (1923–2003), who also theorized Venice's future,

5 Max Risselada and Dirk van den Heuvel, eds., *Team Ten, 1953–81: In Search of a Utopia of the Present* (Rotterdam: NAi, 2005), 184.

6 Le Corbusier, "Rapport technique," trans. Lucia Allais, in Sarkis, *Case*, 45 (emphasis mine).

7 Daniel A. Barber, *Modern Architecture and Climate: Design before Air Conditioning* (Princeton, NJ: Princeton University Press, 2020), 2–21.

7

8

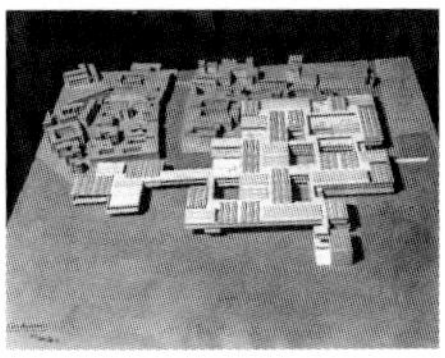

9

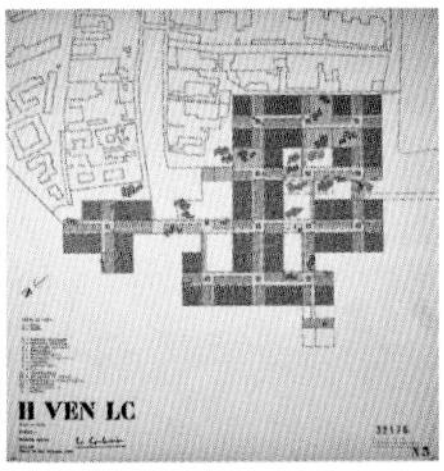

10

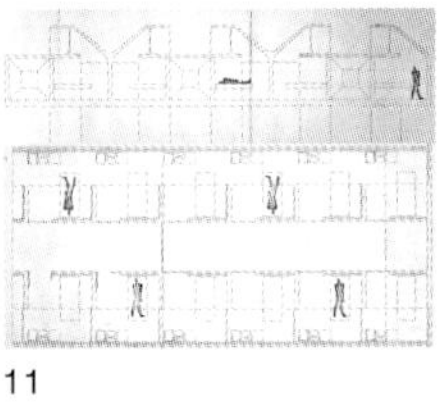

11

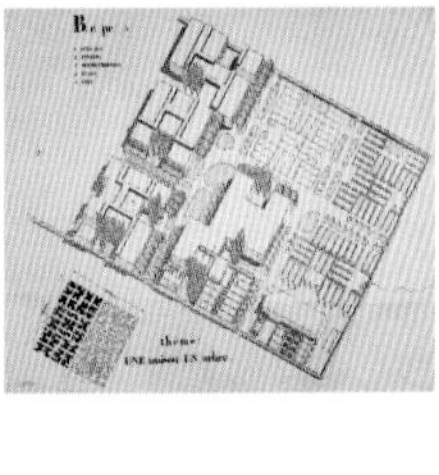

the mat building — an interior form of urbanism — was a meditation on the labyrinth, an archetype associated with exploration and captivation.[8] More a cinematic journey than a building, they theorized, it would initiate productive, iterative learning, mental attentiveness, and considered awareness — in other words, a spatial awakening.

However, disorientation also produces confusion, and a mat building could equally be experienced as a tortuous maze with no exit, a puzzle with no resolution. The vast interior climates and convoluted wayfinding within hospitals already created confounding, anxious, and frustrating experiences, especially when users sought urgent care or specific treatments. It was easy to get lost in a hospital; in a horizontal, formless, and nonhierarchical hospital, the problem would likely be exacerbated.

Mat buildings were labyrinthine not by intention but as a product of their specific formal concerns. Other architects in the 1960s, seeking forms that would excite the mind and create unique journeys, took on the labyrinth intentionally. One example of such a design is the Erich Lindemann Mental Health Center in Boston. A beautiful, fully authored labyrinth, it was designed to resist the institutionalization of users by the medical machine and intended to spark joy and enchantment.

Erich Lindemann Mental Health Center, Boston

The Erich Lindemann Mental Health Center, designed by Paul Rudolph (1918–1997) and completed in 1971, is a critique of alienation and institutionalization in health care. With its heavily authored interiors and exteriors, it is also an attempt to insert the total work of art back into the architecture of health care (fig. 13). Much maligned by the public and admired by architects, Rudolph's anthropomorphic building is his most psychedelic (figs. 14, 15). A winding, bridging hydra, Lindemann was designed to house a government-funded mental health facility that aimed to be "a way station where the deinstitutionalized could acclimate to Boston."[9] The program included temporary housing, a theater, a gymnasium with an Olympic-size pool, a chapel, and spaces to retreat, eat, receive therapy, and socialize.[10] Inspired by the scenographic urbanism theorized by Camillo Sitte in the late nineteenth century, Rudolph believed that a building should be experienced scene by scene, like a cinematic moving image. In Lindemann, he designed a series of spatial vignettes and curvilinear eddies to counter the sense of alienation that large-scale master plans often produce. The building's non-orthogonal geometry was designed to "stimulate people and bind them together," Timothy Rohan wrote, through a therapeutic internal experience of awe, magic, confusion, and disorientation.[11]

Lindemann hosted family treatment, group therapy, individual care, care for children, and research, and Rudolph thought critically and sensitively about its different users. Departments served those suffering from addiction, from emotional abuse and trauma, and from the social and ecological impacts of debilitating mental health conditions, and the building was also a place of work for state employees. Each user had different needs, Rudolph theorized, and therefore deserved a different experience. His solution was to reconsider the entrance, eliminating a

8 Smithson, "How to Recognise and Read Mat-Building."

9 Timothy Rohan, *The Architecture of Paul Rudolph* (New Haven, CT: Yale University Press, 2014), 125.

10 Rohan, *The Architecture of Paul Rudolph*, 125.

11 Ibid.

12

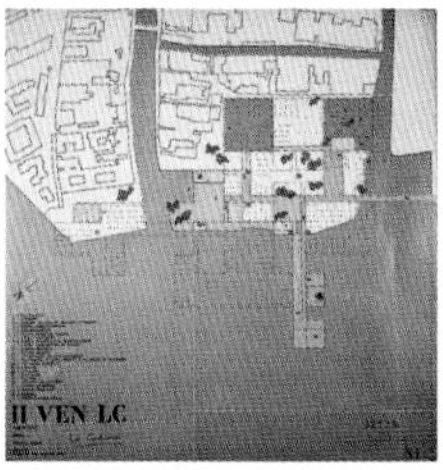

13

14

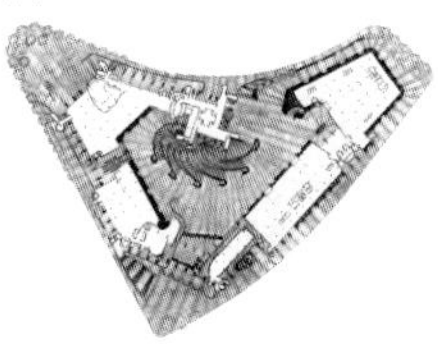

15

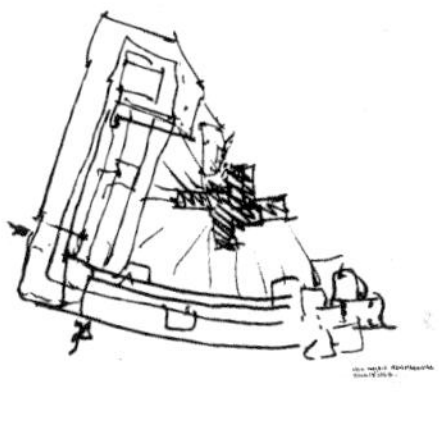

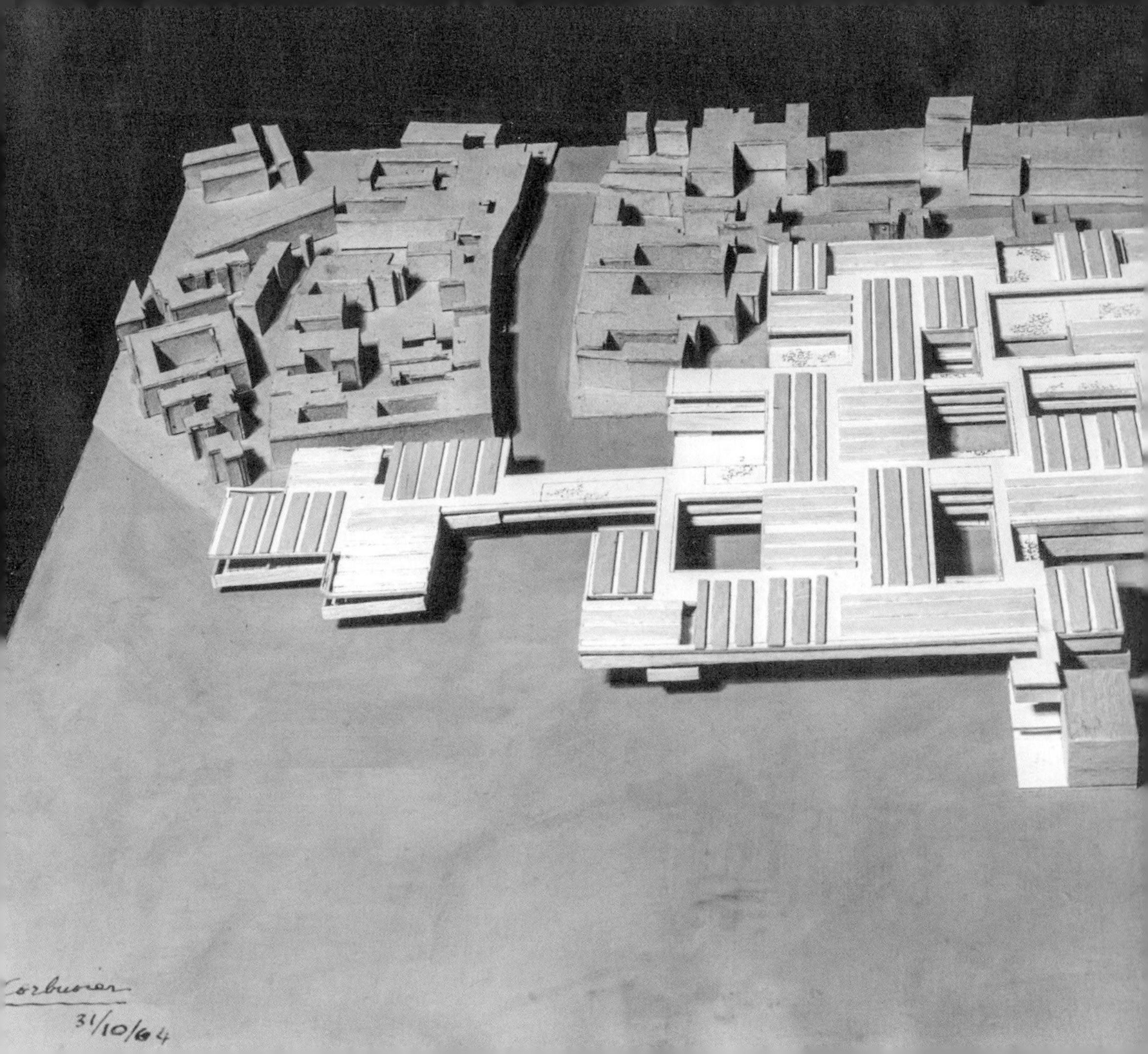
Corbusier
31/10/64

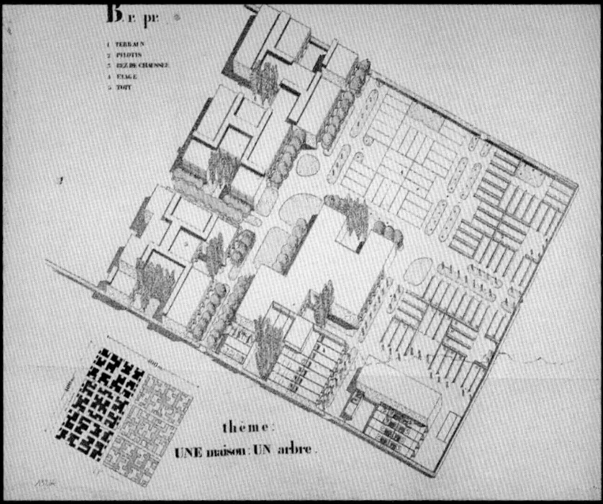

B. r. pr.
1 TERRAIN
2 PILOTIS
3 REZ DE CHAUSSEE
4 ETAGE
5 TOIT
thème:
UNE maison : UN arbre.

1 - Gondoloport
2 - Autoport
3 - Arrivée malades et secours d'urgence
4 - Entrée administration
5 - Administration
6 - Entrée médecine sociale
7 - Entrée visiteurs
8 - Entrée obstétrique, gynécologique
9 - Entrée infirmières et soeurs
10 - Entrée Chapelle
11 - Entrée service
12 - Gondoloport approvisionnement
13 - Passerelle de raccordement à la route de voitures
14 - Pharmacie centrale
15 - Cuisine
18 - Magasin
20 - Eglise et morgue
22 - Entrée
23 - Hôpital pédiatrique
II VEN LC
PLAN N° 6276
NIVEAU 1
Le Corbusier
32173

central hierarchical distribution point in favor of a distributed strategy of multiple entrances. The most circuitous entranceway was the long, unrolling tongue of a staircase that began at the building's front plaza, at the intersection of Staniford and Merrimac Streets, and wound its way up through the pilasters of the elevated upper floors **(fig. 16)**. This was the family-therapy entranceway. A long and winding journey of discovery was required just to reach the door.

Rudolph sought a form that was "particular," not "universal," Mark Pasnik has recounted.[12] He fought against the rationalist modernism he had once favored and instead sought humanity and sensuality in an inflexible and unadaptable design. Patient rooms featured custom built-in wood furniture, including rounded benches to encourage conversation, and hallways were curved and winding to spark delight and movement. Corners were rare **(figs. 17–19)**. But the building's brilliance lay in its acknowledgment that different communities will have different experiences. There was no front or back door, no servant or served spaces, just multiple approaches for a variety of needs and lived conditions.

Rudolph resisted the interiority of the universalizing institution. Exterior courtyards, playgrounds, and entrances were integral to the multiple experiences and approaches the building provided **(fig. 20)**. These spatial strategies lightened the weight of the facility, at least conceptually. Rudolph understood that the institution was inherently dominating, and he attempted to spatially empower the individual from the outside in. A lesson in discovery, with every curve and crevice designed to provide a respite from bureaucracy, his building was human centered, aspirational, and functional and yet also deliberate, personalized, and intentional.

After Functionalism

Lindemann took a stance in contemporaneous debates around function and form and the role of the ever-evolving medical machine in shaping the spaces of health care. Due to the building's rigid construction in concrete, its functionality is limited by its form, but its form is fully authored and designed to serve, with generosity, the humanity of the individual. Here is Rudolph seeking intentional forms in the labyrinth and the chapel, the altar and the bed. By focusing on the journey, he designed the medical center from the inside out, in the process authoring a statement about the inherent individuality of health care. In Lindemann, Rudolph did not look for universal forms but instead sought a universal truth: each person's dignity matters. The result is a building that is poetic, spiritual, and designed by and for humans rather than the machine.

Despite — or because of — this, the building has not aged well. The problem was not decomposition — the materials are sturdy and high quality, and the structure is well built — but rather, new approaches in the state's treatment of the sick.[13] When the program shifted and the care paradigm changed, the building could not respond. In the 1960s, progressive changes in mental health care in the United States (notably the Community Mental Health Act of 1963) transferred services from large state institutions to local treatment programs that involved patients' families and communities. This shift was exacerbated in the

16

17

18

19

20

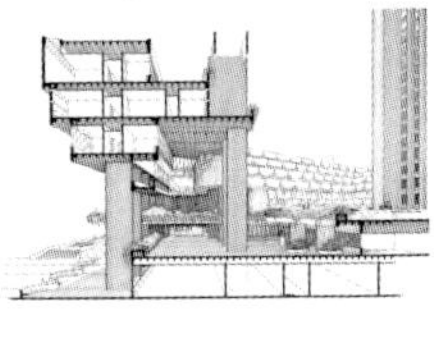

12 Mark Pasnik, "Concrete Therapy: Paul Rudolph's Architecture of Mental Health," *Harvard Design*, no. 40 (Spring–Summer 2015), 160.

13 Pasnik, "Concrete Therapy," 161.

1980s with the deregulation of mental health services, which moved patients into privatized treatment centers. These changes in the care paradigm had spatial implications. They rendered buildings such as Lindemann less and less necessary, and some spaces within the building fell into disuse. Later, security concerns and further changes in program led to the consolidation of Lindemann's entrances into one centralized point that is accessed through gates and checkpoints, and the generous courtyards were chained off from public use. Like Prentice Women's Hospital — built in Chicago at the same time and demolished between 2013 to 2014 (see introduction) — Lindemann is rigid and inflexible. Although the building was a valiant attempt at dignifying the care experience, its flaw is its failure to strike a balance with the ever-evolving realities of health care. Its strength is how specific it was in meeting the needs of those whom it was designed to serve. Like Prentice, Lindemann is an unforgettable piece of architecture. And, like Prentice, it has faced threats of demolition and redevelopment and has been defended by architects and preservationists proclaiming the beauty and poetry of the unadaptable.

Among the most poetic spaces in Lindemann is the chapel (fig. 21). Arguably one of the loveliest in all architecture of this period, it is hidden within the building, the only sign of its existence from the street a small, circular chimney rising above the rooftop. The chapel is hard to find from inside as well, but once you are there it nourishes as only an authored space can, with every detail crafted. It is the transcendent, spiritual center of the labyrinth. The layered enclosure is curved around itself in plan, like a spiral eddy, and its walls evoke a stage encircled by folding curtains of bush-hammered concrete. At its heart, on a dais, is an altar, illuminated by light pouring down from a skylight and projecting shadows and solemnity into the spaces around it.

In Filarete's Ospedale Maggiore or Nightingale's pavilion wards, the altar was an observation point, a locus of control. This, by contrast, is a space to be sought out individually, as desired. What was once the hub of the hospital is now a pocket, hidden deep inside the folds of the labyrinth. Rudolph showed reverence for the divine and for its spaces. He acknowledged that spiritual health and physical health are intertwined in the mysteries of the heavens and also grounded in the spaces of physiological recuperation. Walking into this space would make a preservationist out of a doubter. Here, the building opens up to become something greater, a timeless reflection of the healing power of hope.

Spaces of care can dignify us or they can create a sense of subjugation. Their users can never be fully liberated from the power the spaces have over them, and so that power must be deployed with care — sparingly, humbly, and realistically. If these spaces give agency to the user, their success relies on maintaining a harmony between that agency and the systems that keep the building functional. To create spaces that users may traverse with dignity, it is necessary that beauty, craftsmanship, and the experience of the individual be considered.

We are, all of us, in episodic journeys of both dignity and alienation among the buildings around us. To navigate the health care system is to surrender, ambivalently, to a loss of control, with the hope that this vulnerability will improve our lives. In this way, the hospital reveals

21

Rudolph understood that the institution was inherently dominating, and he attempted to spatially empower the individual from the outside in. A lesson in discovery, with every curve and crevice designed to provide a respite from bureaucracy, his building was human centered, aspirational, and functional and yet also deliberate, personalized, and intentional.

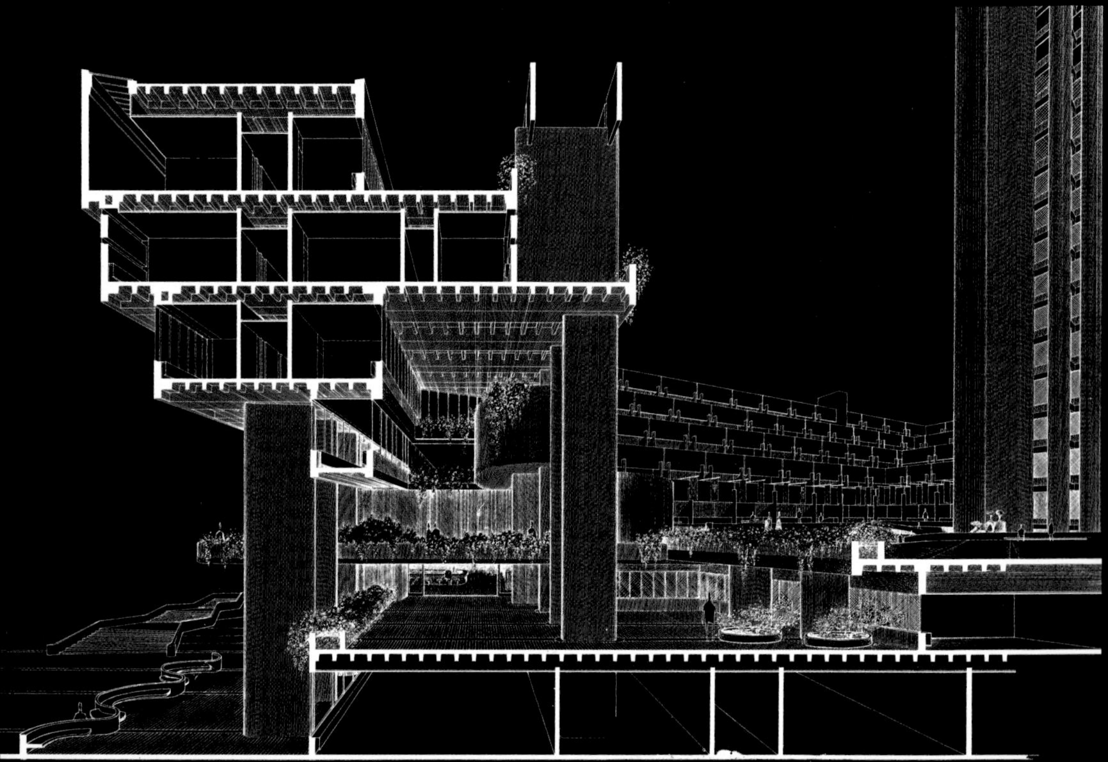

Perspective section, Erich Lindemann Mental Health Center, Boston, designed by Paul Rudolph, 1963 [fig. 20]

Presentation model, Erich Lindemann Mental Health Center, Boston [fig. 13]

Project sketch, Erich Lindemann Mental Health Center, Boston [fig. 15]

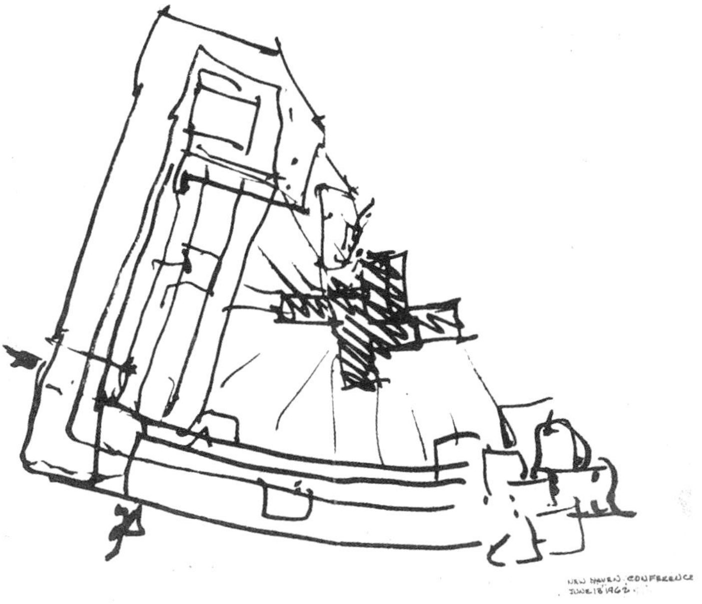

the paralyzing contradiction of architecture and its foundational truths: that no matter how liberating a space might proclaim to be, it still will shape our behavior and experiences. As a space of public charity, the hospital cannot hide behind its primary function, to give care to those who may not be able to request it. And yet, in this proscriptive, authored, and intentional realm, such as in Lindemann, there is the ideal of liberation too: through form itself.

Staircase at the Erich Lindemann Mental Health Center, Boston [fig. 16]

Rendered plan drawing, Erich Lindemann Mental Health Center, Boston [fig. 14]

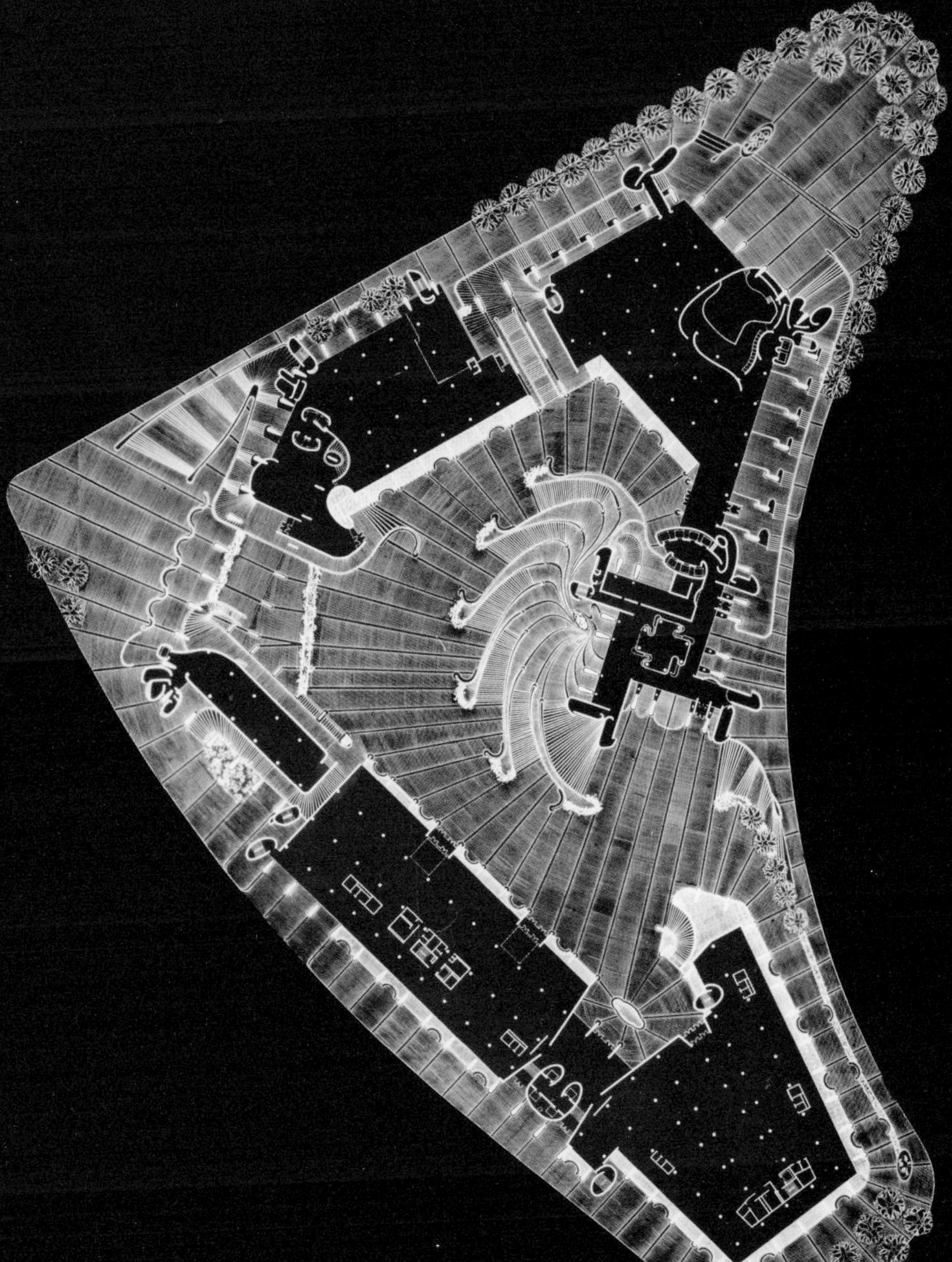

Plaza at the Erich Lindemann Mental Health Center, Boston [fig. 17]

Staircase at the Erich Lindemann Mental Health Center, Boston [fig. 18]

The chapel at the Erich Lindemann Mental Health Center, Boston [fig. 21]

Chapter 8
Hospital City: The Pathology of Form

Boston is home to some of the richest hospitals in the United States, and it has been a leading center of medical education, research, technology, and architecture since its founding. When the Erich Lindemann Mental Health Center was completed, in 1971 (see chapter 7), the Harvard Affiliated Hospitals, across town in the city's Mission Hill neighborhood, were in the process of consolidating into one expanded institution, a major undertaking that required careful planning. They hired the progressive Chicago architect Bertrand Goldberg (1913–1997), fresh from his work in Illinois, to create a vision for the institution's future.

Goldberg's research into medical facilities had already garnered him the first of his many medical commissions, Elgin State Hospital in Elgin, Illinois (figs. 1, 2), which was completed in 1967. Its rounded towers (a trademark of his work) were a solution to the "ganglia" of medical machinery that were then taking over hospitals.[1] In an effort to create patient-centered spaces, Goldberg designed what he called "village clusters," formal arrangements that allocated each patient a window and either a private or a double room, all in close proximity to a central nurses' station. Goldberg's fourteen-year engagement with Harvard Affiliated Hospitals would lead to his largest composition, a merger of three teaching hospitals — the Peter Bent Brigham Hospital, the Robert Breck Brigham Hospital, and the Boston Hospital for Women — into the new Brigham and Women's Hospital (completed in 1980): four cylindrical bed towers whose legs puncture a large rectilinear base (figs. 3, 4).

If Goldberg's 1975 Prentice Women's Hospital in Chicago was an almost pure articulation of the midcentury struggle between the machine and the individual, between charity and control (see introduction), the Brigham exemplifies the health care structure as a living, regenerative cephalopod, constantly experiencing amputation and regrowth. In this model — the amalgam hospital — the institution is no longer defined by a single style or form; instead, it is composed of many assembled forms that change repeatedly over time, growing from a single, identifiable building into a massive amorphous campus with many authors and many distinct appendages and divergent programs.

Brigham and Women's Hospital, Boston

The Peter Bent Brigham Hospital was founded by charitable donation in 1913 in Boston's Mission Hill, an immigrant neighborhood that was home to a booming beer-brewing industry. The hospital, originally designed by the firm Codman and Despradelle, consisted of several pavilion wards laid out on parallel tracks with lawns between them (figs. 5–7).

A centralized, three-story passageway, partially below grade, connected the wards to one another (figs. 8, 9). The ward design was similar to Nightingale's, with the addition of roof cupolas and chases in the walls that forced air vertically as well as horizontally (fig. 10). To maximize natural daylighting, operating theaters were all sited on the same side of the corridor, and an airing balcony on the top floor and a solarium at the end of the ward provided sunlight during the day (fig. 11). During the influenza pandemic of 1918, the solariums and outdoor zones were converted to external treatment wards in a bid to increase access to fresh air by patients (fig. 12), who were offered extra blankets and hats to protect them from the frigid Boston winter.

1 Bertrand Goldberg, quoted in "Bertrand Goldberg: Architecture and Invention; Goldberg Variations: Hospitals and Health Care," Art Institute of Chicago, https://archive.artic.edu/goldberg/Hospital/.

1

2

3

4

5

6
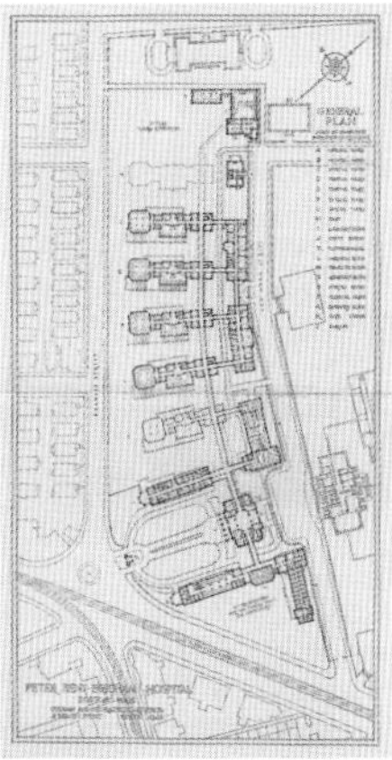
7

8

9

10

11

12

Structural detail of the
Medical Surgical Building,
Elgin State Hospital,
Elgin, Illinois, designed
by Bertrand Goldberg,
completed 1967 [fig. 2]

In the hospital, where life so often begins and ends, architecture can be a machine that moves us along an assembly line, or a space that uncovers latent meaning — a vessel to shepherd us over life's thresholds with dignity.

Elevation drawing, Peter Bent Brigham Hospital, Boston from Codman and Despradelle, 1914 [fig. 10]

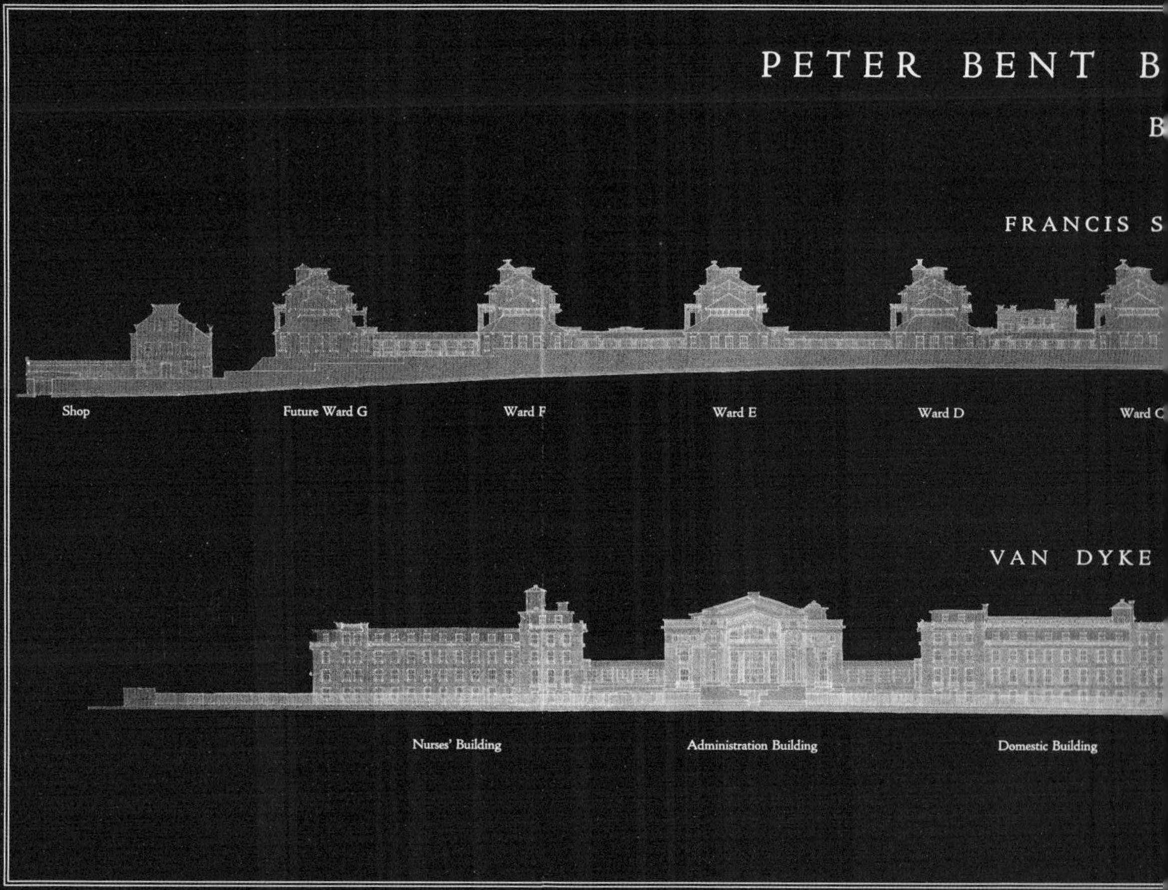

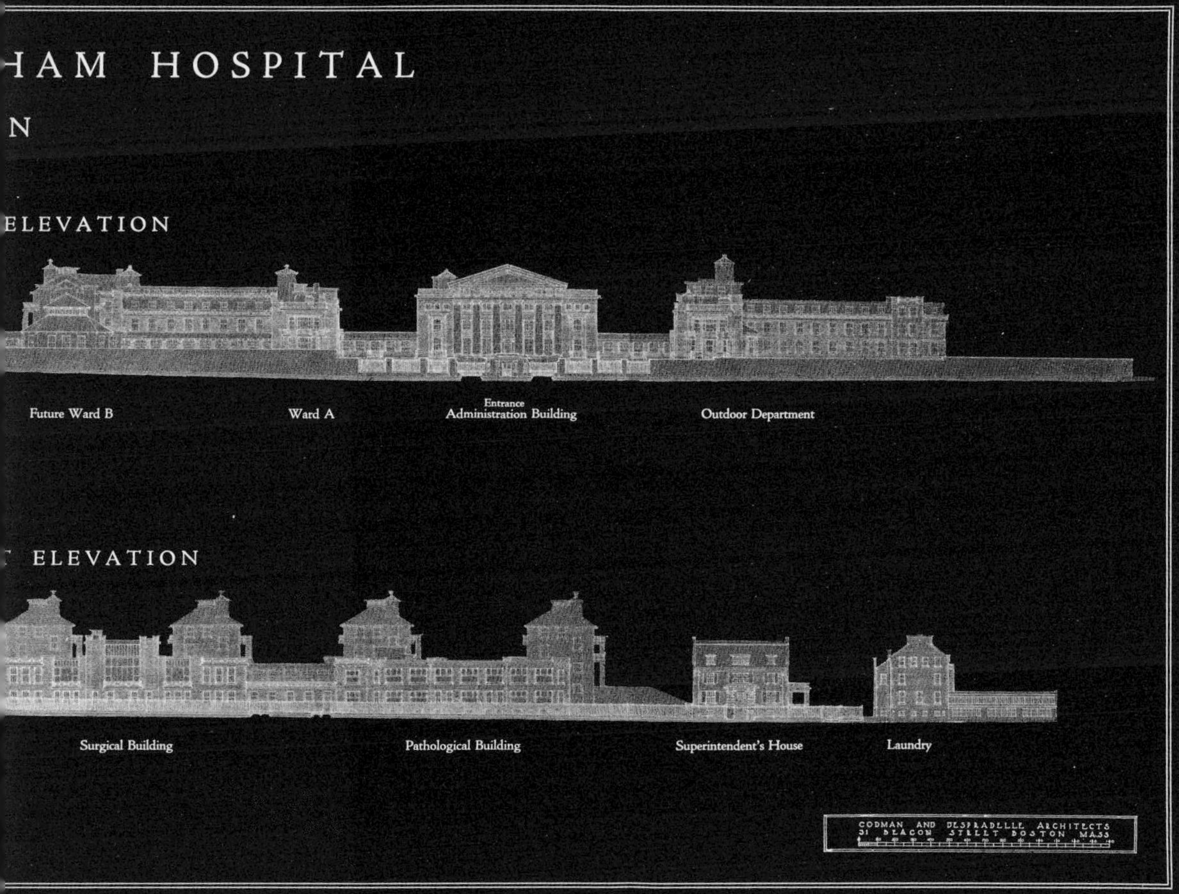
HAM HOSPITAL
N
ELEVATION
Future Ward B
Ward A
Entrance
Administration Building
Outdoor Department
ELEVATION
Surgical Building
Pathological Building
Superintendent's House
Laundry
CODMAN AND DESPRADELLE ARCHITECTS
31 BEACON STREET BOSTON MASS

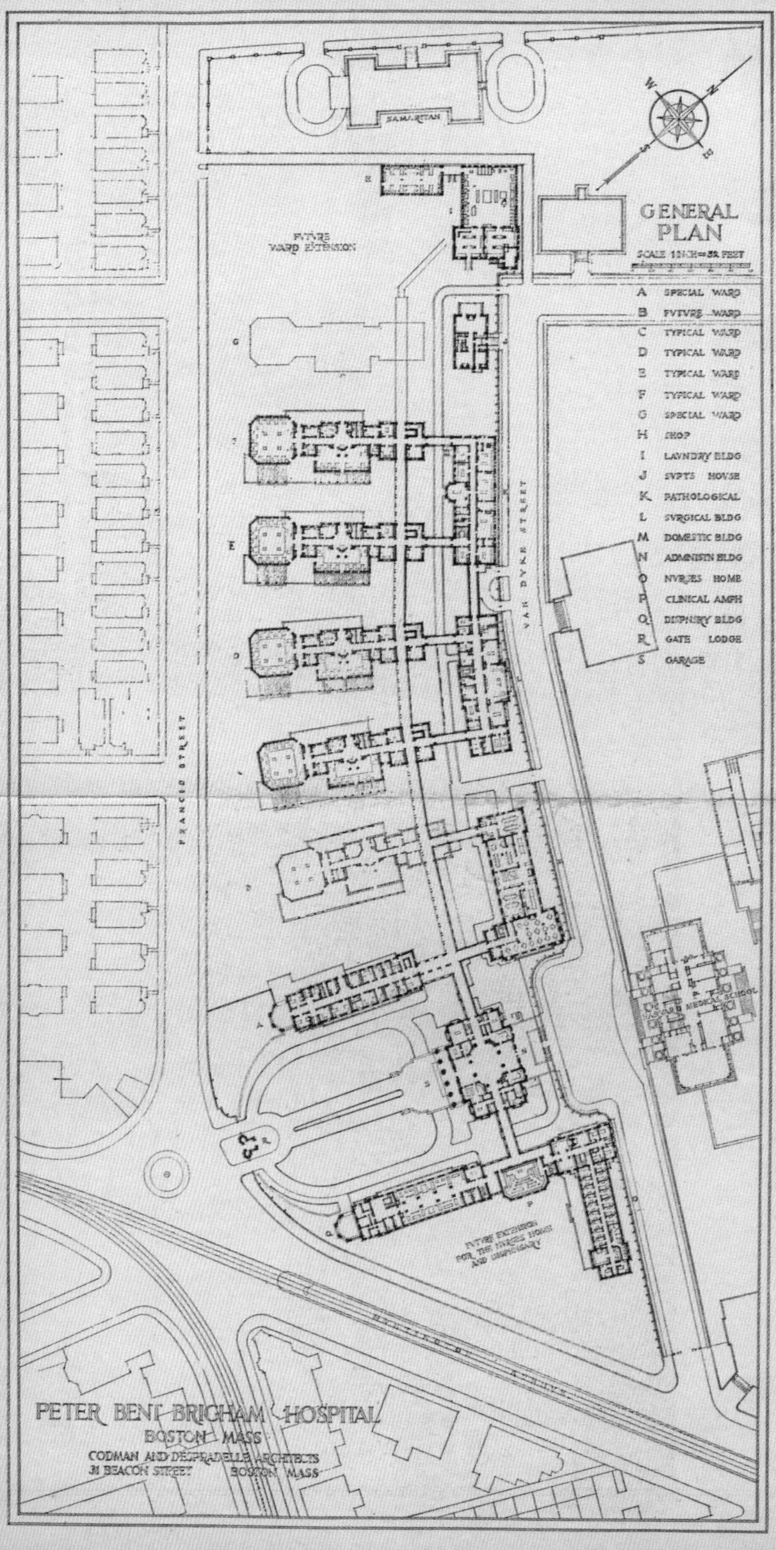

Campus plan, Peter Bent Brigham Hospital, Boston, designed by Codman and Despradelle, c. 1914 [fig. 6]

Airing balcony, Peter Bent Brigham Hospital, Boston [fig. 11]

Outdoor beds during the 1918 influenza pandemic, Peter Bent Brigham Hospital, Boston [fig. 12]

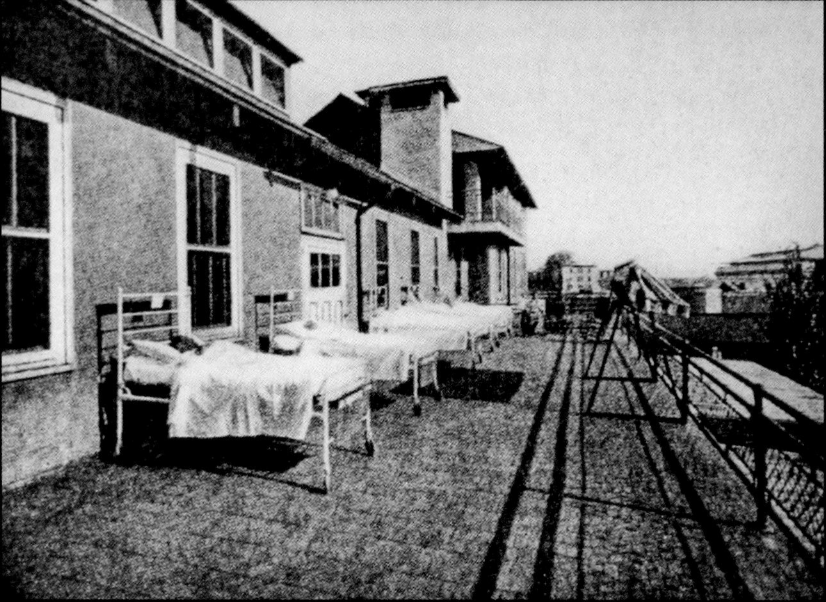

Elevation view, Peter Bent Brigham Hospital, Boston, designed by Codman and Despradelle, c. 1914 (redrawn by MASS Design Group) [fig. 9]

Peter Bent Brigham Hospital, Boston, 1918 [fig. 7]

As the Brigham expanded — through growth, acquisition, and the agglomeration of multiple Harvard-affiliated institutions — its original organizing structures were obscured. As in almost all hospital campuses, the design performance of the original buildings lost precision as new structures were added to them and around them. Private patient rooms and centralized laboratories planned by Coolidge, Shepley, Bulfinch, and Abbott were implemented in 1937, and cardiovascular and geriatric centers were constructed in the 1940s and 1950s, respectively. Pavilion inpatient rooms were modernized and air-conditioned around 1950, and Walter Gropius's late-career firm, The Architects Collaborative, planned and built a clinical research center in 1961 and a new inpatient building with private rooms in 1963. Technological spaces followed, such as the 1968 radiology wing, designed by Dr. Herbert L. Abrams, chief of the Department of Radiology, and new operating suites (figs. 13, 14).[2]

Through institutional mergers and physical growth, the Brigham tripled in size in the 1970s. To connect its disparate parts, a ground-level tunnel, referred to as "the Pike" — after the Massachusetts Turnpike — was configured from existing hallways to link all the buildings from a central distribution point (fig. 15). This consolidating planning strategy, with its clear, centralized pathway, gave the hospital a rhizomatic structure. James Stoller, a resident doctor at the Brigham between 1979 and 1981, fondly described the Pike as the site of "curbside consultations" — informal interactions and educative opportunities between junior and senior staff — as well as private alcoves for confidential conversations.[3]

When construction began on Goldberg's new bed towers and blocklike plinth in 1977, the original pavilion wards were finally demolished. Unlike Prentice's glass-walled block building, the podium Goldberg designed for the Brigham is almost windowless, its facade composed of precast concrete panels that shift in plan to admit slivers of natural light to the interior. Like St. Mary of Nazareth Hospital in Chicago (see chapter 5), the building, seen from the street, is forbidding. The entrance was shifted from the original grand and approachable 1913 neoclassical building to Goldberg's box, where multiple new entrances were created along the residential Francis Street, including a main drop-off location slipped underneath what appear to be solid, windowless walls.

The new growth extended vertically rather than horizontally, compromising the rhizomatic character of the hospital. In this reorganization, the Pike, the campus's central conduit, was severed, rendering the overall composite space more maze-like and institutional. One effect of this, Stoller reported, was a diminishment in the formerly rich interactions among staff. In the elevators, the basis of the new circulatory structure, confidential and casual "curbside" consultations were discouraged.[4] The hospital's capacity and its inpatient capabilities had grown, but the overall impression of the multibuilding institution now verged on the piecemeal.

Hospital planners and staff had acknowledged the challenges they faced at midcentury, when they were "bursting at the seams."[5] To be a leading institution, they concluded, it was necessary for the Brigham

2 "Site Development, Past and Future: The Brigham and Women's Hospital, 1911–Present," slide deck presented at Brigham and Women's Faulkner Hospital and Brigham and Women's Hospital Boards of Trustees dinner meeting, January 18, 2006.

3 James K. Stoller, "A Physician's View of Hospital Design," *Architecture* 77, no. 12 (December 1988): 121.

4 Stoller, "A Physician's View," 121.

5 "Site Development, Past and Future," slide 27.

13

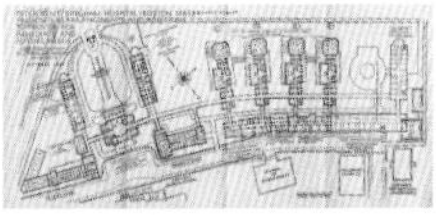

14

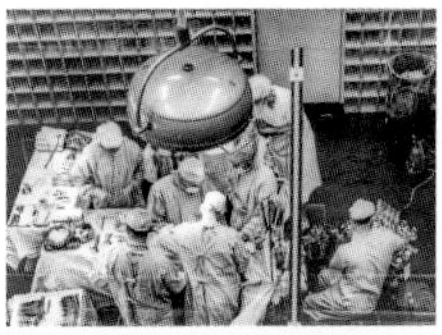

15

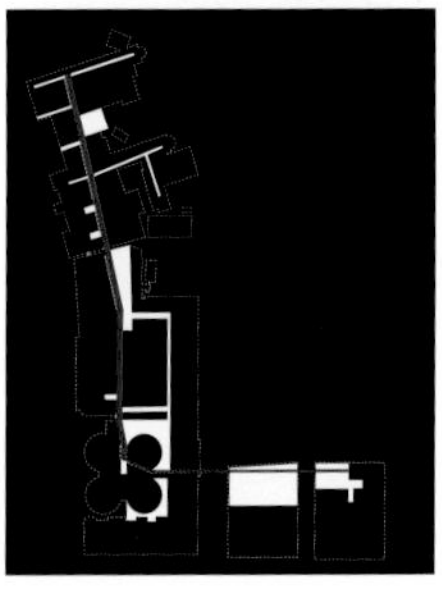

to expand its research capabilities and grow its clinical infrastructure. At the same time, it shouldn't reach that point "where a hospital becomes too large."[6] They recognized that their path forward was a "precarious" "thin ridge" with an "abyss on both sides": one a future in which the institution is merely a modest clinical care facility, and the other in which it has become an "unattractive" research institution. To be successful, they concluded, they would have to balance "the economies of a large hospital, with the intellectual richness of a small unit."[7] According to Stoller, the Goldberg buildings tipped the Brigham out of balance. Growth was necessary, but the new vertical behemoth compromised clinical culture. Breaking the Pike had been an elemental miscalculation. The Goldberg expansion diminished staff interactions and stood in the way of a more productive and dignifying experience for both staff and patients.

However, new designs were already in motion. A research tower was completed in 1984, an ambulatory-care building was unveiled in 1986, and a new lobby and courtyard opened in 1994 alongside a reconstituted Pike that connected Goldberg's towers to the rest of the campus, restoring balance by reversing the diminishment of the user experience. The "thin ridge" seemed to have been straddled once again. In 2008, the Pike took on a new, structural form, breaking through the Goldberg plinth to form a bridge over Francis Street that linked the campus to a new cancer treatment center (fig. 16). In confronting an inflexible form, the amalgam hospital found a way to strike a balance, maintaining functionality while also respecting the specificity of Goldberg's design. In late 2014, the Brigham completed a renovation of the 1913 neoclassical building, integrating a public lawn with much-needed parking below. In 2016, a new center for transformative medicine opened beyond the cancer treatment center.[8] Soon another building will rise in the distance.

The Brigham's evolution demonstrates a truth: the hospital cannot be static; it is a living, impermanent architectural system that must always be under construction. At the Brigham, each new care paradigm received a related architectural response. These were not all perfect as individual architectural forms, but the hospital's evolution overall is a historical record of the ever-evolving relationship between form and function, rigidity and flexibility. The Brigham spans these binaries.

A Living System

Louis Sullivan's law of architecture — "form ever follows function" — is self-evident in the hospital. But so is another law, which Sullivan did not mention: function evolves, and therefore so must form. As the architect Giancarlo De Carlo wrote in the late 1970s, buildings are "processes," not objects.[9] Nowhere is this more obvious than in the hospital.

When the machine altered the DNA of the hospital, it jeopardized both form and function. In response, architects proposed megastructures — authorless, purely functional armatures — and fully authored labyrinths that risked abandoning functionality to chance. But neither extreme could resolve the complex challenges of health care delivery. Goldberg's Prentice Women's Hospital was one response to the challenges of its era; it was entirely unique but also inflexible to changes in

6 "Site Development, Past and Future," slide 33.

7 "Site Development, Past and Future," slide 32.

8 Both of these new structures were by designed NBBJ, while the restoration was by Bruner/Cott Architects.

9 De Carlo wrote, "Contemporary architecture tends to produce objects while its real role should be that of generating processes. This distortion has very serious consequences for it confines architecture to a very narrow strip of a whole spectrum, so segregating it, leaving it open to the risks of dependency and megalomania, and leading it to social and political indifference." See "Opening Editorial," *Space and Society*, no. 1 (1978): 5.

16

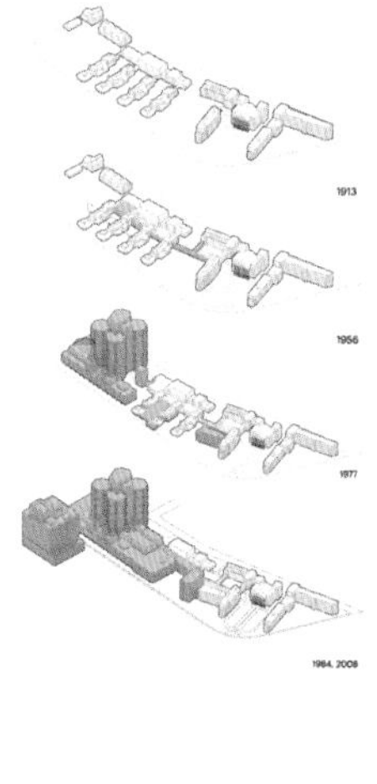

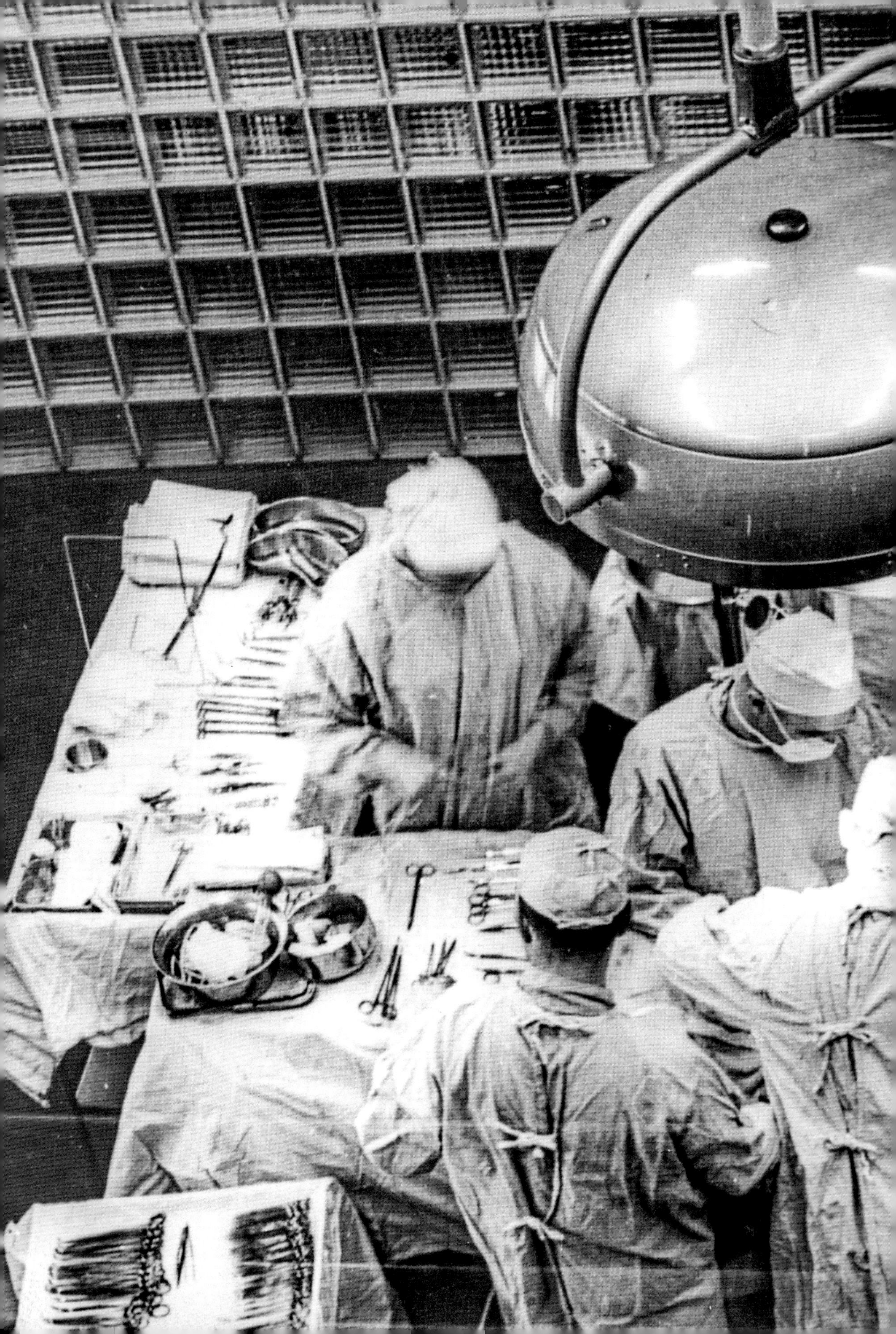

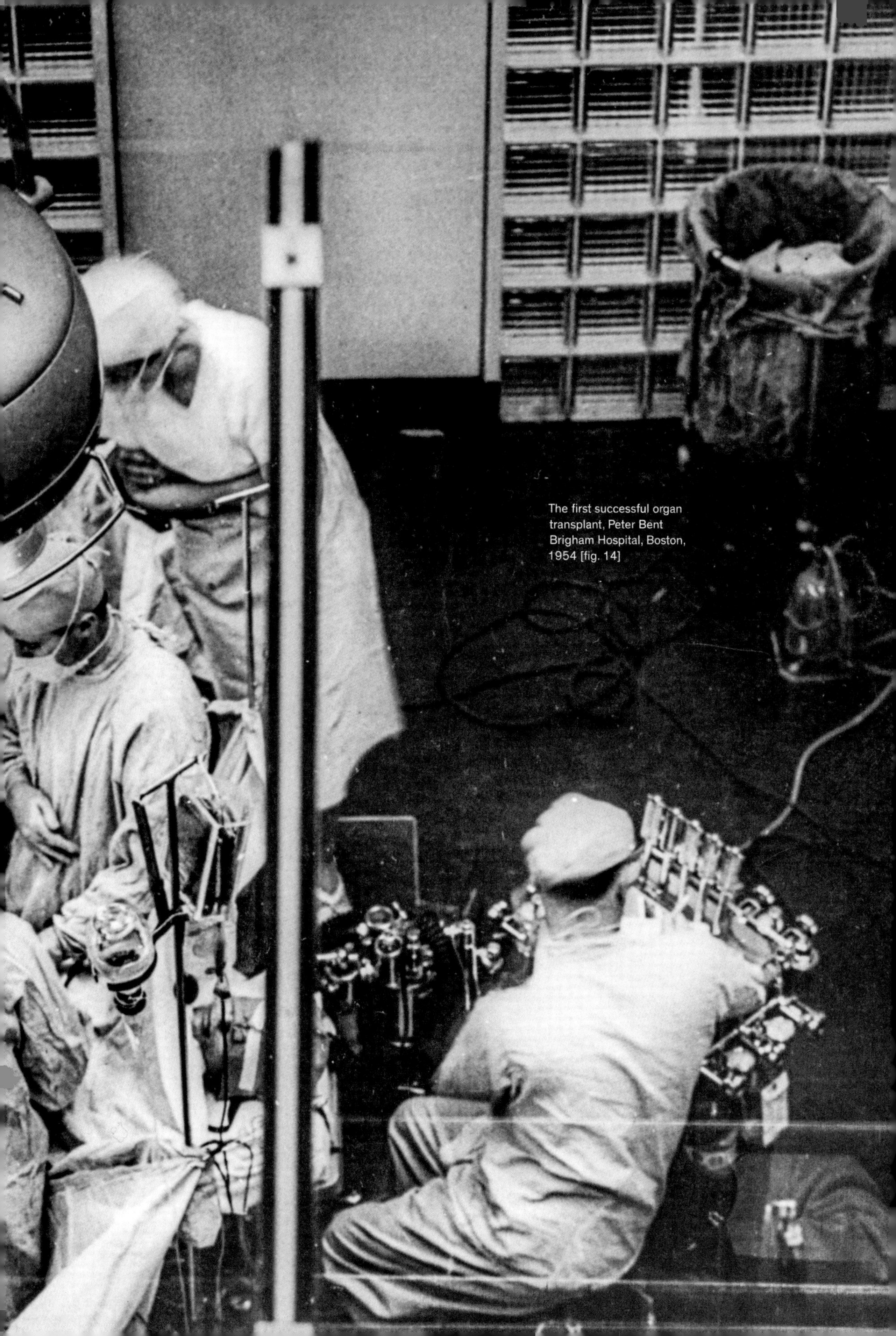

The first successful organ transplant, Peter Bent Brigham Hospital, Boston, 1954 [fig. 14]

10 "Site Development, Past and Future," slide 33.

function. Prentice's demise — it was demolished in 2014 — shows that attention to form can result in a beautiful and dignifying experience, but also that, without flexibility, such dignifying forms may not survive. Only those formally bold and creative enough to attract preservationists (to whom functionality is irrelevant) will avoid destruction.

The Brigham, with its incremental additions, provides another model. Jumbled together in an evolving campus, the individual architectural intentions may get lost, but the Brigham proves that a combination of authored forms can be functional. If the system is pushed out of balance, it can be adjusted to once again "walk the thin dividing line" that constitutes a harmony between quality medical care and the advancement of human dignity.[10] In the Brigham, this adjustment was achieved by listening to the voices of its users.

In the hospital, where life so often begins and ends, architecture can be a machine that moves us along an assembly line, or a space that uncovers latent meaning — a vessel to shepherd us over life's thresholds with dignity. In either case, the architecture of health cannot succeed without a harmony between the needs of its users and the needs of this living system. The forms and functions of our built world are not fixed. Architecture must adapt to unknown futures and, over time, serve the lives of many publics. Function changes. This is the law.

Expansion sequence, 1913 to 2008, Brigham and Women's Hospital, Boston [fig. 16]

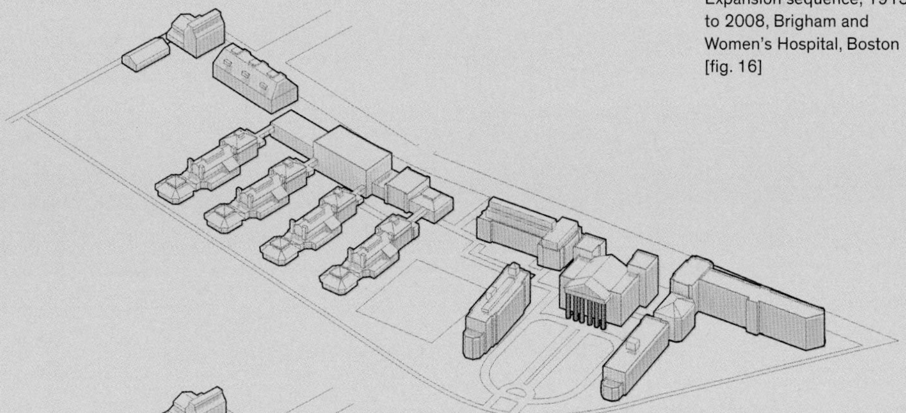

1913

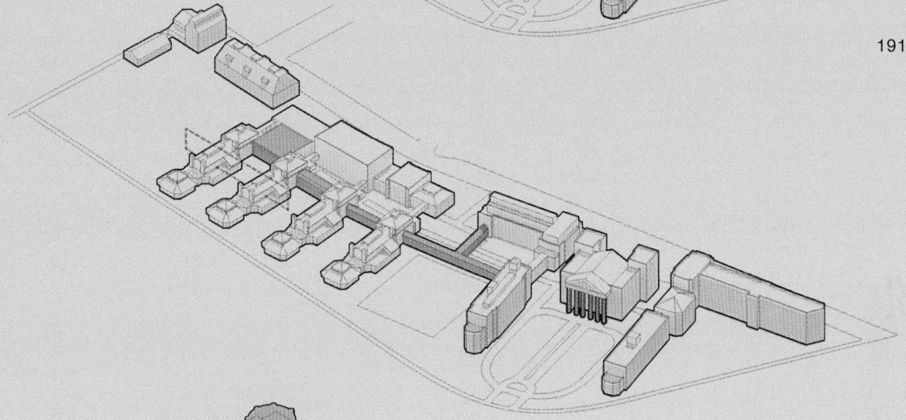

1956

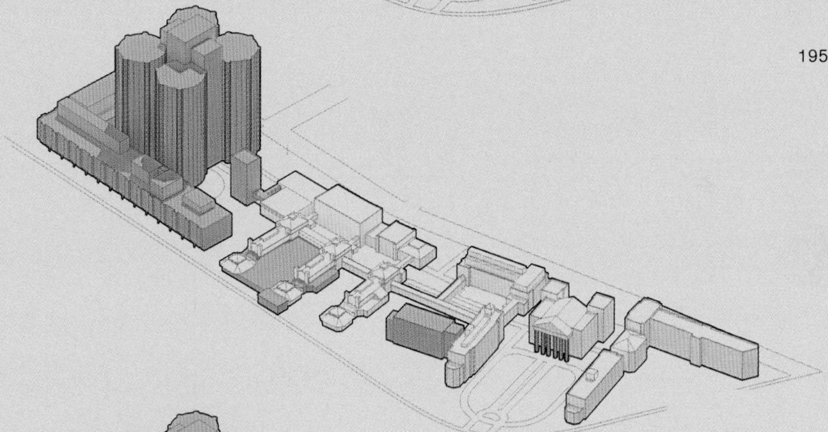

1977

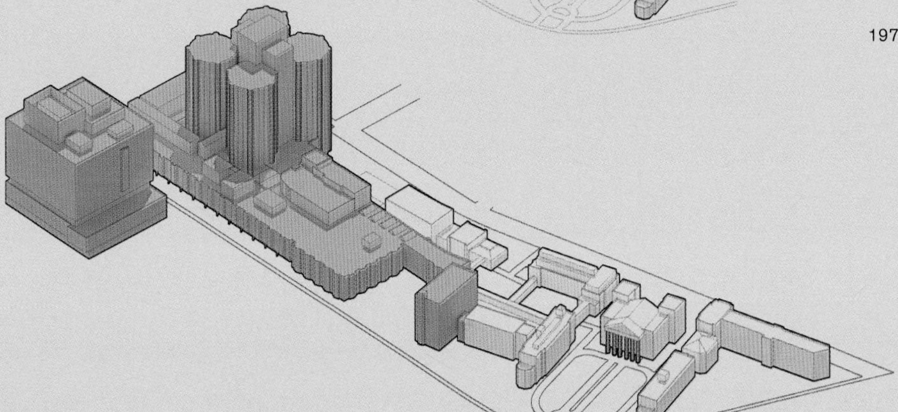

1984, 2008

Brigham and Women's Hospital,
Boston, 1980 [fig. 4]

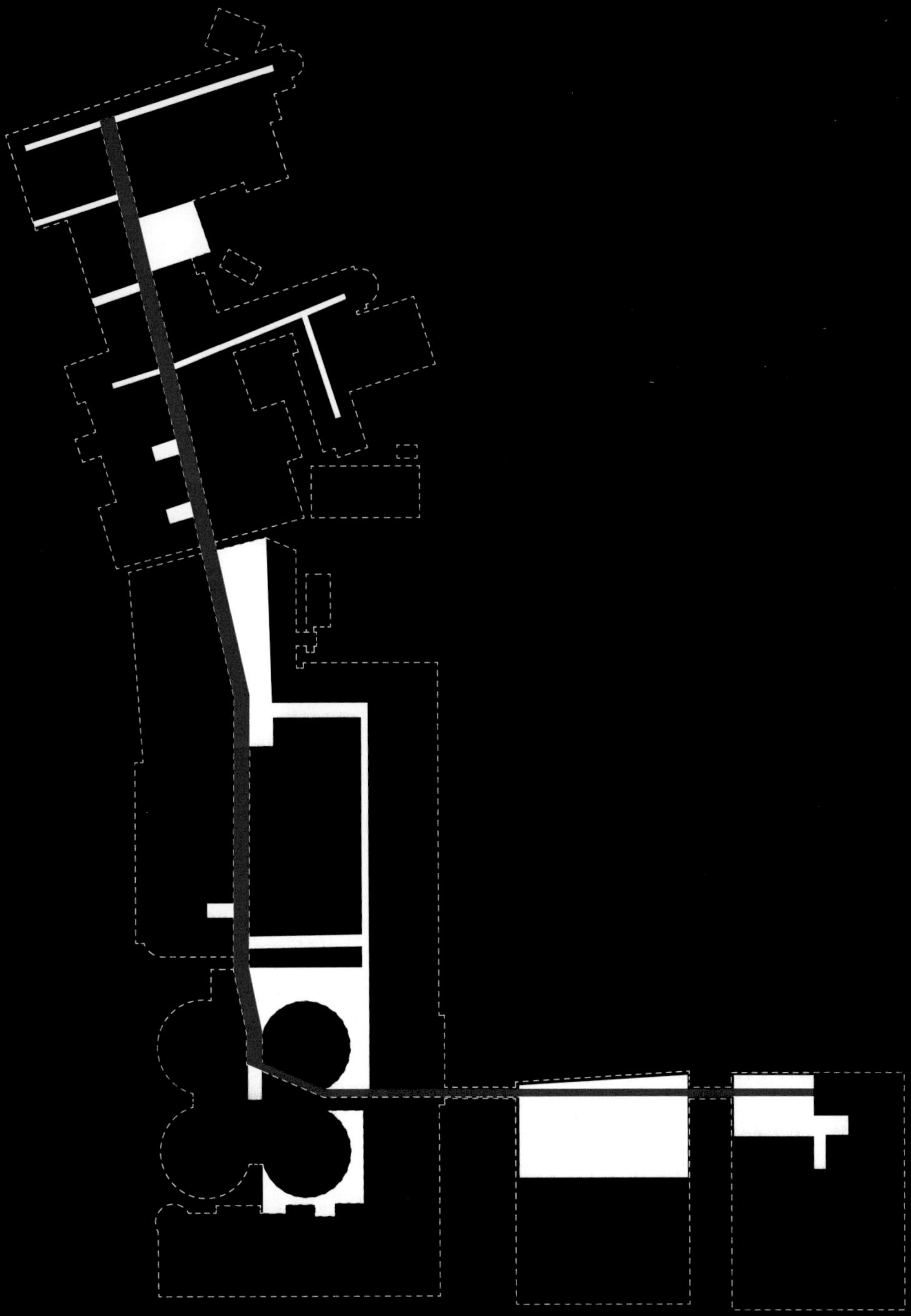

"The Pike," Brigham and Women's Hospital, Boston [fig. 15]

Coda
The COVID Pandemic

In the spring of 2020, during the writing of this book, the COVID-19 pandemic stretched hospitals around the world beyond capacity **(fig. 1)**. The infection of doctors and nursing staff showed early on that the virus was airborne, and the movement of air, that age-old hospital problem, became a dominant criterion in the prevention of contamination. As in the Crimean War field hospital in Renkioi, 170 years ago (see chapter 2), it became essential to ensure the separation of beds, to provide protected observation points for nurses, to prevent the contamination of equipment, and to isolate patients. And as was true both in Crimea and at the Brigham during the influenza pandemic of 1918, the window and the flow of air received the most attention.

Medical professionals at Mount Sinai Hospital in New York moved COVID patients from modern air-sealed buildings to a 1930s bed tower that had windows designed to be opened, retrofitting those spaces with in-room filters and fans **(figs. 2–4)**. Suddenly, the hospital's reliance on machine air-conditioning was a weakness, a reminder to planners that certain universal, spatial principles — notably that buildings must provide access to uncontaminated air — should not be designed around. The machine, in this way, had broken a primary law.

Like all crises that reveal cracks in the system, the pandemic has prompted a public reckoning with the role of buildings in shaping our health. Recent reporting is waking up to the crisis of breathability in buildings, raising questions about our dependence on mechanical systems and the lack of access to fresh, natural air.[1] Why are so many buildings filled with inoperable windows? How did we not foresee the dangers of creating an airtight seal around entire city blocks? Is it really acceptable that our built surroundings are entirely dependent on ever more complex mechanical systems that pollute the environment and, if they should fail, prevent us from breathing? At our peril, we have ignored Nightingale's prescriptions. The history of the hospital contains clear lessons about the importance of air movement through buildings, the public health risks of poor design, and the dangers of technological reliance. Architecture professionals should look back to see what else has been forgotten or ignored in the race to merge art and technology. Whose lives might be at stake if they don't?

1 See Philip Kennicott, "Designing to Survive," *Washington Post Magazine*, July 13, 2020; Justin Davidson, "How Do We Rethink Public Space after the Pandemic? Start with Rolls of Tape," *New York*, April 27, 2020; and Sarah Zhang, "We're Just Rediscovering a 19th-Century Pandemic Strategy," *Atlantic*, February 22, 2021 (web).

1

2

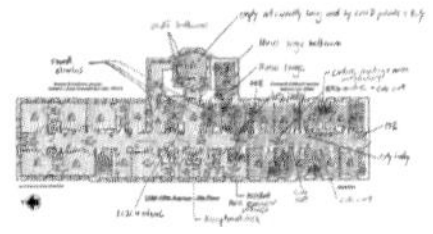

3

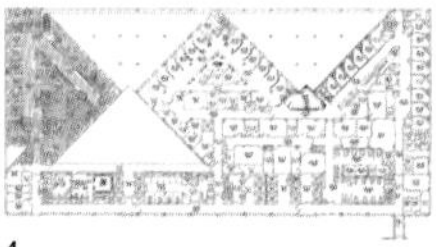

4

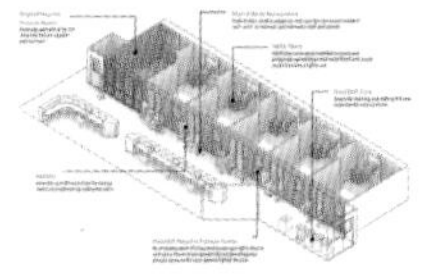

clinicians at Mount Sinai Hospital, New York, 2020 [fig. 2]

Heat maps of ICU units drawn by clinicians at Mount Sinai Hospital, New York, 2020 [fig. 3]

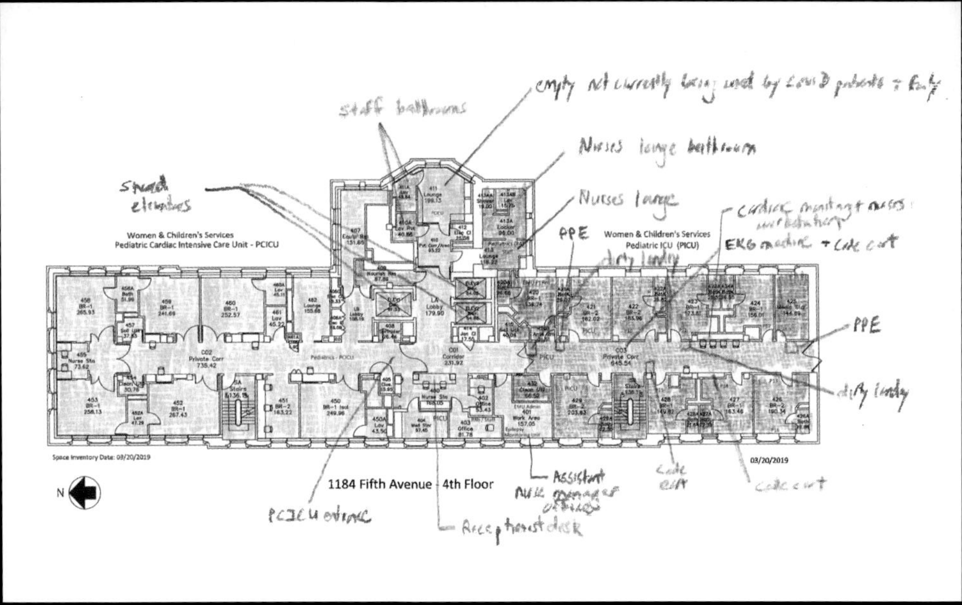

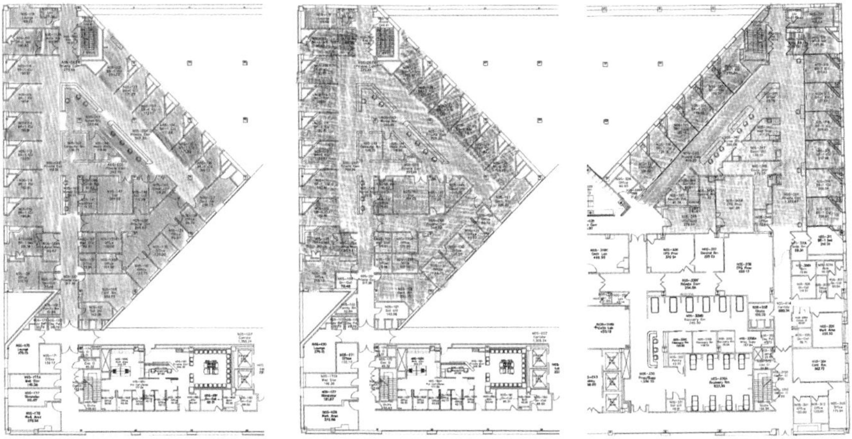

The Jacob Javits Convention Center, New York, converted into a temporary hospital for COVID-19 patients, 2020 [fig. 1]

Diagram showing interventions made to convert an adult ICU wing into an ICU ward for COVID-19 patients, Mount Sinai Hospital, New York, 2020 [fig. 4]

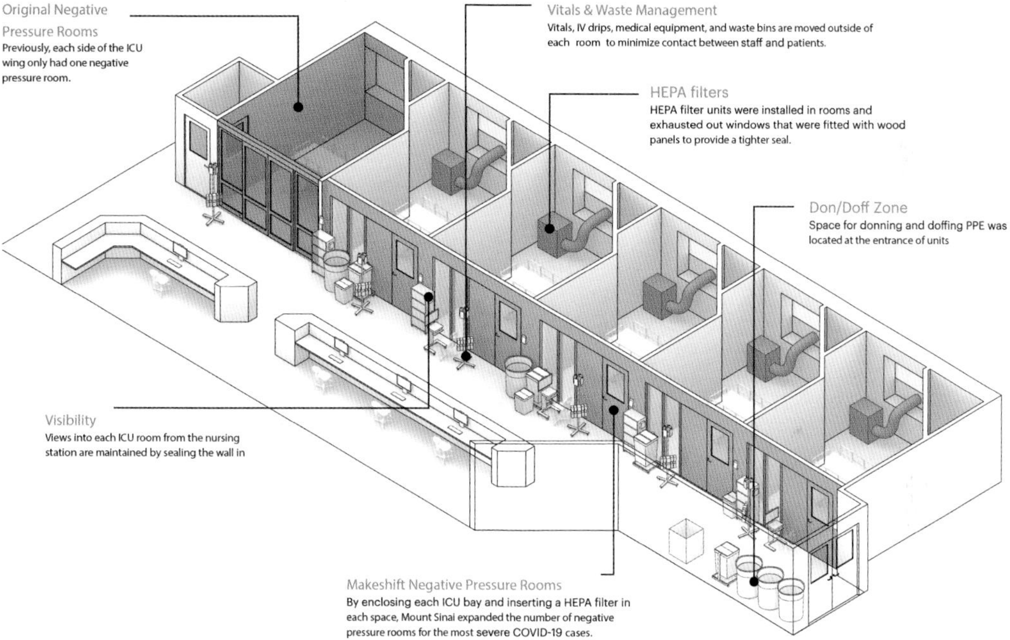
Original Negative Pressure Rooms
Previously, each side of the ICU wing only had one negative pressure room.
Vitals & Waste Management
Vitals, IV drips, medical equipment, and waste bins are moved outside of each room to minimize contact between staff and patients.
HEPA filters
HEPA filter units were installed in rooms and exhausted out windows that were fitted with wood panels to provide a tighter seal.
Don/Doff Zone
Space for donning and doffing PPE was located at the entrance of units
Visibility
Views into each ICU room from the nursing station are maintained by sealing the wall in
Makeshift Negative Pressure Rooms
By enclosing each ICU bay and inserting a HEPA filter in each space, Mount Sinai expanded the number of negative pressure rooms for the most severe COVID-19 cases.

Epilogue
The Right to Breathe

Butaro District Hospital, Rwanda

In 2008, Rwanda was freshly tilled soil. Streets were swept, lawns were manicured, and education and health care were guaranteed. The genocide of 1994 had stripped a people of dignity and destroyed a generation of lives; the country had seen the depths to which humanity could fall. But fourteen years later, after focused investments in health, education, housing, economic reconstruction, and reconciliation, Rwanda was abundant and hopeful. It was shedding histories of colonialism and ethnic division and recalibrating its future toward shared economic and social progress. To assist in strengthening the country's health care system, Dr. Paul Farmer (fig. 1) and his organization Partners In Health were asked by the Rwandan government to consult. After two decades of providing visionary medical services to the world's most underserved communities, Partners In Health had shown that health care systems could be designed to meet patients where they are. A key element of the collaboration between the Rwandan government and Partners In Health would be a new purpose-built hospital in the remote northern hamlet of Butaro.

At that time, I was studying architecture. After hearing Farmer lecture, I asked him which architects he was working with and how I might be of service. He told me that few had ever reached out to him, and his organization was often left to design and build by itself, with just the resources it already had. He described the failure of Western "experts" as a remnant of colonial power. Outside designers working on projects for the underserved, he said, were intoxicated by modern emergency clinics in shipping containers. They never stopped to ask if people *wanted* to receive health care in an industrial waste product.

He also described the dystopia created by modern technology, with its ostensibly cheap, easily deployable medical care, panacea solutions to drinking water, and procedural hacks. He called this equipment "junk for the poor" and described it filling storage closets, sitting broken in hallways, or lingering, inoperable, in medical clinics the world over. There is no one-size-fits-all solution to the health care problems of the poor, he said. To deliver health care was to "accompany" the community and listen to its needs, serving the system from within instead of designing from outside.

Farmer's lead engineer in Rwanda, Bruce Nizeye, needed help designing the hospital in Butaro, and he invited me to join him there in 2008. I jumped at the chance. Most of the clinics and hospitals Partners In Health had previously built were additions or renovations to hospital

1

campuses. The Butaro hospital was, at the time, the largest project it had ever designed and constructed from the ground up. The client was the government of Rwanda, and the hospital needed to address current problems, such as the epidemic of tuberculosis that was ravaging poor communities around the globe.

Dr. Michael Rich, an expert on tuberculosis and its multidrug-resistant variants, was then the director of Partners In Health's Rwanda operations (through its sister organization Inshuti Mu Buzima) and an architecture junkie. Hospital hallways, he explained, were the major problem in the transmission of multidrug-resistant tuberculosis. Patients waiting in these spaces without windows or airflow would cough on each other, become coinfected with drug-resistant variants, and then bring them back to their communities. In the hallways of hospitals, buildings meant to heal, the epidemic had begun.

"We have been trying to design hallways out of hospitals for years," Rich told me. Naïvely, I asked, "Shouldn't a modern hospital use a mechanical system to ventilate its spaces?" Like a patient teacher, he explained that mechanical systems never work as designed. And sometimes, he said, they are too expensive to maintain. When they break or are turned off for budgetary reasons, the spaces have worse airflow than those with simple windows or outdoor waiting areas. Better mechanical systems do not meet patients where they are.

Dr. Edward Nardell, another tuberculosis expert at Partners In Health, pointed me to a study in Peru that showed how older, colonial-era hospitals, built with generous windows, tall ceilings, and open-air waiting areas, were better able to prevent the transmission of tuberculosis than newer ones designed to keep mechanically conditioned air from leaking out.[1] Nardell also introduced me to Florence Nightingale's *Notes on Hospitals* (1859) and her spatial strategies to increase airflow and reduce disease transmission, and I realized that there were universal principles of building function that transcend culture, context, and time. We sought to locate more of these truths and insert them into the design of the Butaro hospital.

The Right to Breathe

We took Rich at his word, and proposed a hospital without hallways. In the new structure, all patient, staff, and public movement and waiting takes place outdoors (fig. 2). Rwanda's temperate climate allows for comfortable exterior waiting throughout most of the year, but when it rains, covered outdoor areas provide respite. When it gets cold, we should fetch blankets, Farmer said, unknowingly replicating a lesson from both the Paimio Sanitorium (see chapter 4) and the Peter Bent Brigham Hospital in Boston during the influenza pandemic of 1918 (see chapter 8). Exterior hallways necessitated a distributed multibuilding design rather than a centrally loaded institution, and the buildings had to be thin (so air could move through them). Doctors would walk between buildings dispersed in a campus setting, so we created covered pathways surrounded by lush landscaping and gardens to brighten their journey (fig. 3).

1 C. J. Noakes et al., "Use of CFD Analysis in Modifying a TB Ward in Lima, Peru," *Indoor and Built Environment* 15, no. 1 (February 1, 2006): 41–47. See also Alan Short and Sura Al-Maiyah, "Design Strategy for Low-Energy Ventilation and Cooling of Hospitals," *Building Research and Information* 37, no. 3 (2009): 264–92; Kevin John Lomas and Yingchun Ji, "Resilience of Naturally Ventilated Buildings to Climate Change: Advanced Natural Ventilation and Hospital Wards," *Energy and Buildings* 41, no. 6 (June 2009): 629–53; A. R. Escombe et al., "Natural Ventilation for the Prevention of Airborne Contagion," *PLoS Medicine* 4, no. 2 (February 2007): 309–16; and W. Jiamjarasrangsi et al., "Inadequate Ventilation for Nosocomial Tuberculosis Prevention in Public Hospitals in Central Thailand," *International Journal of Tuberculosis and Lung Disease* 13, no. 4 (April 2009): 454–59.

2

3

Butaro District Hospital,
Butaro, Rwanda [fig. 2]

Butaro District Hospital,
Butaro, Rwanda [fig. 3]

Elevators often break, and in rural areas the maintenance required is too specific for proper upkeep. We needed a facility that would be accessible without elevators, one that a patient in a wheelchair could fully traverse. Rwanda's zigzagging hillside footpaths were a useful precedent; we layered the hospital across the crests of a hill to ensure that multiple stories would be accessible at ground level. This had the additional benefit of leaving space for future campus growth (fig. 4).

The trend in both infection control and patient experience was to isolate patients in single rooms. But in rural settings, Rich told me, patients were dying more often in isolated rooms because there were not enough staff to monitor them. Nurses had to see the patients, and the patients had to see the nurses: there was a reciprocal relationship of care and trust. Without complicated monitoring devices, it was necessary to have a visual relationship between the nurses' station and the patient. This was less a form of control or dominance, we learned, than a way of ensuring that everyone was attentive to the needs of the patient. We designed open wards with nurses' stations in the center, low walls to ensure the visibility of the entire room and all the beds, and few corners to block the view between staff and patient (fig. 5). Glass-doored isolation rooms for actively contagious patients are located at the end of each ward. Adjacent bathrooms are equipped with their own venting and entrances off the wards to reduce the spread of odors and bioaerosols.

Nightingale's design principles were based on wards that could hold a carefully balanced load of twenty to thirty beds: no less, no more. In Rwanda, we saw wards designed for two dozen patients holding well over thirty, sometimes with two to three people per bed or with patients lying on mats underneath. With few medical facilities in the country, this was understandable: doctors were trying to use all the available space. But Paris's Hôtel-Dieu had taught us how dangerous overcrowding and unregulated scale could be (see chapter 1), and we wanted to ensure that the wards in Butaro would not overfill during times of stress to the system.

4

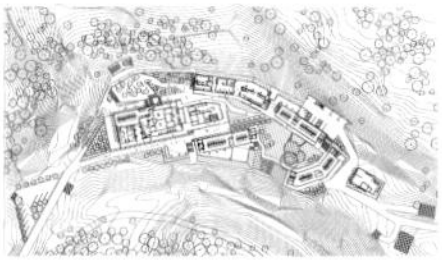

5

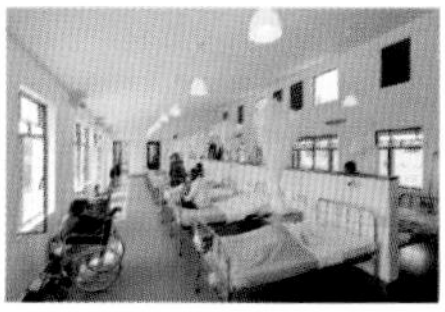

6

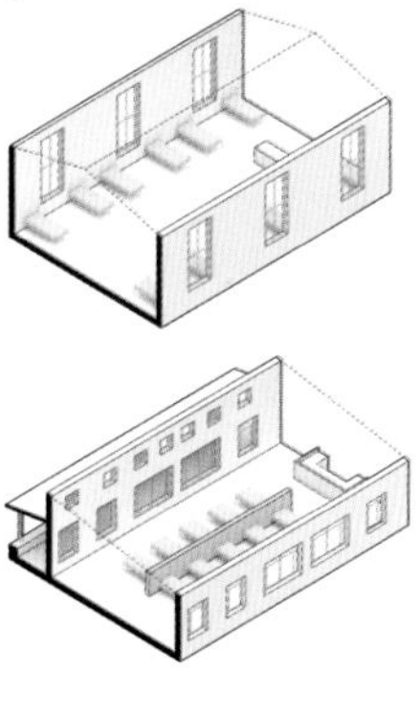

Nightingale's prescriptions, I learned, defined a parametric relationship among people, spaces, and services. When one of those elements is out of balance, the system can break down and patients can get sicker. To target overcrowding, we amended the Nightingale ward slightly, replacing the central hallway with a half-height wall. Patient beds project out from this central wall, facing the windows (fig. 6), and the pathway encircles the ward rather than cutting through the center of it. This provides three complementary benefits. First, with an immovable wall in the center and smaller hallways on the perimeter, staff can't overfill the ward without disrupting the nursing rounds. In this way, we designed against the downside of flexibility. Second, this central wall consolidates electrical outlets, call buttons, and oxygen sockets, which are placed in the headboard. Its colored panels are removable to allow for the addition of future systems and for repair.

The third benefit taught me about the deeper role of architecture. With their beds oriented to face the windows, patients can see the breathtaking landscape outside. Scholarship has shown that a simple view reduces patient stay times and pain medication requests.[2] Plus, it was quite obvious that it would be preferable to look out a window

2 Robert S. Ulrich, "View through a Window May Influence Recovery from Surgery," *Science* 224, no. 4647 (April 27, 1984): 420–21.

rather than gaze at a roomful of other sick people. With beds no longer ranged along the periphery of the ward, we were able to increase the window sizes, lowering the sill below headboard height, and thus bring more light, views, and air into the space. This simple move demonstrated that when architectural design is human centered, it can be in harmony with function, form, and experience **(fig. 7)**.

"With limited resources," Farmer once said to me, "people get resourceful." This seemed to be the case in Butaro. The new ward design, now called the Butaro ward, is written into national guidelines, and it has been replicated in hospitals throughout Rwanda and beyond. I am sure we will see the Butaro ward adjust and recalibrate as new services and systems take over these hospitals. But I was reminded that when doctors fight for their patients' access to health care, they are also fighting for their right to breathe clean, uncontaminated air. Nightingale changed a lot of things, but most important to us was the revelation that architecture is an essential, rights-based discipline. I learned this on that hill in Rwanda.

Constructing Dignity

Designing the Butaro hospital was not without difficulties. My colleague David Saladik and I lived in Butaro in a district building that had housed a prison cell during the genocide. We shared a room off the kitchen. Our colleagues Alan Ricks, Sierra Bainbridge, and others were working remotely and sending iterations over an unstable internet connection.[3] We drew all day and then presented the plans and ideas to the doctors at night. The budget was incredibly tight and the timeline was even tighter, and so many ideas had to be rethought. And not all the stakeholders welcomed a young design team taking up crucial space in this hospital far in the hinterlands of northern Rwanda. One prominent visiting doctor asked, "Aren't more equipment and more beds a better investment than fancy buildings?" Scarce resources require sacrifices, he seemed to suggest. He was a surgeon working in field hospitals, and perhaps this equation made sense in his work, and saved lives. Or was he repeating that adage by Marc-Antoine Laugier, that "houses designed to lodge poor people, ought to taste something of it.... The poor should be lodged as poor"?[4] In either case, I could sympathize with his suspicion. Until they were built, our proposals were just empty ideas. We had to prove that they were ideas worth investing in — including our proposal to clad the entire campus in volcanic rock harvested from the surrounding hills.

Many houses and garden walls in that region of Rwanda are built from basalt, a volcanic rock — the result of eruptions of lava — that is found between layers of soil in the ground **(figs. 8, 9)**. Butaro is in the foothills of the Virunga mountain chain, and this black, porous rock similar to pumice is a perfect building material, soft and very malleable. Local homes made from basalt feature thick mortar joints and sometimes hand-applied cement over the stone, creating a polka-dot pattern **(fig. 10)**. We wanted the hospital cladding to look more like the garden walls, which were dry stacked with no visible signs of mortar, highlighting their texture and the fact that the materials came from this

3 See Michael Murphy and Alan Ricks, *Justice Is Beauty* (New York: Monicelli, 2019), 52–67. Original team members included Alda Ly, Marika Shioiri-Clark, Ryan Leidner, and Justin Brown. They were joined by others, including Andrew Brose, Garret Gantner, Ebberly Straithairn, Sarah Mohland, Christian Benimana, Commode Dushishimana, and Maura Rockcastle.

4 Marc-Antoine Laugier, *An Essay on Architecture*, 2nd ed. (London: T. Osbourne and Shipton, 1755), 191. See also chapter 1 in this volume.

7

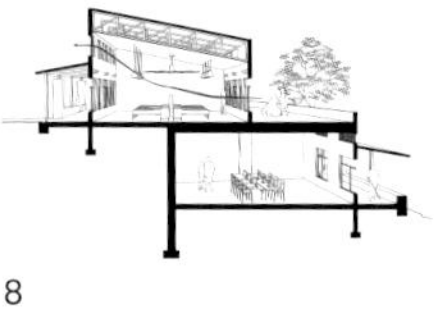

8

9

10

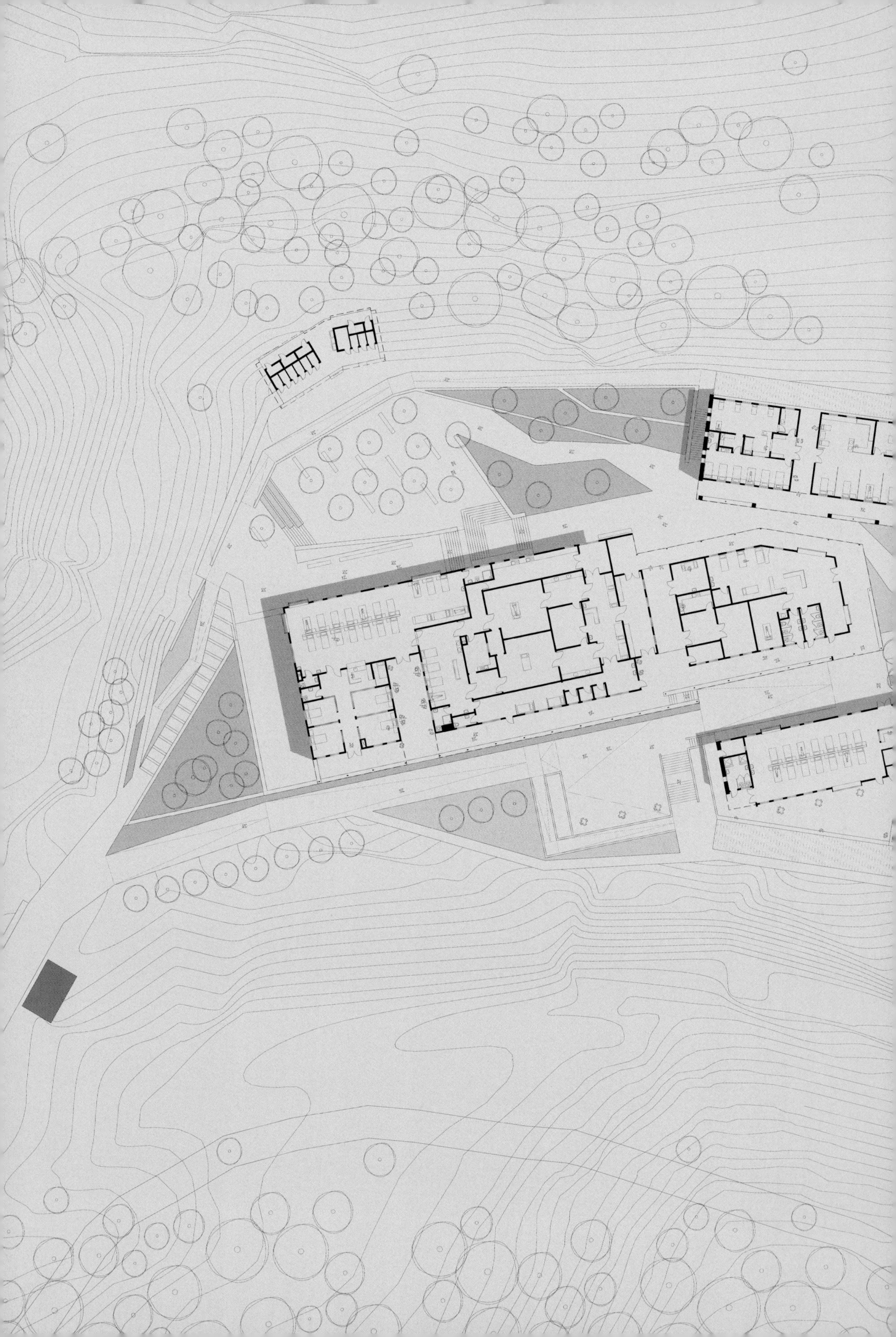

Site plan for Butaro District Hospital, Butaro, Rwanda, designed by MASS Design Group, 2011 [fig. 4]

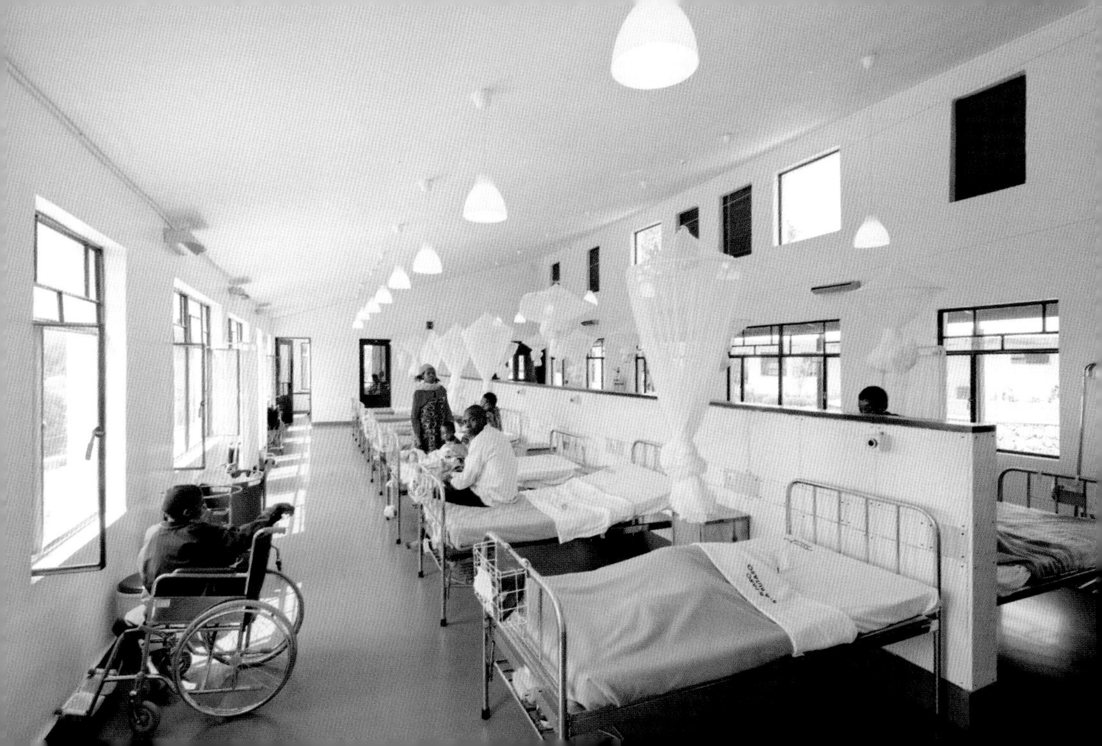

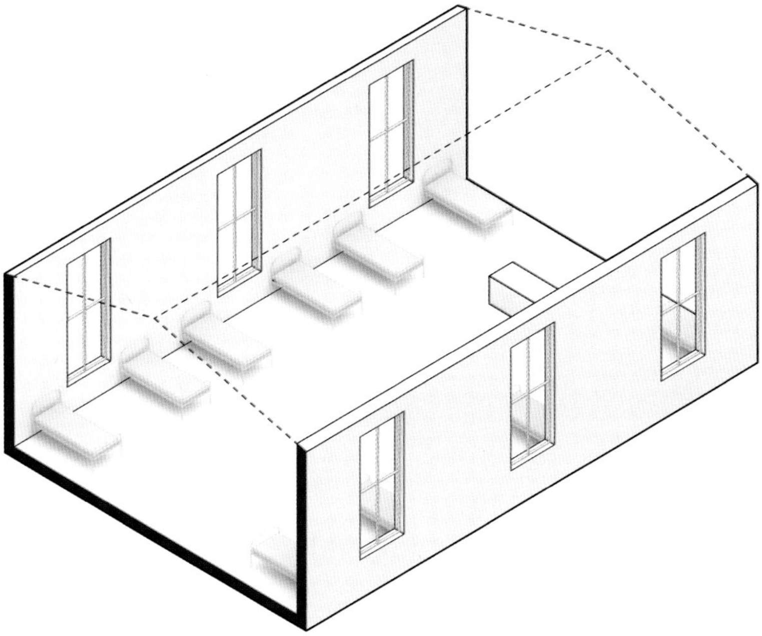

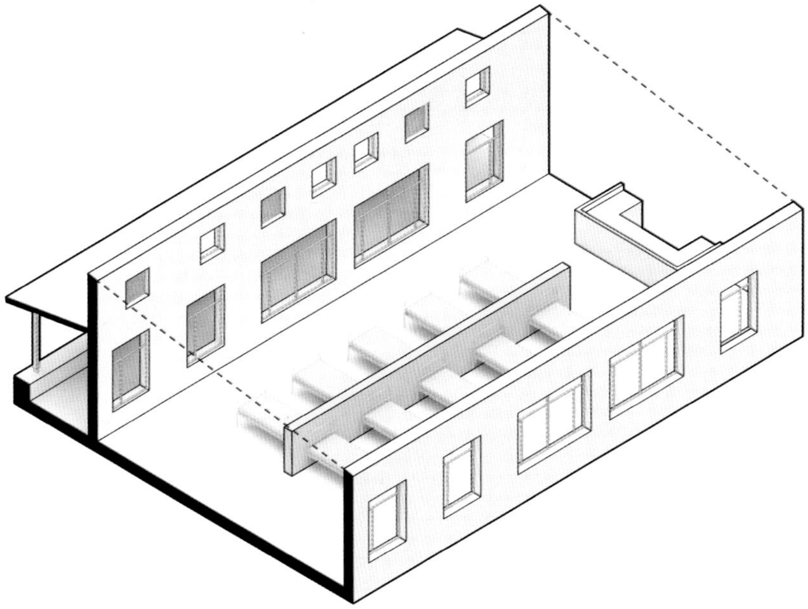

Volcanic stone piled along property lines near Butaro, Rwanda [fig. 9]

A "polka dot" wall, composed of volcanic stones covered with plaster and mortar, Butaro, Rwanda [fig. 10]

Section drawing of Butaro District Hospital, showing airflow through a ward [fig. 7]

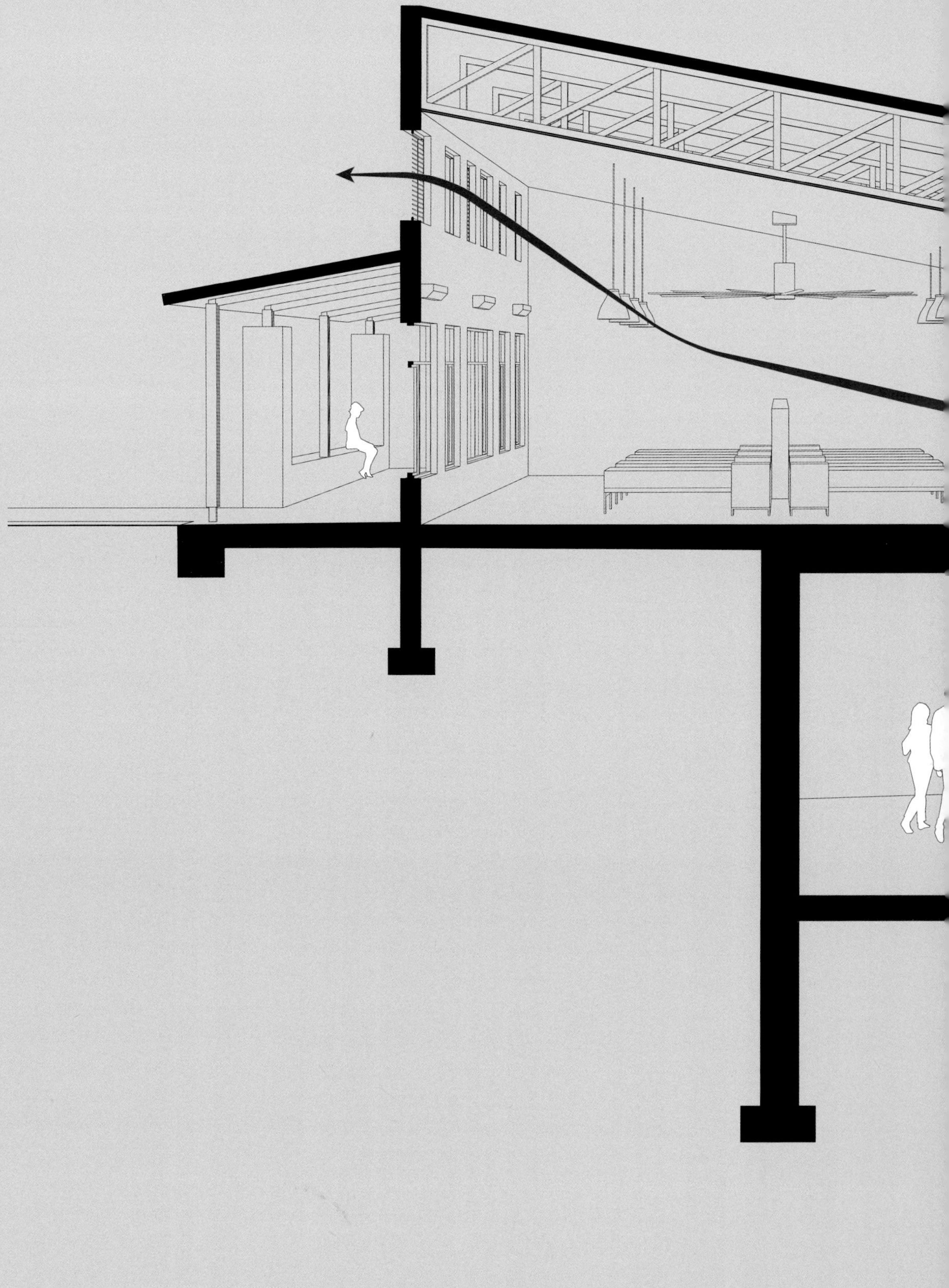

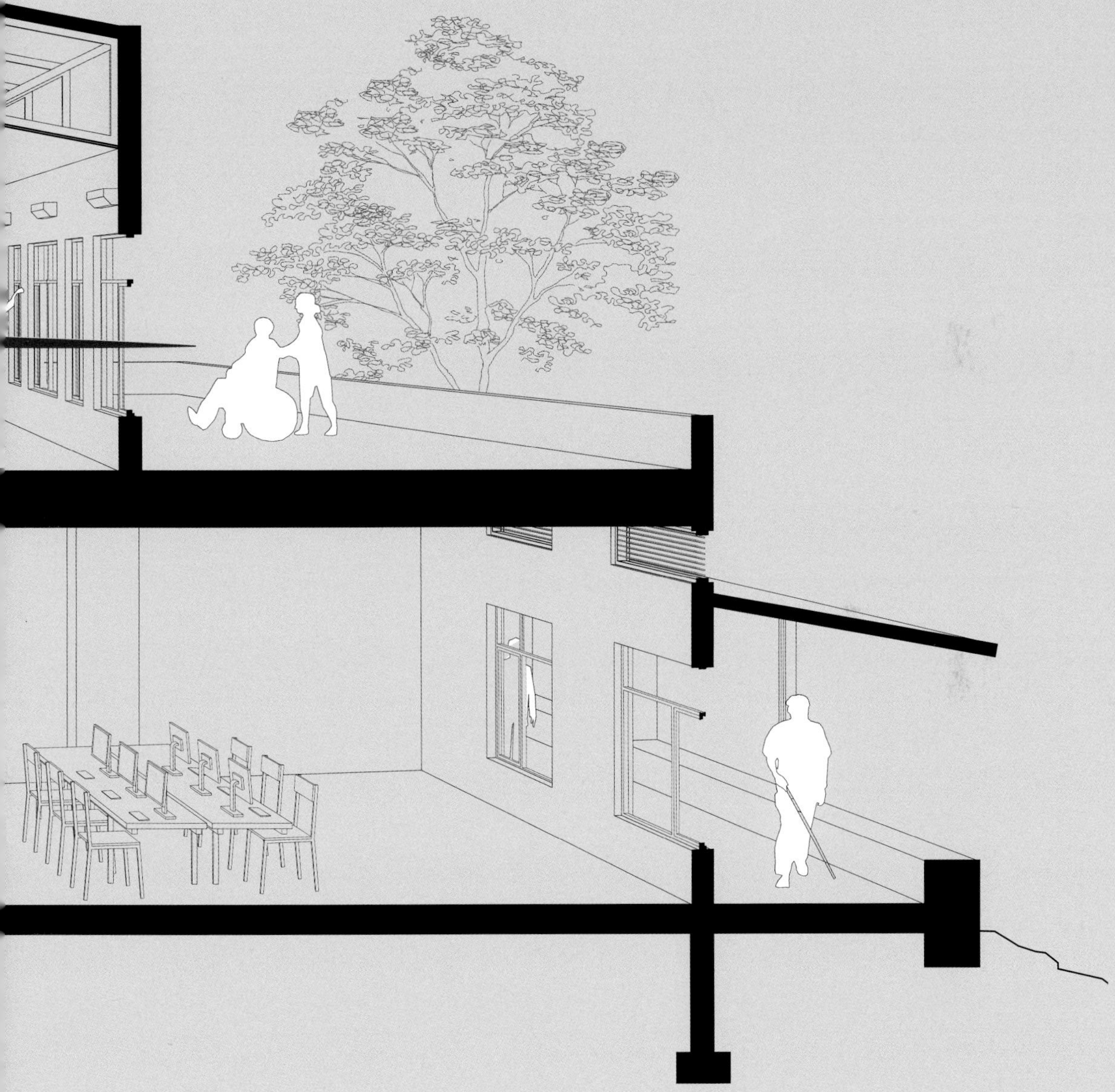

very ground. To fit the stones together in this way, like a jigsaw puzzle on the surface of the building, required both innovation and a high level of skill.

Nizeye, the lead engineer and builder, insisted that we make a number of mockups, and he hired the best masons he could find to assemble various iterations. We got to the mockups late at night; it was pitch black, but construction had to start in the morning. We beamed car headlights on the samples and perused our options. Some had too much mortar, and the stones in others were too uniform. The last mockup was perfect, a puzzle of rock well configured into unique shapes, with tight joints that showed very little mortar. Our choice was made.

The next morning, the masons got to work. One of them, Anne Marie Nyiranshimiyimana, had started a guild of female masons; she made the two-hour journey from her home to show off their skills. Emmanuel (Hakiza) Hakizama was training as a mason at the time. They and their colleagues began covering the walls of the hospital, including the first main building, which houses the outpatient waiting areas, laboratory, pharmacy, and operating room sequence areas. This building is the largest, and the first one encountered by patients: it had to be right.

When the masons began their work, the stones looked great assembled on top of each other. Minor variations in joint sizes would disappear in the image of a massive stone wall, I thought. But slowly, as the weeks went by, their calibration got tighter, the joints narrower, and the stones more unique. One mason developed a method of bending a clothes hanger to approximate the shape of the stone they needed to fit to next. Their speed picked up, as did their precision, and the massive, nearly thirty-foot foundation wall began to tower over the campus. By the time Hakizama, Nyiranshimiyimana, and their teams worked their way around to the entrance corner where they had started, there was a noticeable difference in quality between where they had begun and where they ended. The masonry team asked if they could take down the original corner and rebuild it so it matched more precisely, and although it caused a small delay, Nizeye agreed.

Local artisans assembled every piece of the hospital, from the walls to the furniture to the windows, and the result is a total work of art. This hospital is greater than the individuals who worked on it; it is a symbol that transmits purpose and intention. This has nothing to do with the subjective debates about form and sculpture I weathered in school. Nor is it the misplaced "sumptuousness" or "magnificence" Laugier warned us about. It is, rather, the formation of the most foundational architectural element — the wall — from the original tools of construction: the hand and the stone (figs. 11, 12). This, I realized, was the composition of beauty.

A year after the hospital opened, the skeptical field surgeon cornered me at an event. "I thought what you were doing was an enormous waste of time and resources," he admitted. "We doctors look for proof and evidence; it is hard to quantify the value of design. But when I saw the stone walls, I realized we needed this too. The unquantifiable, the beautiful, is in the service of our patients and our beliefs."

On that hilltop in Rwanda, Nizeye, the stonemasons, and that doctor taught me something I had not learned in architecture school. They taught me that architecture can both impede and advance our collective rights — such as the right to health care or the right to breathe. But they also taught me that buildings, made with great care, can help us locate ourselves within the sometimes dizzying and alienating pressures of the world around us. They locate us and ground us, and through this they give us hope (figs. 13, 14). Buildings can fulfill our most elemental right — the right to dignity.

11

12

13

14

Butaro District Hospital,
Butaro, Rwanda [fig. 13]

Exterior wall of volcanic stone, Butaro District Hospital, Butaro [fig. 12]

Interior of Butaro District Hospital [fig. 11]

Butaro District Hospital,
Butaro, Rwanda [fig. 14]

Index

Page numbers in *italics* refer to photographs or illustrations and captions. Those followed by n refer to notes.

Photo Credits

Credits are listed by figure number unless otherwise noted. Any figure not listed is believed to be in the public domain or the copyright holder was unable to be identified. Any errors in crediting will be corrected in subsequent editions.

Introduction: The Rise and Fall of Prentice Women's Hospital

1–2: C. William Brubaker Collection, Special Collections and University Archives Department, University of Illinois at Chicago.

3: Ryerson and Burnham Art and Architecture Archive, The Art Institute of Chicago.

4: © David Schalliol.

5–10: Ryerson and Burnham Art and Architecture Archive, The Art Institute of Chicago.

13–14: Ryerson and Burnham Art and Architecture Archive, The Art Institute of Chicago.

16: © David Schalliol.

Typologies: A Taxonomy of Type

(listed by page number)

41: MASS Design Group.

44: Wellcome Collection, Attribution 4.0 International (CC BY 4.0).

46: Albert Kahn Associates, Inc. / Bentley Historical Library, University of Michigan.

47: MASS Design Group.

48: From *Hospital Modernization and Expansion* (1971), Edward Todd Wheeler Estate.

49: © Craig Zeidler Strong (Zeidler Architecture Inc.: ongoing practice).

50: MASS Design Group.

51: © The Estate of Paul Rudolph and the Paul Rudolph Heritage Foundation.

Chapter 1: Charity and Control: The Birth of the Hospital

2–3: Wellcome Collection, Attribution 4.0 International (CC BY 4.0).

7: © The Courtauld Institute of Art, London.

9: Tango Images / Alamy Stock Photo.

10: Rare Book / Special Collections, Library of Congress.

11: © Archives Charmet / Bridgeman Images.

13: Bibliothèque nationale de France.

15: Division of Rare and Manuscript Collections, Cornell University Library.

16–17: Wellcome Collection, Attribution 4.0 International (CC BY 4.0).

Chapter 2: Sanitation and Experimentation

1: The Metropolitan Museum of Art, Gilman Collection, Purchase, Harriette and Noel Levine Gift, 2005.

2: Mary Evans / Pharcide.

3: Roger Fenton, J. Paul Getty Museum.

5: Courtesy of the Brunel Institute, a collaboration of the SS Great Britain Trust and the University of Bristol.

6: Digital Public Library of America, Courtesy of David Rumsey.

7: Wellcome Collection, Attribution 4.0 International (CC BY 4.0).

8: Department of Epidemiology, School of Public Health, UCLA.

9: British Library / Granger.

10: Wellcome Collection, Attribution 4.0 International (CC BY 4.0).

11–12: Digital image courtesy of the Getty's Open Content Program, J. Paul Getty Museum.

13–14: Wellcome Collection, Attribution 4.0 International (CC BY 4.0).

15: MASS Design Group.

16: Wellcome Collection, Attribution 4.0 International (CC BY 4.0).

17: Arxiu Fotogràfic de Barcelona.

18: © Jaume Ribera Llopis / Arxiu Històric de l'Hospital de la Santa Creu i Sant Pau.

19: © Robert Ramos / Fundació Hospital de la Santa Creu i Sant Pau.

20–21: © Arxiu Històric de l'Hospital de la Santa Creu i Sant Pau.

22: © Robert Ramos / Fundació Hospital de la Santa Creu i Sant Pau.

23–25: © Arxiu Històric de l'Hospital de la Santa Creu i Sant Pau.

Chapter 3: Imperial Forms and the Medical Mission

3: The National Archives, UK, CO1069/214.

4–8: MASS Design Group.

9–10: French Ministry of Culture.

11–12: MASS Design Group.

13: University of Southern California Library.

16: MASS Design Group.

18: Courtesy of Hilton Teper.

20–21: Wellcome Collection, Attribution 4.0 International (CC BY 4.0).

24: MASS Design Group.

27–28: Erica Anderson / Albert Schweitzer Fellowship.

29: Hôpital Albert Schweitzer Collections.

30: Science History Images / Alamy Stock Photo.

31: Service protestant de mission Défap.

32–33: Erica Anderson / Albert Schweitzer Fellowship.

34: MASS Design Group.

35: Hôpital Albert Schweitzer Collections.

36: MASS Design Group.

37: Erica Anderson / Albert Schweitzer Fellowship.

38: W. Eugene Smith / Black Star.

Chapter 4: Modernism and the Factory

1: Nuremberg, Germanisches Nationalmuseum, Deutsches Kunstarchiv.

2: MASS Design Group.

3: Frankfurt am Main, Institut für Stadtgeschicte.

6–7: Albert Kahn Associates, Inc. / Bentley Historical Library, University of Michigan.

8–9: Gustaf Welin, Alvar Aalto Foundation.

10: Alvar Aalto Foundation.

11: Gustaf Welin, Alvar Aalto Foundation.

12–13: Alvar Aalto Foundation.

Chapter 5: The Medical Machine

1: Photo by Robert French, National Library of Ireland, The Lawrence Photography Collection.

3: Granger.

4–5: MASS Design Group.

6: Stephen Barnes / Medical / Alamy Stock Photo.

7: Ryerson and Burnham Art and Architecture Archive, The Art Institute of Chicago.

8: BNP Media.

11: Massachusetts General Hospital.

14–15: MASS Design Group.

Chapter 6: The Mega-Hospital

1: Natalini Superstudio Collection, Beinecke Rare Book and Manuscript Library, Yale University.

2–5: From *Hospital Modernization and Expansion* (1971), Edward Todd Wheeler Estate.

6: Historic Images.

7: Chicago History Museum.

8: Steven Zucker, CC 4.0.

9: Photo by Malcolm Smith, Louis I. Kahn Collection, the University of Pennsylvania and the Pennsylvania Historical and Museum Commission.

10: Photo by Mildred Schmertz, Louis I. Kahn Collection, the University of Pennsylvania and the Pennsylvania Historical and Museum Commission.

11: Daniel Lu, CC 4.0.

12: MASS Design Group.

13: MASS Design Group.

14: David Dent.

15–18: © Craig Zeidler Strong (Zeidler Architecture Inc.: ongoing practice).

19: © Arata Isozaki, digital image © The Museum of Modern Art / Licensed by SCALA / Art Resource, NY.

20–28: © Craig Zeidler Strong (Zeidler Architecture Inc.: ongoing practice).

Chapter 7: The Mat and the Labyrinth

2: Academie van Bouwkunst, Amsterdam.

4–5: MASS Design Group.

7–12: Fondation Le Corbusier / ADAGP.

13: Ezra Stoller / ESTO.

14–15: © The Estate of Paul Rudolph and the Paul Rudolph Heritage Foundation.

16: © Matthew Ireland.

17: Paul Rudolph Collection, Library of Congress, Prints & Photographs Division, LC-DIG-ppmsca-32701.

19: Justin Kerr Scheckler, CC 2.0.

20: © The Estate of Paul Rudolph and the Paul Rudolph Heritage Foundation.

21: © 2021, Edua Wilde Photography.

Chapter 8: Hospital City: The Pathology of Form

1–4: Ryerson and Burnham Art and Architecture Archive, The Art Institute of Chicago.

5: MIT Museum, Cambridge, MA.

6–7: Brigham and Women's Hospital.

8–9: MASS Design Group.

10: Brigham and Women's Hospital.

11: The Reading Room / Alamy Stock Photo.

12: The Center for the History of Medicine and the Brigham and Women's Hospital Medical Library.

13–14: Brigham and Women's Hospital.

15–16: MASS Design Group.

Coda: The COVID Pandemic

1: "New York National Guard" by The National Guard is licensed under CC BY 2.0.

2–4: MASS Design Group.

Epilogue: The Right to Breathe

1: Partners in Health.

2–3: Iwan Baan.

4: MASS Design Group.

5: Iwan Baan.

6–7: MASS Design Group.

8–9: Iwan Baan.

10: MASS Design Group.

11: Iwan Baan.

12: MASS Design Group.

13–14: Iwan Baan.

Acknowledgments

This project has been over a decade in the making. It began in 2008 with research on medical facilities during the design of the Butaro District Hospital in Rwanda, when the founding members of MASS Design encountered a rich history of architectural strategies for managing airflow and infection control that predated the introduction of air-conditioning. It continued in 2013 with a two-year research grant from the Robert Wood Johnson Foundation to fund the study of the history of hospitals around the world. In the spring of 2016, Alan Ricks, Jeffrey Mansfield, and I led a seminar at the Harvard Graduate School of Design called The Architecture of Health: Power, Technocracy, and the Hospital. Many students and faculty members helped us think critically about this unexplored history. Thanks are due to Stephen Verderber, Matthew Basilico, Edward Nardell, Mark Careaga, Lachlan Forrow, Jean Comaroff, Mohsen Mostafavi, and Rahul Mehotra for their participation in teaching the course. The students were exceptional, and I am grateful to them for inspiring us: Taylor Brandes, Ellie Lee, Whitney Hansley, Kelley Hess, Yina Ng, Linda Maytan, Sama El Saket, Jason Kim, Andrew Nahmias, Johanna Faust, Insu Kim, Yubai Zhou, Matther Murray, Jia Gu, Andy Rauchut, Chi Yoon Min, Albert Wang, Fan Wang, Enoch Wong, and Nadia Perlepe.

In 2017 I attended a writing retreat at the Santa Fe Art Institute. I am indebted to the amazing people there, namely, Jamie Blosser, Toni Gentilli, Kourtney Andar, Joseph Kunkel, and Nuttaphol Ma, for giving me the space to draft this material into a legible project.

Without the brilliance, patience, and clarity of thought of my writing partner, Jeffrey Mansfield, this project would never have started or finished. I must also thank Daniel Murphy, who rolled up his sleeves and rewrote this book with me, sentence by sentence. I love you, my brother, and your genius in putting words on paper. Alan Ricks is a partner in all my work, and his friendship, fairness, and kindness are impossible to fully acknowledge. Thank you, Alan, for all you do for so many people.

To Pamela Horn, Matthew Kennedy, Ellen Lupton, Julie Pastor, Yvonne Gomez, Molly Engelman, and the amazing staff at the Cooper Hewitt, Smithsonian Design Museum: I am deeply appreciative of your indelible contributions in making this book and the exhibition *Design and Healing* a reality. Thanks are due to Rebecca Roberts for exceptional editorial support; to Bud Rodecker, Rick Valicenti, and Alyssa Arnesen, who designed this book with grace and fortitude; and to the brilliant and generous advisers who read through early drafts: Alexander Arroyo, Sara Carr, Regina Chen, Mark Pasnik, Jonathan Massey, and Maggie

Jacobstein Stern. I am particularly grateful to Daniel Barber for his contribution to the book and for his inspiring writing, which both drove and challenged many of my inquiries and ideas. I extend a special appreciation to Paul Farmer, Paola Antonelli, Neel Shah, and Sara Carr for lending their expert perspectives, voices, and support to this publication.

In the course of research and teaching, we have been blessed by the contributions of so many collaborators. I am indebted to all the MASS people, past and present, who in one way or another worked on this project: Jeffrey Mansfield, Regina Chen, Rinika Prince, Maggie Jacobstein Stern, Lauren DiLoreto, Emily Ebersol, Erin Huang, Sophia Angelis, Sierra Bainbridge, Kyle Barker, Thatcher Bean, Christian Benimana, Andrew Brose, Justin Brown, Emma Colley, Christopher Conway, Jonathan Evans, Ana Fernandez, Patricia Gruits, Garret Gantner, Rosie Goldrick, Emily Goldenberg, Arash Guity, Christopher Hardy, Carolina Kammel, Christopher Kroner, Joseph Kunkel, DeeDee Kim, Anton Larsen, Nancy Mendoza, John Maher, Ashley Marsh, Sarah Mohland, Sarah McKeever, Nadia Perlepe, Karima Peermohammed, Nicki Reckziegel, Jack Rodat, Julie Rhoad, John Rudikoff, David Saladik, Adam Saltzman, Christopher Scovel, Amie Shao, Ashita Sivakumar, Matthew Smith, Katie Swenson, Caitlin Taylor, Peter Torrebiarte, Jean Paul Sebuhayi Uwase, Jean Paul Uzabakiriho, Annie Wang, Jhanea Williams, Jody Adams, Karen Conway, Donald Kimelman, Neil Mahapatra, Paul Nakazawa, Marc Norman, Diana Ramirez-Jasso, Pardis Sabeti, Jean Shia, and Jay Wickersham. To our photographer and friend Iwan Baan: thank you for making so much of our work visible to the world. And to our friends and colleagues at Partners In Health, Michael Rich, Paul Farmer, Agnes Binagwaho, Bruce Nizeye, Peter Drobac, and Edward Nardell: thank you for giving us the opportunity to question what and how we have been taught.

To Zeidler Architecture, Art Institute of Chicago, University of Illinois Chicago, Hospital de la Santa Creu i Sant Pau Foundation, University of Pennsylvania, Massachusetts General Hospital, Brigham and Women's Hospital, Alvar Aalto Foundation, University of Michigan, Le Corbusier Foundation, and Défap Protestant Mission Service Library, thank you for your visual contributions that brought this book to life.

To my mother, Patricia Murphy Lynch, and my stepfather, Peter Lynch: thank you for your love. To Kenn Guimond and Jennifer Guimond: thank you for giving us a house in which to write this book; it would not have been possible otherwise. Finally, to my wife, Monique Guimond, and our son, Wilde Murphy, for giving me a reason to write and for supporting me every day: I love you.

Colophon

A Note on the Type

The headings, footnotes, and captions in *The Architecture of Health* are set in Theinhardt, a typeface designed by François Rappo and released by the foundry Optimo in 2009. Inspired by the sans serif typefaces of the late nineteenth and the early twentieth century, it is named after Ferdinand Theinhardt (1820–1906), a Berlin-based punchcutter and typeface designer whose radical innovations significantly shaped the development of modern typography. It is similar to the typefaces available to Alvar Aalto in the early 1930s when he designed his Paimio Sanitorium, including the "noiseless washbasin" reproduced in chapter 4.

The body text is set in GT Sectra and the display text in GT Flexa, both typefaces from the foundry Grilli Type. GT Sectra, designed by Dominik Huber, Marc Kappeler, and Noël Leu and released in 2013, is a serif typeface that, as described by Grilli, "combines the calligraphy of the broad nib pen with the sharpness of the scalpel knife." GT Flexa was designed by Huber with Kappeler and released in 2020. "Instead of the traditional view of a typeface as a collection of static styles," Grilli writes, "GT Flexa embraces the idea of a fluid design space.... From thin to thick, narrow to wide, and upright to italic—along its three axes, GT Flexa dynamically responds to any given format." In this way, the typeface addresses one of the key animating tensions in hospital design and a major theme of this book: the relationship between flexibility and utility, form and function, a conundrum illustrated in the introduction by the story of Chicago's Prentice Women's Hospital.

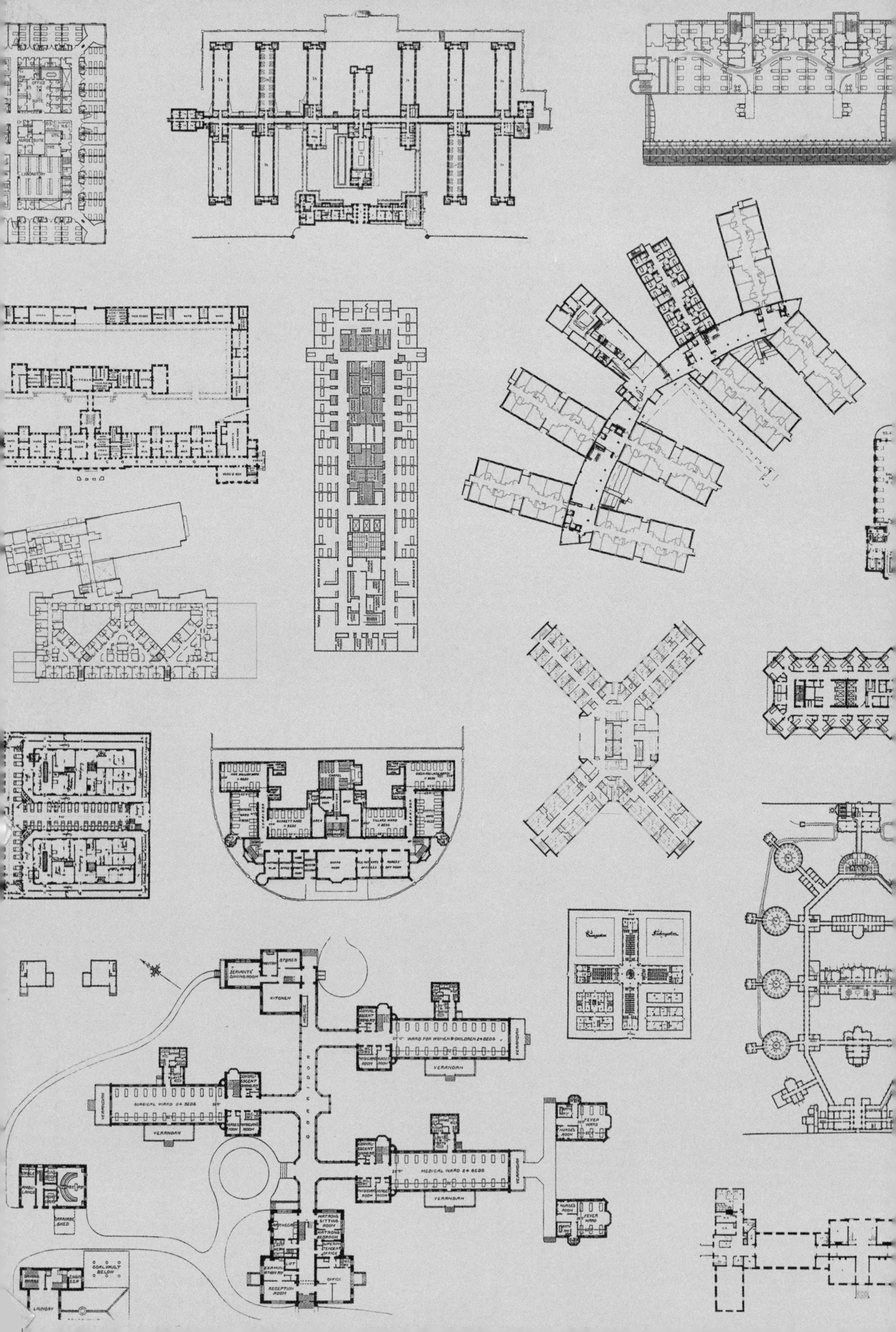

SERVANTS' DINING ROOM
STORES
KITCHEN
WARD FOR WOMEN & CHILDREN 24 BEDS
VERANDAH
SURGICAL WARD 24 BEDS
CORRIDOR
MEDICAL WARD 24 BEDS
FEVER WARD
NURSES ROOM
MATRONS SITTING ROOM
MATRONS BEDROOM
RECEPTION ROOM
OFFICE
CARRIAGE SHED
COAL VAULT BELOW
LAUNDRY
BOARD ROOM
CHAPEL